Always

With Best Wishes on your 70th birthday

Meryola   Alan   Fili

Edited by Giles Foden
Foreword by Alan Rusbridger

The **Guardian**
Century

First published in Great Britain in 1999 by The Guardian,
119 Farringdon Road, London EC1R 3ER.

Copyright 1999 by Guardian Newspapers Limited

The rights of Giles Foden to be identified as editor
of this work has been asserted in accordance with the
Copyright, Design and Patents Act 1988

A catalogue of this book is available from the British Library

ISBN 1 84115 236 6

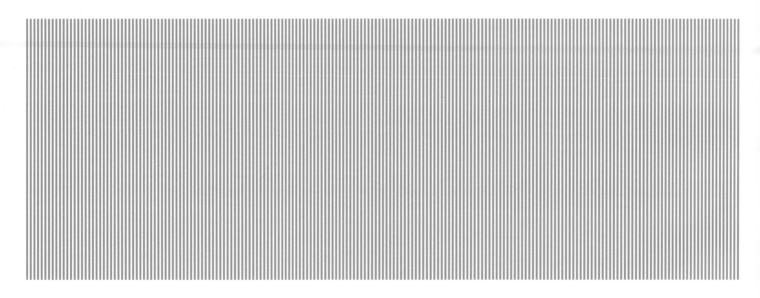

Design: Mark Leeds
Assistant editors: Lisa Darnell, Karen Windmill

Picture research: Tracey Tomlin
Additional assistance: Sidonie Beresford-Browne, Mathew Clayton

Production: Dave Kirwan, Oliver Spratley
Printed and bound in Great Britain by the Bath Press

Foreword & Introduction

FOREWORD

BY ALAN RUSBRIDGER, EDITOR OF THE GUARDIAN

"A HUNDRED YEARS is a long time; it is a long time even in the life of a newspaper, and to look back on it is to take on not only a vast development in the thing itself, but a great slice in the life of the nation, in the progress and adjustment of the world."

The words are those of CP Scott, editor of the *Manchester Guardian* for a remarkable 57 years, published to mark the centenary of the paper in 1921. They open perhaps the most famous article ever written on journalism in this country, with its timeless and much quoted (at least to his successors) dictum: "Comment is free, but facts are sacred." Now, 78 years later, comes this volume, which looks at another hundred years of history through the eyes of that same newspaper.

This is not a magisterial retrospective of a turbulent century. There will be a millennial rash of that elsewhere. And besides, we are journalists, not historians. This is simply that "great slice in the life" as we saw it at the time — with all that that implies. Not all of its contemporaneous judgements are, as things turned out, flawless. Sometimes the tone can be a touch overheated, sometimes almost comically underwhelmed, sometimes passionately right, sometimes righteously wrong. But, taken as a whole, it is more often right than wrong. On most of the big issues of the century, from the Boer War to Suez, from the suffragettes to apartheid, from Ireland to the internet, the *Guardian* can take some pride that its first draft of history will not be so very different from the final draft.

Newspapers are thrown together at great speed. Information is gathered, sifted, tested, written, analysed, edited, printed and distributed with impossible haste against near impossible odds. At its worst the hurry shows: clichés, mistakes and veneer. At its best journalism beats anything a historian can manage decades later with time and hindsight in plentiful supply. Some of the reporting we've re-read while compiling this book crackles with drama and narrative immediacy. Some of it is also astonishing for its cool-headed judgement and the sheer quality of writing.

That literary quality is one thread throughout this book. Scott himself needed no convincing about the ability of the journalist to write as powerfully as any novelist or author: "People talk about 'journalese' as though a journalist were of necessity a pretentious and sloppy writer: he may be, on the contrary, and very often is, one of the best in the world." The other thread is a unity of outlook and of tone. The "heretoforeness" is, I think, tangible throughout this volume. "Heretoforeness?" It refers to the instruction to each Editor as he takes over at the *Guardian* — to edit the paper "as heretofore". The imperative is partly, but only partly, political. 19th-century Manchester Liberalism is, after all, a distant relative of late 20th-century progressive liberalism — whether upper or lower case "l". It is as much to do with tone and with a style of writing and editing. It is a style which, when it

works best, allows individual writers to write freely about what they observe, what they feel and what they believe. That was true of our special correspondents in the Boer War, it was true of Malcolm Muggeridge's and Arthur Ransome's sometimes uncomfortable coverage of the early years of the Soviet Union. It was true of Alistair Cooke and James Cameron as it is today of Maggie O'Kane and Nick Davies.

Safeguarding the "heretofore" is made a good deal easier by the ownership structure of the paper — which has, extraordinarily enough, remained in the hands of one family since the beginning (strictly speaking, two: but the Taylors, who founded the paper, married the Scotts, who established the Scott Trust, which owns the paper today). The owners have been indulgent towards their Editors, and there have been only eleven of them since 1821. Compare this with, say, the *Times*, which this century alone has managed to notch up five different proprietors and 13 editors. Or compare the *Independent* which in its first dozen years of life got through no fewer than three different proprietors, and as many Editors as the *Guardian* managed in its first 110 years. Constant, enlightened, non-interfering ownership matters. An absence of profit-obsessed shareholders matters. A sense of continuity and shared purpose matters. All these things translate directly into ethos, and ethos into words.

It would be a foolish successor who attempted to emulate Scott's magisterial essay on the moral purpose of journalism in general, and the *Guardian* in particular. Those who have never read it in full will find it at the end of this book and can appreciate for the first time its clarity, power and wisdom. The great man is particularly good on the character of a newspaper — how it results from "the slow deposit of past actions and ideals". This book is a partial record of that slow deposit. It would be an even more foolish successor who tried to predict future deposits, less still what form the *Guardian* will take by the end of the century. One predecessor, Alastair Hetherington, found that the reporters' room had no phones when he joined the *Guardian* in 1950, "because the people who edited the paper cared about rational thought, good writing and peace to concentrate". We stretch to the odd phone these days, and each reporter now has high-speed internet access on their desktop machines. No-one I've met can predict where technology will lead us. Will the *Guardian* still be a broadsheet in 100 years — inky words on paper, driven through the night with small boys prodded from their beds to drop it through letter boxes? Or will readers print the paper themselves: or download it onto pocket palmtops which update the news every 10 seconds? Who knows, and how silly these questions will doubtless look in 100 years time. All one can say with certainty is that words will survive. And as long as words survive the *Guardian* will survive. The physical manifestation may change, but in spirit and in all other important respects the *Guardian* will live on, and thrive, as heretofore.

GUARDIAN CENTURIES, GUARDIAN DAYS

INTRODUCTION

BY GILES FODEN

"GLACIAL EPOCHS ARE great things," Mark Twain once observed, "but they are vague, vague." The same goes for anything one might want to say about the character of a smaller span of time, a single century. Epochal generalisations are often dangerous in that way. Even after selecting the articles included here, sifted from over a million words of the *Guardian*, I feel that to venture something introductory along those lines would be a mistake.

Better instead to quote three writers who all figure in this anthology. The first is DH Lawrence, who describes the mechanical horror of artillery fire on page 30: "Not I, not I, but the wind that blows through me! / A fine wind is blowing the new direction of Time."

The second is TS Eliot, one of whose book reviews from the paper is reprinted on page 38: "Time present and time past / Are both perhaps present in time future, / And time future contained in time past."

Finally, Samuel Beckett, whose *Waiting for Godot* is reviewed on page 160: "The sun shone, having no alternative, on the nothing new."

Each of these quotations has some bearing on the architecture of a book such as this. When one reads, in the 1899 chapter, a parliamentary sketch raising the matter of how old-age pensions will be paid for in the future ("Cooking An Uncaught Hare", page 14), Beckett's view seems in the ascendant.

But as Lawrence knew so well, change does take place, and on a scale outstripping individual lives: which is why at the heart of this book are pieces illustrating the seismic social, cultural and technological shifts that have shaped our world. Yet however massive those changes might be, the devil is in the detail: Time's wind is "fine" at the same time as being powerful.

In this millennial moment, that wind sweeps up each one of us, even more than it did at the moment this book begins its journey, at the passing of the last century — although the *Guardian*'s reporter in Manchester in 1899 clearly sensed the weight of that occasion: "As the last minute of the century drew near thousands of men and women thronged into the Square before the great clock of the Town Hall . . . Hanging high above, in the light fog, the clock's yellow face was signalling Time's great news — that another year was far advanced in its last hour, and that the sand of another century ebbed low in the glass. The clock face, with its sweeping minute hand, made a centre for the eyes and thoughts of the multitude" (page 4).

To give the heavier blows of the clock their due, as one must, is to pursue an essentially Marxist view of history. AJP Taylor gives a masterclass in this in his 1950 *Guardian* article on the turn of the half-century (page 129). It is a view in which the acts of great men and great women are the instruments rather than the vehicles of change.

But one must also take account of individuals — of figures such as Winston Churchill, Nelson Mandela and, from another view entirely, Adolf Hitler. The lines from Eliot's *Four Quartets* quoted above were, probably, more concerned with personal destiny than the larger patterns of human (or, as we are increasingly aware, other) types of life. But in both views they seem to have a direct bearing on an enterprise such as this; at least that is how I felt when making the selection. The instinct to trace causes, developments and consequences was almost overwhelming — the basic human urge towards narrative, a deep need to make sense of events.

Events, news stories major and minor, are the backbone of newspapers and of this book too. But 20th-century history didn't just "happen", it was mediated through culture, or cultures — which is why reviews of books, films and music have also been included. And sometimes the culture too made the news, as with *Lady Chatterley's Lover* or a work by another writer who contributes a piece here, Salman Rushdie's *Satanic Verses*.

At other times, the culture is seen working through less evident byways, as witnessed by entertaining curiosities such as "Golf: Its Importance to the Empire" (page 18) or Norman Shrapnel's article on the Milk Bars of the 1950s (page 152). This, incidentally, seems to be the way with history more and more these days, as Church and State and the other *grands récits* give way to the postmodern peepholes of books like *Longitude* or *Cod: A Biography of the Fish that Changed the World*.

Newspapers have always been able to alter their focus in such a way, to open up the narrow byways of history as well as its trunk roads and motorways. A part of the culture, they also mediate it in their own particular way. Whatever else it does, the chosen content of this book demonstrates the *Guardian*'s distinct perspective.

For while *The Guardian Century* is by no means a history of the *Guardian* over the past hundred years, it is obviously informed by that history (not least the part played by writers such as Neville Cardus, Alistair Cooke, Michael Frayn, Jill Tweedie and Nancy Banks-Smith). It is a history we don't often study. Ever concerned with the daily production, newspapers rarely look back, probably quite rightly; but no celebration of a century of news-gathering would be complete without a retrospective look at the news-gatherer itself.

This is doubly appropriate at the moment, for as I write, the paper is mourning Alistair Hetherington, editor from 1956 to 1975. He himself had occasion to write a retrospective when the *Guardian* celebrated its 150th anniversary in 1971. In that article, Hetherington conjured up a powerful picture of his predecessor, the young Manchester radical and cotton merchant who founded the paper in 1821.

"When John Edward Taylor wrote the first prospectus 150 years ago, he was preoccupied with a world recovering from the Napoleonic wars, struggling and suffering under the dark pressures of the Industrial Revolution, and yet trying (or so he hoped) to extend a healthier life and better education to more of its citizens."

Originally a weekly, and then a bi-weekly, the *Manchester Guardian*, as it then was, made rapid progress. By 1842, its circulation of 6,600 made it the largest selling paper outside London. Its readership would have been very much larger, since in those days a single copy might have 25 readers. On its launch the paper cost seven pence an issue, of which a whopping four pence comprised government stamp duty. After the repeal of that punitive and free-speech crushing tax in 1855, the *Manchester Guardian* was able to launch as a daily.

Making a success of the daily proved difficult indeed, and the 1850s and 60s were troublesome years for the *Guardian*. Only with the arrival on the staff of a young man called CP Scott in 1871 did it come into its own again. Within twelve months, aged 26, he was editor and the *Guardian* was once more combining crusading journalism with commercial success, as well as expanding the remit of the paper in terms of news service and into what we would now call "features". Scott is known as an uncompromising, if not stern character, but he was also as full of the innovation, irreverence and originality that have been as much a part of the *Guardian* tradition as have seriousness of purpose and freedom of expression.

As Hetherington points out in his retrospective, although conditions change, the preoccupations of a paper do have some continuity over the years. Those preoccupations are at the centre of one of the greatest statements ever made on the ethics and ideals of the press, in the shape of Scott's 1921 centenary essay on newspaper ideals, which is printed as an Afterword at the end of this book.

Between Scott (who retired in 1929) and Hetherington came the "initialled editors", ET Scott, WP Crozier and AP Wadsworth, and after Hetherington, Peter Preston and the present editor Alan Rusbridger. Each of them added his own ingredient to the Guardian mix, together with riding a series of practical changes:

1. The reorganisation of the paper along symmetrical lines around 1900 and, over the next three decades, the extension of its coverage

2. The replacement of advertisements on the front page with news in 1952

3. The dropping of the name Manchester from the title in 1959, and other typographical changes

4. London printing in 1960, acknowledging the established fact that the bulk of circulation and advertising targets now lay, for better or worse, in the south

5. The weathering of a commercial crisis in 1966, which nearly broke the paper and lead to the laying off of staff

6. Moving to London in 1970, to Gray's Inn Road, and then to the current site in Farringdon Road six years later

7. The introduction of modular design in 1978 (as opposed to run-on vertical columns)

8. A major redesign in 1988, in which David Hillman introduced the sans-serif helvetica font which is at the heart of the *Guardian's* contemporary look. The same year saw the launch of the Saturday magazine

9. The introduction of the G2 tabloid section from 1992

10. The purchase of the *Observer* and related publications from Lonrho for £27 million in 1993

11. Another major redesign in 1999, together with new sections and the launch of Guardian Unlimited, the paper's internet service (on which a more extensive view of *The Guardian Century* is available).

THESE WERE THE staging-posts which made the modern *Guardian*. Its hinterland was the creation of the Scott Trust in 1936, whereby JR Scott (elder son of CP) divested himself of beneficial interest and formed a trust to which all the ordinary shares of The Manchester Guardian and Evening News Ltd were assigned. Any income of the trust must either be given to charity or be applied to furthering the interests of the newspapers. It is the removal of the element of private profit and ties to individuals or shareholders which gives the *Guardian* its unique position in today's cut-throat media world. By sacrificing a personal fortune for himself and his family, JR Scott tried to ensure that the papers would preserve their independence and integrity.

If the immense public benefaction of the Trust is the instrument by which today's *Guardian* became possible, it is the editorial, commercial and production staff which make it happen day to day — the "friendly company" of which CP Scott speaks in his essay. This book, and its larger parent, the *Guardian Century* supplements published weekly with the paper between October 9 and December 11 1999, bear witness to that quotidian but often extraordinary effort over the past 100 years.

In truth, quotidian as a term needs no amelioration for journalists, since the business of a newspaper is the stuff of days, not the wider weave of time. The pages in this book represent just a few of those days. It is indeed tempting to resolve them into wider meanings . . . but instead I refer readers to one last quotation from another writer who contributes to the book, Philip Larkin. His words form the codicil to David McKie's excellent piece on "The Coming of Para-Religion" (page 272) — something of which we may have heard a lot more by the time the next 100 years are out.

What are days for?
Days are where we live.
They come, they wake us,
Time and time over.
They are to be happy in:
Where can we live but days?

Ah, solving that question
Brings the priest and the doctor
In their long coats
Running over the fields.

Contents

Chapter 1 1899 - 1914

Chapter 2 1914 - 1918

Chapter 8   1970 - 1980

Chapter 9   1980 - 1990

Chapter 10   1990 - 1999

1899 | 1914

DOWN TO THE SEA AGAIN

JOHN MASEFIELD

BUT I MUST be leaving Portsmouth, with her sailors and ships and her street posts made of sea-cannon. She is an unchanging town, full of character and charm and jolly people. They have started electric cars, but there is even now a merchant service brig in her little dock. They cannot change such a town, for the nature of her inhabitants cannot change. But I must be leaving Portsmouth. In the grey, silent streets upon which I gaze move certain figures, vague figures in clothes of an unreal blue. They are phantoms of her ancient sailors, ghosts of a press-gang, each beautiful with a special pig-tail. If I do not get away at once, goodness knows —.

OCTOBER 23, 1905

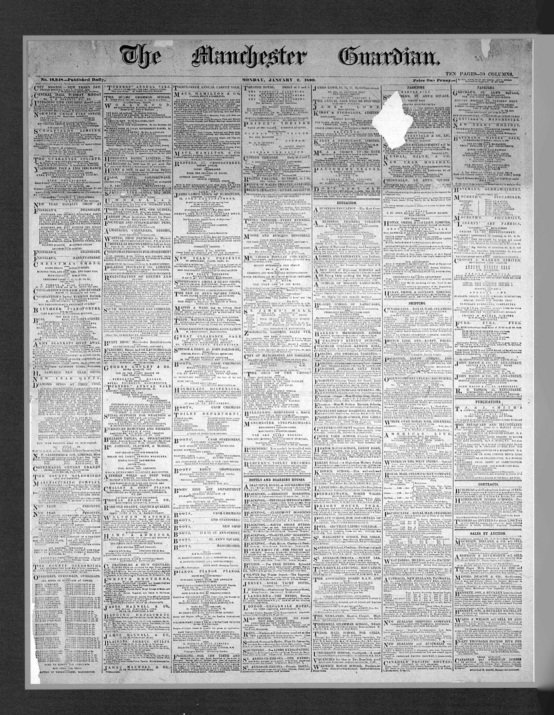

BOUND FOR THE SEAT OF WAR

BY JOHN BLACK ATKINS

WAR WEARS A double face. One face is a mask which has been thrust upon it, and this face is all laughter; the other is the natural face of war, and it is all tears. The two are not seen as alternatives, but always side by side. At Waterloo Station, there it was — the eternal double face of war. Next a bawling, singing, hatless, perspiring, triumphant face, a face straining, clinched, stricken, speechless — a face of unfathomed woe. As the train moved out of the station the long frieze of faces was drawn past one's carriage, the higher faces crushed into the architrave formed by the top of one's carriage window. The first few faces were distinct — sad and glad; but the platform was incredibly long, the train quickened, we said goodbye to a composite picture. At Southampton again the double face of war. It filled the wharves as, the oldest captain said, they had never been filled before, and, surging, craned itself up to the vessel's decks; and the face in the one character urged us on, in the other it beckoned us back.

At last we were off, and then a cry of farewell crackled below the ship and spread; along the lines it went — such a shout as the oldest captain had never heard at Southampton before. And then we on the *Dunottar Castle* glided away till the screen of faces was watered down into the vague solidity of the quay walls.

On the monotony — or what we choose to think the monotony of a modern voyage it were useless to dwell. Really a sea voyage is almost the only means left by which we may easily and suddenly escape from end-of-the-century life; it is a time to be prized and cherished and used in a new and wholly peculiar way; it is a secret door for our convenience and our profit. Yet most of us inexcusably neglect to appreciate it; our intolerance of the days spent at sea becomes continually greater as science makes a modern voyage continually shorter. We reckon time by our meals — it is so

long after breakfast or before dinner — and the daily miracles of the changing latitudes are performed in vain.

On Monday, October 23, we overtook the Aberdeen White Star vessel, the *Nineveh*, south of the Equator.

On Sunday, October 29, the *Australasian*, again of the Aberdeen White Star Line, came in sight. It is strange how different associations breed different practices. Men and women who would not stop in Regent Street if a hansom fell in pieces before them will spend hours watching a speck on the horizon when they are in mid-ocean; will stream up from the saloons and the cabins to see a poor mean little brig shuffling and drifting through the doldrums. But the meeting with the *Australasian* was more important than that; it was the most dramatic encounter at sea that any of us could call to mind, or is likely to experience again. When we sighted her she quickly came near to us. She was coming form the Cape, not going to it, and since she was coming from the Cape, why she must have news — news only three days old. Think of the days we had fed only on speculation; think what it is to be without news of the war for two weeks; remember that we had the brains of the army on board, and then realise the curious mixture of voracity, impatience, excitement and emotion with which we altered our course to come quite near the approaching vessel, burst out our signals from the mast, tumbled down the companions to our cabins for glasses and cameras, returned and — waited. I, for one, will always believe that the *Australasian* slackened almost to dead slow as she approached us; but there is the captain's evidence to the contrary, that she never altered her speed. At all events we came side to side with her at last, and then someone discovered that she had a long black board hung on her ratlines, and on the board there was — was it? — yes, not a doubt of it — writing.

NOVEMBER 20, 1899

THE PASSING OF THE CENTURY

BY FILSON YOUNG

AS THE LAST minute of the century drew near thousands of men and women thronged into the Square before the great clock of the Town Hall. To be one of the crowd was to take part in a purely sentimental function — one of the few occasions upon which the great British public plays formal homage to the influence that plays so great a part in its national life. No spectacle attracted the throng; nothing was about to happen that should entertain their eyes or ears; each unit in the mass must have a private sensation in his own mind which he held in common, although he could not share it, with others. There was no spectacle, it has been said; yet that is hardly true. Hanging high above, in the light fog, the clock's yellow face was signalling Time's great news — that another year was far advanced in its last hour, and that the sand of another century ebbed low in the glass. The clock face, with its sweeping minute hand, made a centre for the eyes and thoughts of the multitude. All such crowds have a pulse; thoughts and sensations and ideas are in the surrounding air, contributed to and drawn upon by all — by the man who holds the bottle to his mouth no less than by him who stands alone with his thoughts, by old fourscore who looks sadly backward upon the years that have fallen away from him, and by the sweethearts who look to the clock to usher in their years of happiness. To share the common thrill of feeling one needed but to leave one's thoughts to themselves, when they would vibrate in true unison to the prevailing note of one's fellows.

Yes, the clock was the thing. A steady stream of thought flowed upwards through the gloom to where the bells were jangling, hammering, beating, chasing echoes abroad over the city; the small noises of the people were obliterated by the metallic clatter and the resultant strife of harmonics and over-tones in the air; Time, who as a rule slips by us almost disregarded, was passing in a pageant of savage music, and dominating for once the expectant crowd. Remember that it was a crowd composed largely of people not much accustomed to meditate on abstractions, that half of them sought in the witching midnight movement an opportunity for, and a stimulus to, conviviality; that a third of them were the poor outcasts of a city who flock to the companionship of a crowd as sea-birds in a storm gather round a lighthouse — remember this, and you may realise the significance of that upward stream of thought. It flowed towards the belfry, where the bells were swinging in the shadow and scaring spiders in their webs and mice in their holes; higher still towards the lighted chamber where the wheels and cogs and weights invented by man to measure out the movements of eternity were clicking, catching, revolving on their solemn business; and out again to where the great minute-hand, now not far from the perpendicular, marched round the lighted dial, two strides to the minute.

The bells ceased ringing some minutes before twelve; and these last minutes were long. They were tasted and examined separately, held close before the eyes, as it were, and magnified; their slow passage suggested an image of Time tottering yearly on the verge of extinction and yearly drinking a youthful elixir. This apparent delay, or rallentando of the hour, was not the least vivid of the night's impressions, and, hallucination though it might be, it was surely of value to poor hurried toilers. Anything that gives foothold even for a moment amid the current of time is a benefit to people who although they are sometimes accused of living only in the present are in reality hardly ever conscious of it. We realise easily the past and the future; the one is kept alive by memory; imagination plays with the other and projects it fearlessly into a space that contains no contradictions; only the present is hard to make real. So for people who pass today in dreams of yesterday and tomorrow a division of years, however arbitrary, cannot but be precious, since it gives them a few moments in which they may come up with Time, make his shadows tangible, and consolidate his triple life.

All this, or the essence of it, was in the air; and what were the people doing who thronged the pavement? Most of them who were not gazing at the clock were disposed in little groups of men and women keeping a kind of rude festival. Small and impotent instruments, such as the mouth-organ, the accordion, and the penny whistle, were urged by their players to adorn with a thin and florid counterpoint the *cantus firmus* of the bells; circles of merry-makers were formed, in which a few couples made shift to dance to the rhythm of a sobbing concertina; but on the whole the crowd was quiet, awed, perhaps, by the domination of the clock and the solemnity of the hour. The bottle, indeed, travelled round convivial circles; pale-faced youths gulped and shuddered over raw and nauseous spirits under a vague impression that a crisis was approaching for which they needed to be strung up; those whom liquid comfort had already overcome sang loud snatches of song that died away suddenly into murmuring soliloquy, while the singers leaned and pondered upon their fellows or failed to avoid the dizzy pavement; but all this added to rather than took away from the portent of the travelling minute-hand. It was pointing, an emblem of the things that go on whether we live or die, to the words written somewhere above the dial: "So teach us to number our days." No one could see the words; some knew they were there, but even the dullest could hardly fail to read their message in the two creeping hands now almost merged in one. An old man remarked that he had seen

Tempus fugit ... the Manchester Town Hall clock tower

twenty years come in and go out on that spot, "and," he added with sorrow, "I suppose they'll come in just the same when I'm gone." He expressed our common amazement that the world should have the heart to outlive us. Yet thousands stood there as surely under sentence of death as prisoners in the condemned cell; admonished by a clock fashioned by dead hands — a clock that probably will proclaim the last hour of every creature who listened to it yesterday; and the strong tower will stand when the clock shall have worn out; and Time will outlast——

But the last minute had fled before the end of these meditations, and the uplifted hands of the clock touched the hour. A deep note swelled and filled the air with mellow thunder; Big Abel was striking twelve. After two or three stokes the atmosphere and the buildings and the telegraph wires had all attuned themselves to the great vibration, and

gave it back to the bell in a clinging echo, so that for about a minute his diapason prevailed over all other sound. The crowd stood for a moment irresolute, as though waiting for some great outward thing to happen and forgetting to look inwards for its sensation. But in a second or two the people broke out into cries that seemed feeble enough beneath the now ear-splitting cannonade of the bells; the bottles, travelling their last round, attained an almost perpendicular elevation; everyone who had an instrument caused it to utter its voice; but the noise of the bells was so great that united song was impossible. A little boy near me who had twice attempted to "raise" a tune and had been beaten down by the jangling bells looked up at the tower with an air of injury, saying "It should play tunes — 'Auld Lang Syne' an' that." But even that great song of fellowship failed to establish itself; instead of singing it, the

more demonstrative people embraced each other, and all gave expression to some kind of good wish. In these exercises some minutes passed, and when people looked again at the clock they found the minute-hand well started on its voyage into the new century. The old scroll was rolled up, then, and the new one opened fair and clean and — uninteresting; a sudden flatness fell upon the crowd, and the square began to empty itself through the adjacent streets. For perhaps half an hour the clatter of bells pursued the throng and mingled with the cries and laughter of cheerful celebrants; for perhaps an hour or two the pavement still echoed to the step of a belated reveller and then, for the little while in which the unresting city takes on the appearance of rest, the square lay vacant under the stars of a new January sky, and the drama of the clock went on in an empty theatre.

JANUARY 1, 1901

THE BATTLE OF SPION KOP

AN ACRE OF MASSACRE

BY JOHN BLACK ATKINS

WERE THOSE ROCKS or men in khaki up there on the side of that kopje? Rocks! No, they move — they are men. They advance. General Hart, with the strongest brigade, was ahead of the others. One inferior height after another was put behind him in the series of kopjes that rise to the sky. And the Boers? They were invisible. Jagged schantzes against the sky showed where a few hundreds were. The rest had become part of the rocks and the brown grass. Soon even our own infantry became invisible from Three Tree Hill — invisible unless you had the true eye for infantry, which can pick out its object, as the fisherman can in a stream, when another eye sees nothing. These are not the days in which a line four deep in men marches up to a similar line, and when both have discharged their weapons point-blank the line that remains the less thin marches through the other. Weapons, we are told today, are too terrible for wars to continue. What an ironical thing is fact! Soon, if the Boers cannot be dislodged by the long-range skirmishing imposed by modern weapons, we may really return to the practices of the terrible old days. If we attack with a sufficient number of men — how many Heaven only knows! — some must get through and be alive at the end of the day. Shall we emulate Grant in the American Civil War and launch a mass of men against a mass of men, and disregard losses when we call the issue of the day a victory? We may come to that. But we have not yet.

I saw one man (in the enjoyment of one of those trifling licences which are permitted on active service) trudging happily to the firing line with a puppy under his arm. The naif act was somehow characteristic, and I scarcely know whether to think it amusing or pathetic. I wonder how the man and the dog spent that day. Did the dog return yapping at the heels of stretcher-bearers?

On our extreme left a headland ran out from the range of hills southward into the plain, and the mounted infantry were opposite the southern face of it. Bastion Hill it had been suitably named. "Go a little way up it. See what sort of place it is and who is there. If it is strongly held, come back; but if it is not, go on, take it, and hold it." That was the sense of the order given to Lord Dundonald. When an officer is told to go on if he can, he finds in most cases that he can: and that is just what Lord Dundonald did that day.

The South African Light Horse were told to go first. They dismounted and drew open like a fan into their line of advance. Now there was one man called Tobin — a sailor — and he sprang at the hill as though it were the familiar rigging of a ship. Up he went hand over hand, up an ascent like the slope of a bell-tent. Everyone who watched held his breath for a man to fall — not from the steepness but from a bullet. Ten minutes before all the others he reached the top. There he stood against the sky and waved his helmet on his rifle. No Boer was there, and the hill in a few minutes was ours. "It was splendid to watch," Lord Tullibardine said the next day. "It was a VC thing, and yet, if you know what I mean, it wasn't."

On the evening of Tuesday, January 23, it was clear that we could get no further with the frontal attack. Sir Charles Warren had all the time had Spion Kop, of which the general direction is north and south, in his eye, as likely to be useful. If we could get on to the southern crest of it we could probably push on to the northern end, and once there we could open a flanking fire on the Boer lines which ran east and west. Spion Kop, properly used, was the key of the position, and the key that would open the door of Ladysmith. Patrols had reported that there were only a few Boers on it. Therefore Sir Charles Warren presented his scheme for capturing it, and it was accepted by Sir Redvers Buller, when it had been all but decided to bring the whole left wing back to Potgieter's. Soon after dusk on Tuesday a party set out to make a night attack on the hill. There were Thorneycroft's Mounted Infantry, the Lancashire Fusiliers, the Lancaster

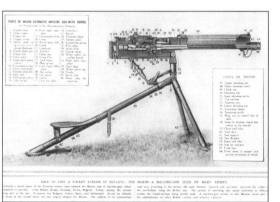

The Maxim-Nordenfelt — one of the deadly new guns

Regiment, two companies of the South Lancashire Regiment, and a company of Engineers. General Woodgate commanded. It was a hand-and-knee march up the southern face — a climb over smooth rock and grass. It was necessarily slow; it is to the great credit of the party that it was steady. The force was three-quarters of the way up before it was discovered. Then a Boer sentry challenged it for the password. "Waterloo!" said an officer. The sentry turned to flee, but fell bayonetted where he turned. Thorneycroft's were on the left, the Lancashire Fusiliers on the right of the front line. "Fire and charge!" came the order. The Fusiliers went forward at the deliberate, conventional trot; Thorneycroft's, with the untrained, admirable enthusiasm of volunteers, rushed forward in a frenzy. Only a picket was behind the sentry, and it vanished. But the crest was not reached till dawn. Colley made scarcely a longer or steeper march up Majuba. When dawn came the party found that it was in the clouds. It could see nothing but the plateau — 400 yards across — on which it stood. Trenches were made, but it was difficult to determine the right place for them. The Boers were invisible; our own troops below were invisible; for three hours the party lived on a fog-bound island in the air. At last the mist lifted. The curtain rose upon the performance of a tragedy. The Boers — need I say, on another ridge of Spion Kop? — began to fire heavily, and our men seemed to have no sufficient protection in the trenches. The space was small; they were crowded together. I will describe the scene as I saw it from below. I shall always have it in my memory — that acre of massacre, that complete shambles, at the top of a rich green gully, with cool granite walls (a way fit to lead to heaven), which reached up the western flank of the mountain. To me it seemed that our men were all in a small square patch; there were brown men and browner trenches, the whole like an over-ripe barley field. As I looked soon after the mist had risen (it was nine o'clock, I think) I saw three shells strike a certain trench within a minute; each struck it full in the face, and the brown dust rose and drifted away with the white smoke. The trench was toothed against the sky like a saw — made, I supposed, of sharp rocks built into a rampart. Another shell struck it, and then — heavens! — the trench rose up and moved forward. The trench was men;

British dead at Spion Kop

the teeth against the sky were men. They ran forward bending their bodies into a curve, as men do when they run under a heavy fire; they looked like a cornfield with a heavy wind sweeping over it from behind. On the left front of the trenches they dropped into some grey rocks where they could fire. It is wonderful to see a man drop quickly for shelter when he has to; his body might be made of paste, and for the first time in his life he can splash down in an amorphous heap behind a rock. Spout after spout of dust bounced up from the brown patch. So it would go on for perhaps half an hour, when the whole patch itself bristled up from the flatness; another lot of men was making for the rocks ahead. They flickered up, fleeted rapidly and silently across the sky, and flickered down into the rocks, without the appearance of either a substantial beginning or end to the movement. The sight was as elusive as a shadow-show.

The Boers had three guns playing like hoses on our men. On the west of the hill they were firing a Maxim-Nordenfelt, in the middle a large Creuset gun, on the east of the hill another Maxim-Nordenfelt. It was a triangular fire. Our men on Spion Kop had no gun. When on earth would the artillery come? Guns were the only thing that could make the hill either tenable or useful. When on earth would they come? No sign of them yet, not even a sign of a mountain battery; and we who watched wriggled in our anxiety. The question now was whether enough men could live through the shelling till the guns came. Men must have felt that they had lived a long life under that fire by the end of the day, and still the guns had not come. From Three Tree Hill the gunners shelled the usual places, as well as the northern ranges of Spion Kop, where the Boer riflemen were supposed to be. Where the Boer guns were we did not know. If only they had offered a fine mark, like our own guns, we should have smashed them in five minutes. The British gunner is proud of the perfect alignment and the regular intervals which his battery has observed under the heaviest fire; the Boer gunner would be sorry to observe any line or any intervals. He will not have a gun in the open; he is not proud, but he is safe. You might say that in this war the object of the Boer gunners is to kill an enemy who cannot see them; that of the heroic British gunners is to be killed by an enemy whom

Boer soldiers await the Battle of Spion Kop

they cannot see. The European notion of field guns is that they should be light enough to be moved about rapidly in battle and not hamper the speed of an army on the march. Now, does it not appear that the Boers will change all that for us? They have dragged heavy long-range guns about with them and put them on the tops of steep hills, and we, of all people, know that they have not hampered the speed of their army. Some dunderhead, perhaps, proposed that such guns should be taken by the army into the field — some fellow who had never read a civilised book on gunnery. But how many fools in history have led the world? Let us make ourselves wise men by adding another to the list.

Reinforcements were ordered to Spion Kop. They were needed. The men on Spion Kop were crying out for them. I could see men running to and fro on the top, ever hunted to a fresh shelter. Some Boer riflemen crept forward, and for a few minutes fifty Boers and British heaved and swayed hand to hand. They drew apart. The shelling did not cease. The hollow rapping of the Maxim-Nordenfelts was a horrid sound; the little shells from them flapped and clacked along the ground in a long straight line like a string of geese. But the reinforcements were coming; already a thin line corkscrewed up the southern slope of Spion Kop. Their bayonets reflected the sun. Mules were in the column with ammunition, screwing themselves upwards, as lithe as monkeys. The Dorsets, Bethune's, the Middlesex, the

Imperial Light Infantry — volunteers destined to receive a scalding baptism — were on the climb. From left to right of the field, too, from west to east, infantry moved. Hildyard's Brigade and the Somersets emerged from behind Three Tree Hill in open order, and moved towards the Boer line on the north and towards the west flank of Spion Kop. The Boers sniped into them. A man was down — a shot rabbit in the grass with his legs moving. The infantry went a little way further north and east, halted and watched Spion Kop the rest of the day. General Woodgate had been hit over the left eye about ten o'clock in the morning; the command came by a natural devolution to Colonel Thorneycroft. And this big, powerful man, certainly the best mark on the hill, moved about fearlessly all day and was untouched. The reinforcements poured up the steep path which bent over suddenly on to the plateau at the top. It was ten steps from shelter to death.

A doctor told me of the scene on Spion Kop on Thursday morning. A great proportion of the wounds had been made by shells; therefore they must not be described. A Boer doctor looked at the dead bodies of men and horses, the litter, the burnt grass where shells had set fire to it — at the whole sad and splendid scene where the finest infantry in the world had suffered. "No!" he said, with double truth, "we Boers would not, could not, suffer like that."

FEBRUARY 27, 1900

WHAT MISS HOBHOUSE SAW

BY EMILY HOBHOUSE

SOME PEOPLE IN town still assert that the camp is a haven of bliss. Well, there are eyes and no eyes. I was at the camp today, and just in one little corner this is the sort of thing I found. A girl of 21 lay dying on a stretcher — the father, a big, gentle Boer, kneeling beside her; while, next tent, his wife was watching a child of six, also dying, and one of about five drooping. Already this couple had lost three children in the hospital, and so would not let these go, though I begged hard to take them out of the hot tent. "We must watch these ourselves," he said.

I sent —— to fetch brandy, and got some down the girl's throat, but for the most part you must stand and look on, helpless to do anything because there is nothing to do anything with. Then a man came up and said, "Sister, come and see my child, sick for three months." It was a dear little chap of four, and nothing left of him but his great brown eyes and

white teeth from which the lips were drawn back, too thin to close. His body was emaciated. The little fellow had craved for fresh milk, but of course there had been none until these last two days, and now the fifty cows only give four buckets. I can't describe what it is to see these children lying about in a state of collapse. It's just exactly like faded flowers thrown away. And one has to stand and look on at such misery and be able to do almost nothing.

JUNE 19, 1901

BUFFALO BILL'S WILD WEST

BY OUR CORRESPONDENT

UPPER CHORLTON ROAD continues to be one of the busiest thoroughfares in Manchester, and after a fortnight of abnormal tramway traffic, constantly crowded footpaths, an army of zealous hawkers and a generous provision of police, the residents have almost forgotten the former secluded character of their district.

The Wild West Show has achieved something very substantial in drawing so many Lancashire people to a suburb which is two miles from the railway stations and which is not easily reached by an almost unlimited number of persons within a limited period — say an hour in the afternoon and an hour in the evening — even with the assistance of the splendid electric car service. For, as always,

everybody wishes to go by car at the same time, and, however long the procession of cars may be, it must have a limit, and that this limit has left the demand unsatisfied has been shown by the fact that the sixpenny buses and waggonettes from the city, not to mention the cabs, have done excellent business . . .

It ought to be acknowledged that notwithstanding the succession of so large and miscellaneous a population as is attached to the Wild West — Red Indians, Mexicans, cowboys, Cossacks, negroes, and so forth — the good character of the neighbourhood has undergone no deterioration. The behaviour of our passing visitors of so many races and from so many lands has been excellent.

APRIL 28, 1903

MR KIPLING'S NEW BOOK

| STALKY AND CO. |

IT IS A common complaint of fathers that they are out of sympathy with their sons, because they have forgotten their own boyhood and they are unable to understand the dangers and the pleasures of school life. To them we can recommend *Stalky and Co.* (Macmillan and Co., 6s.), the book that all the world was reading when Mr Rudyard Kipling was so dangerously ill, as an exact reproduction of certain phases of average school life.

It is true that the school here described is not strictly in all respects a public school. It is obviously a small school, with some of the advantages and some of the defects that pertain to a small school. But the "boy" is described to the life.

A BOY'S SECRET HEART

Mr Kipling has been able to remember, or perhaps it is truer to say that he has never forgotten, what he seemed and what he was as a boy, that incomprehensible and elusive being, as various as a woman, so stubborn and intractable in wrong hands, so malleable in right hands, so penetrating and cunning that he takes his master's measure in a day, so difficult and secretive to those who have not been gifted to see, so transparent and simple to the few who understand him.

Mr Kipling not only understands the boy as a unit, but, what is far rarer and more difficult, he understands him as one of a crowd. And this is the great secret. The boy is the slave of his milieu, of his traditions. He is a ridiculous idealist, with a sense of honour that is magnificent but often totally wrong; he is at once cruel and affectionate, clinging and proud. In his secret heart he responds readily to appeals to elementary principle; he is easily moved by patriotism, by duty to his parents and to his school. But he will never show this, and if you do not understand him you will never guess it.

Mr Kipling remembers it all. It is wonderful how little his picture is marred by his literary craft; how very seldom his boys talk his language instead of their own. He makes us see the masters from the boys' point of view, and we are amazed at the justness of their insight.

DECEMBER 3, 1900

MEMORIAL NOTICE

| MR OSCAR WILDE |

MR OSCAR WILDE died at Paris last Friday, in his forty-fifth year. He was the son of Sir William Wilde, an eminent Irish surgeon, and his mother was a woman of considerable literary ability. In 1874 he entered Magdalen College, Oxford, where he won his two "firsts" in the Classical School, and also the Newdigate Prize for English verse. But the bent of his mind was not academic or scholarly. Even while he was at Oxford he was the most prominent leader in the new "aesthetic" movement, as it was called.

The aestheticism of the day was largely a misreading of the spirit of Hellenism. The modern world is apt to draw a false antithesis between the good and the pleasant, and to make hard and fast distinctions between the moral, intellectual, and physical sides of life.

The Greek knew nothing of this antithesis. Moral and physical excellence were alike "beautiful"; moral and physical defects were alike "ugly". Hence the philosophic basis of the new aesthetic movement, or cult of the beautiful. The beautiful in life was the only thing worth pursuing; ugliness was the thing to be avoided . . .

He had great literary gifts. His romance *The Picture of Dorian Gray*, which embodies his philosophy of aestheticism, is a book of unmistakable tragic power. In 1892 he appeared as a writer of comedies with *Lady Windermere's Fan*. This was followed by *A Woman of No Importance* and *An Ideal Husband*.

His plays were witty, paradoxical and perverse. There was little variety in the characterisation, but the work in other respects was technically admirable. In 1895 Wilde disappeared from public life. Two years later, on his release from prison, he published *The Ballad of Reading Gaol*, perhaps his most powerful piece of writing. Wilde's life is one of the saddest in English literature. His abilities were sufficient to win him an honoured place as a man of letters, but they struggled in vain against his lack of character.

DECEMBER 3, 1900

DEATH OF THE QUEEN

RECEPTION OF THE NEWS BY THE PUBLIC

BY OUR LONDON STAFF

"DEATH OF THE Queen!" was suddenly called in raucous tones as I descended upon Charing Cross, having only a moment or two before heard the dread news. At that very moment even the bell of St Martin's-in-the-Fields tolled forth its knell. Hearing it, a working girl beside me, with grief in her voice, explained, "Then it's true! Dear old lady! Is she really gone?" This was the keynote to the feeling in London tonight, as I discovered it in a walk through some of the principal streets. I am anxious not to put it too high, for exaggeration in such a case is foolish; but everywhere there is the same quiet, subdued, almost unexpressed sentiment. The Strand, as the news flashed along it with incredible speed, became filled with a crowd, a large proportion of which had been hastening to the theatres and found itself stopped at the doors. Not a theatre was open tonight. Not a theatre is likely to open until after the funeral, and the seekers after pleasure had turned back, looking sad and almost anxious. There was a very easily recognised seriousness upon the multitudes that passed westward down the Strand. They had for the moment only one topic of conversation, and if one had passed through London without knowing the news one must have demanded why the

The funeral cortège reaches Windsor Castle

joy had seemed to leave its people. The universal expression of eye and mouth was all the more impressive as it was so obviously involuntary and without conscious demonstration. Through the whole length of the Strand and Fleet Street an observer listening for it did not hear one laugh. All the glee of a crowded thoroughfare had suddenly ceased. Another smaller matter which struck the imagination was the liking of the crowd to read the news over again. Those

who travelled eastwards seemed to go to each newspaper office window, there to peruse again precisely the bulletins which had been already pondered, and they passed on each time in a curiously eloquent silence.

But the most remarkable sight was that to be seen at St Paul's Cathedral. It is very remarkable that this spot — the heart of the City, as it has been called — seems to be attracting its crowds on great occasions as it was wont to do in the old mediaeval and Elizabethan days. Possibly a more imaginative Churchmanship would have put some purpose into the crowd which stood about the great doors of the London Cathedral, but as it happened "Great Paul" boomed his knell from out a mass of architectural darkness, unrelieved save by a very feeble light from a gas lamp at the small northwest portal. Yet on the steps was an almost silent waiting crowd. On the bases of the pillars boys sat in unboyish patience, and the people spread away to Queen Anne's statue, or crossed the road and gathered on the pavement of what is called the Churchyard. There must have been some thousands there when I first passed, and when I returned an hour later they appeared not to have stirred. The faces of such as were on the steps were all turned westward down Ludgate Hill, and at each stroke of the mighty bell they seemed to wake to full intelligence. But why they had come there, why they stood there for hours when there was nothing to see, nothing to learn — only the monotonous and infrequent knell overhead — they would have been greatly puzzled to explain. Some of them did seem to imagine that Dean Gregory would throw wide the doors and chant some penitential psalms. But there was silence save

Mourners throng the streets

from the belfry, and the lingerers looked sadly into vacancy, the young men among them smoking with serious persistency, and the young women, who formed more than half of this strange congregation, standing almost motionless. And there was another crowd — not so large, of course, and more mobile — about the north door of the Cathedral, at which it seemed to be imagined that some news would be pasted, though none came. On the south side only the ordinary passengers went their way, but during the whole evening the crowd seemed to come up Ludgate Hill, to gather aimlessly where no object was to be attained. In Cheapside the bells of Bow rang out, as in Fleet Street the bell of St Dunstan's. Here, the same seriousness, the same self-repression, the same absence of laughter, the same subdued tone of conversation were observable.

There was another centre of interest at the Mansion House. I reached this neighbourhood at the very moment when, as I judge, the restaurants and cafés were sending forth their bevies of waitresses to their homes. They had all

heard the news, but it did not suffice them. They all rushed to buy the papers which were being thrust on them by the hawkers of Lombard Street. They came on towards the Mansion House, reading, but hardly talking at all. It was strange to note their comparative silence. And when they came to the Lord Mayor's residence they were not content with their news. They must see it posted in front of his home. The crowd at this point was again great, but the police had a very easy task in keeping it from too great congestion. Born of the sadness of the occasion, there was an "obligingness" on the part of everybody — a silent submission. Here, too, the exclamations which one heard were all the same kind, nothing violent or exaggerated, not to say hysterical, nothing even loud — "I am sorry!" or "She's been a good Queen!" or, "Ah! she felt the war too much!" or, "Didn't she do splendidly for her soldiers!" or (to take one saying which I overheard), "What a pity she can't know how sorry we are — she'd be glad to know we were so sorry!" — a very true thing.

JANUARY 23, 1901

COOKING AN UNCAUGHT HARE

> AN OLD-AGE PENSION PASTIME

NATURALLY ONE LOOKED for Mr Chamberlain today when the subject of old-age pensions came up for its annual airing. It was practically the same bill as that on which he made his memorable declaration of a year ago: "I do not think that the old-age pension is a dead question, and I think it may not be impossible to find the funds; but that, no doubt, will involve the review of our fiscal system which I have indicated as necessary and desirable at an early date."

That, however, was at the beginning of the "amateur hurricane". Now that Mr Chamberlain is about to invite a vote of confidence in the Government on the ground that they are actually pledged against a too hasty review of our fiscal system, he seems less anxious than before to augment his hurricane with side winds. More than one member this afternoon echoed the plaint of the Hebrew patriarch: "Joseph, my son, where art thou?" The appeal remained unanswered. Mr Chamberlain was elsewhere, together with all or most of his following, and although he must have known that his presence would be welcome he obstinately stayed away.

In his absence the debate languished. As Mr Crooks put it in the one lively

speech of the day, the subject has become a mere pastime for Friday afternoons. "Oh," said Mr Crooks in his uncomfortably plainspoken style, "it will be so thrilling for working people to read tomorrow that we have again been amusing ourselves with a discussion on this topic. And they will say, as their grandfathers said — yes, and as their great-grandfathers said, for we have been talking about it for 130 years — "Why don't they catch their hare before considering how they'll cook it?"

MAY 7, 1904

HILAIRE BELLOC ON THE SHORT STORY

> A MATTER OF ART

THE SHORT STORY is a very modern thing. What brought it into being has not been discovered, though the subject has been discussed at great length. It may or may not last. Another confused, eager, and creative time, the Renaissance, produced the essay and the essay (though perhaps it is dying today) has had a good three hundred years' run for its money. Perhaps, in spite of prophecies, the short story will survive.

It is in the very essence of a good short story that its metaphors should be clean and sharp, doing a lot of work in a very little space. There is another element. It is the trick of saying a thing once and no more. In most literary work such terseness is an affectation. In much — in lyrics, for instance — it is a vice. But in the short story it is a necessity, and one which a very great many writers forget.

But there is something else. The short story demands poignancy, and there is a great temptation to take short cuts to poignancy — to bring in violent emotions which, precisely because they are violent, are not "matter of art". When men are jaded in their emotions they demand things monstrous to arouse them. Perhaps this demand has created the modern supply of the monstrous in letters, but also largely the facility which is thus afforded to the writer of producing an effect. I repeat, it is not "matter of art". Violent dread, violent cruelty, violent lust — all these things are outside the drama within which humanity is permitted to draw. There is no power of development about them; no recurrent fruitfulness, which in letters as in agriculture, follows upon wisdom and restraint. If I may draw a metaphor from my little farm, they "pull the land". They lead to nothing. You soon reach the end of them, and beyond there is a blank. But you never reach an end of true tragedy, of sublime awe, of pain that is sacrificial and majestic; such "matter of art" is capable of an indefinite extension. There is an endless competition in it between the great masters of the pen.

JUNE 14, 1905

FACTORY WORKERS AND MODERN DRESS

BY ONE OF THEM

WAS IT NOT Douglas Jerrold who said that Eve ate the apple on purpose to dress? At any rate in the matter of outward adornment factory workers never willingly take a back seat. They are no believers in the dictum that "beauty unadorned is adorned the most". "Better be out of the world than out of the fashion" is their motto. For the past two seasons factory workers have trailed their skirts more or less gracefully in the dust of summer and the slush of winter, entirely indifferent to Ruskin's remark that he had lost faith in women since they had taken to be street scavengers. Now that low-necked bodices are considered the thing, they are to be seen at every turn, whether the elements be seasonable or not, and regardless of whether sore throat, bronchitis, or pneumonia be contracted.

Factory workers delight in sudden changes. One year they wear such high, stiff collars to their bodices as almost to threaten suffocation; the next year no collar at all. One year the hats are severely plain in shape, very little trimming, scarcely any brim, and small in size; the very next season the shapes are the most fantastic imaginable. In size they may be near akin to car wheels, and as for trimming — why, they look like walking flower gardens, while the brims flip-flop up and down with every movement of the head. During the past summer lace medallions were much in vogue on the sleeves of dresses, and sometimes they were worn so large that I have known them to be mistaken for the badges of hospital nurses. During the reign of Edward IV, sleeves got to such an enormous width and length that it is recorded of the King that he was driven to the expedient of tying his behind his back to avoid falling over them. At present sleeves are not worn quite so long or so wide, but they are certainly showing a decided tendency in that direction. At any rate they are so wide and fussy that one has the greatest difficult in keeping them out of the way when at meals.

Fashion also reigns in the dressing of the hair. Some years ago a craze for short hair set in, and most factory workers wore their hair cropped like boys. Then fringes appeared, and fringes have remained more or less in fashion up to the present time. Sometimes the hair is parted down the middle and combed smoothly on each side in Quaker-like simplicity, and sometimes it is worn in curls and waves all over the head, suggesting by its appearance that the wearers have been dragged backwards through a quickset hedge. Just now the fashion is to puff it out at the sides and on the top, in imitation of our great-great-grandmothers. Colours, again, have their vogue among the factory workers. At one period greens are all the rage, and they may range from the lightest of pea-greens to the deepest emerald. Not very long ago a peculiar shade of green was much in fashion which often made the wearers look as though they suffered from chronic liver complaint, but it "caught on" all the same. A year or two ago nothing but Coronation red could be seen on every side, and this was worn in spite of numerous complexions that did not match. In recent years heliotrope has been a favourite colour in factory circles, and this ran up the scale from a delicate mauve to what our grandmothers used to call puce. Jewellery, too, has come in again, and factory workers wear rings, bracelets, bangles, brooches, watches and chains, lockets and earrings. Years and years ago, when I was working in the spinning-room, factory workers used to consider themselves "dressed up" in the evenings and on Saturday afternoons if they cleaned their clogs and put a fresh shawl over head and shoulders. But at the present day, every evening in the week as well as Saturday and Sundays, they may be seen parading the streets dressed in the latest fashion. Of course even now in some benighted villages factory workers may occasionally be seen wearing clogs and smart blouses, but in towns no self-respecting factory worker would dream of lowering her dignity by such a display of ignorance of the becoming.

A TRADE IN DREAMS

It is interesting and also amusing to contrast the dress of factory workers as they trudge to and from their daily toil and their attire when "got up" for occasions — regardless of cost. See them setting out cheerfully to their work in the early morning hours. Strong iron-bound clogs on the feet, harden mill-skirts to protect the dress, and warm shawls over the heads and shoulders. Look at the same girls on Saturdays and Sundays, and you would fail to recognise them. Now, smart tailor-made costumes and dainty blouses have taken the place of mill-skirts, hats which are known in the trade as "dreams" and "creations" are in place of woollen shawls, and French kid boots are worn instead of clogs. Indeed, when factory workers are on the warpath, arrayed in all the glory of modern finery, you cannot tell from outward appearances whether they are factory workers or members of some severely respectable middle-class family.

The question may naturally be asked: have not factory workers as much right to spend money on dress as Lady Esmeralda Vere de Vere? Of course they have, always providing that they earn the money honestly and pay for what they get. James Russell Lowell somewhere says that "human nature has a much greater genius for gameness than it has for originality." That being the case, it causes no surprise to find that factory workers love pretty things just as do the women who occupy higher social planes, and they experience the same craving to gratify the instinct.

FEBRUARY 21, 1905

THE REVOLT IN ODESSA

WHY THE MUTINY COLLAPSED

BY OUR SPECIAL CORRESPONDENT

ON FRIDAY THE squadron appeared under Admiral Krieger. And those who saw its approach and its discomfiture will never forget the sight. As the five battleships steamed up slowly over the blue sunlit waters the flagship signalled to the *Potemkin*.

"Madmen, you have mutinied and become traitors to your Tsar and your fatherland. Surrender!"

The *Potemkin*, still anchored off Odessa, replied,

"We have no Tsar, and we understand the word fatherland in a different sense. We will not surrender!"

And the flags on Admiral Krieger's ship spelled out,

"If you will not surrender you must fight."

"We are ready to fight," replied the *Potemkin*, "and we are waiting for you to come."

"Oh, mad *Potemkin*," signalled the flagship, "we shall not fight you near the town, for peaceful inhabitants would suffer. Come out to sea!"

"I will come out," said the *Potemkin*, and immediately steamed out to meet the squadron. The squadron came on, and when well within range prepared to fire. The *Potemkin* directed her guns on her opponents, but, to the amazement of all spectators, not a shot was fired, and the squadron steamed away to a safe distance. Then Admiral Krieger sent destroyers towards the *Potemkin*, but after steaming half the distance they retired in obedience to signals made, not by the flagship, but by the *Potemkin*. And in the end the whole squadron turned to the south and steamed off ignominiously to Sevastopol, their task unaccomplished. The *Georgiy Pobyedonosets*, the last battleship in the retreating line, began signalling to the *Potemkin*, and, slowing down until she was well in the rear, suddenly turned about, joined the *Potemkin*, and steamed back with her to Odessa. There was only one conclusion to be drawn from all these remarkable manoeuvres. The whole

Paying respects . . . mourning a mutineer

squadron had caught the infection of mutiny, and the men had refused to fire. And this was to those on land the source at once of hope and of fear.

On Saturday the two battleships lay off Odessa until the evening. During the day, with a fine coolness, the *Potemkin*'s crew sent ashore two of their number to ask the commandant for medicine and provisions. The men marched resolutely up from the port, passing soldiers and officers without saluting or showing any sign of respect, and the officers, furious at this breach of discipline, could but let them pass and grind their teeth in helpless rage. They made their way into the room of the commandant's aide-de-camp, and having communicated their errand and received from the irate officer a forced promise that everything would be sent, they returned quietly to the ship.

In the evening the *Georgiy Pobyedonosets* proved unfaithful, and cautiously steaming around until a wharf lay between herself and the *Potemkin*, and she was thus safe from the *Potemkin*'s torpedoes, she began negotiating with the authorities ashore. The authorities were not too ready to believe in the crew's willingness to surrender, and it was only on the following day that General Karangazoff, who seems to have been braver than the rest, ventured to board the *Georgiy* and arrange the terms of surrender. The *Potemkin*, perhaps in sorrow or in anger at the desertion of her comrade, left Odessa on Sunday, taking with her her destroyer, the *Ismailia*. On Sunday evening the Prefect of Odessa issued a notice declaring that the danger was over, and that residents might resume their normal occupations. And with the publication of the notice this most dramatic episode in the history of Odessa may be said to have come to an end.

AUGUST 8, 1905

The mutineers aboard the *Potemkin*. Matuchenko, leader of the mutiny, is in the white shirt

GOLF

ITS IMPORTANCE IN THE EMPIRE

BY A SPORTSMAN

THE TYPE OF the hunter is one, the type of the footballer is another, but the type of the golfer, candidly, does not exist. To take the type perhaps most obviously marked, one can distinguish almost at the first glance the man who hunts, for hunting appeals to one particular kind. Again, the young man who plays football is easily distinguishable from his less fully blooded fellow. Each of these two sports has its own clearly defined constituency. That they may both attract the same men in no degree weakens the fact. But with golf it is different. Here is a sport which is confined to no particular type; it is singularly catholic. In proof of this it would seem sufficient to refer to the continuous stream of photographs, likenesses of all sorts and conditions of men, which flows week by week in the pages of a golfing contemporary.

such a man that success of a kind comes, and he knows it. It is patent to you at the outset. The studied care with which the grip and stance are taken, the earnest attention to all the attitudes of swing and finish in the preliminary trials on the tee are convincing. It is the same throughout his round. Most strokes are corrected in subsequent pantomime. He talks but little, and then only about getting his left shoulder well down, his left arm straight out, and the discipline of the eye. Any approach to the social amenities or suggestion of wider topics is ignored. He simply does not hear you. You are asked to play two more and are set down as unaccountably preoccupied or irresolute. In a bunker he is grim, and there is no doubt as to the firmness of his grip. On the green he is a study of emphatic, patient concentration. His attitude to his caddy is that of a field marshal to a subaltern on a

Yet even in golf by consistency in habit and by a more or less ordinary conformity in action men group themselves into classes. The division is in no way affected by their play or based on their handicap. Golf is an attitude which many men assume.

There is one type of golfer who represents too large a class to suggest personalities but is not without his share of human interest. Golf, like everything else, is to him a serious business. For whatever ostensible reason he has "taken it up", whether it be for the sake of exercise, or status or because his friends play, he is determined to make it a success. He is as ambitious and persevering as George Eliot's Tom Tulliver, with a rather less sense of humour. Nothing can seduce him, nothing — not even the hopeless impotence of his novitiate — can turn him from his purpose. It is to

field-day; to his opponent (or rather to his partner, for there is no sufficient personal interest in him to suggest opposition) passive toleration, with a suspicion of the schoolmaster. In the clubhouse, where we might expect him to cast off this stern exterior, he is exactly the same. A little conversation, strictly to the point, but, like his meals, in the nature of a concession. Over his tea he silently studies Badminton or the attitudes in Mr Hutchinson's *Golf and Golfers*. He seldom smokes there, and then always with his hand on his pipe. He may miss much, but he has his certain reward. He is the admired model of purposeful, persevering industry, and it is some compensation for the lack of the more social qualities to reflect that it is to such men that we owe our Imperial greatness.

OCTOBER 31, 1899

THE BRITISH EMPIRE

A BLUE-BOOK was issued last night dealing with the census of the British Empire taken in 1901. The results of the census are summarised in a long report by the Registrar General's Department and the President of the Local Government Board. From this it appears that at the time of the census of 1861 the Empire compromised in round numbers eight and a half millions of square miles. In the next two decennia no important territorial additions took place, but between 1881 and 1891 the extensions in the East Indies and in our Indian dependency and the great annexations of territory in West, South, East, and Central Africa added about two millions of square miles. Since 1891 further expansions have occurred, principally in Africa and in Asia, raising the total as nearly as can be ascertained to 11,908,378 square miles. Thus, in the short space of forty years, the aggregate area of the British colonies, dependencies, and protectorates has increased by about 40 per cent, and now amounts to more than one-fifth of the land surface of the globe. Of this huge territory somewhat more than four millions of square miles are situated in North, Central, and South America, three millions in Australasia, two and a half millions in Africa, and nearly two millions in the Indian Empire and other parts of Asia, while the portion that lies in Europe constitutes a very inconsiderable fraction of the whole, amounting to only 125,095 square miles, of which 121,039 constitute the area of the United Kingdom.

MARCH 9, 1906

RISING IN NIGERIA

A REUTER'S MESSAGE of yesterday's date from Lagos, says: "Two companies of troops, with three hundred carriers, are proceeding to Northern Nigeria to assist in quelling an outbreak at Sokoto, where a company of mounted men and five officers have been killed by fanatics."

FEBRUARY 21, 1906

CAVALRY CHARGE THE MOB

RIOTING BROKE OUT afresh tonight in Belfast and as a result of the extraordinary scenes which occurred, the military were hastily mobilised and marched to the affected locality, which lies between the Grosvenor and Falls Roads — a district mainly occupied by Nationalists. How the trouble arose cannot be ascertained, but several quarrels took place in the course of the afternoon. Towards evening the rows became general and the police found it necessary to interfere. Their interference was the signal for some wild scenes, and repeated baton charges were necessary to restrain the infuriated mob, which numbered several thousand. The rowdies resorted to the throwing of bricks and stones. Windows were smashed and a score of constables were struck. Seven of the injured men were removed to the infirmary.

Towards night, fearing a panic, the authorities summoned the military, and in a short time the Dragoon Guards dashed at a gallop amongst the rioters, followed at the double by detachments of the Essex and Cameron Highlanders. The presence of the military quelled the disturbance, but at a late hour they still formed a cordon round the disturbed area. The scene has not been paralleled since the famous riots of 1886, and but for the arrival of the military this portion of the city would have fallen a prey to the infuriated mob.

AUGUST 12, 1907

A TERRIBLE SEA COOK

TALE FROM THE SOUTH SEAS

MAILS FROM VANCOUVER received at Queenstown last night brought a stirring tale of mutiny and murder on board a South Sea schooner. It appears that an English lad, one of the crew, was in prison at Suva, Fiji, together with the cook of the vessel, a Belgian, charged with the murder of the captain and mate and with piracy. The English lad's story was that when the vessel was two days out from Callao the cook came on deck with a chopper in his hand and attacked the captain and the mate. After dodging him around the deck for some time they were forced to climb into the rigging to save their lives. The cook shouted to them to come down, and as they would not he brought a gun from the cabin and threatened to shoot them if they did not jump into the sea. They begged hard for their lives, but the cook was obdurate, and he had levelled the gun to fire when both men jumped overboard. They must have been drowned.

OCTOBER 29, 1908

WHIRLWIND AT MARPLE

ABOUT EIGHT O'CLOCK last night (writes a correspondent) a sudden whirlwind caused great alarm in Marple. Slates were torn off the roofs and windows rattled, and pedestrians ran to the shelter of walls to keep on their feet. The whirlwind was accompanied by a loud hissing noise, and people ran out of their homes in alarm. The commotion soon, however, passed, but in the east the sky was frequently for a time lit by broad sheets of lightning.

OCTOBER 29, 1908

A BABY SMOKER

A CHILD OF three years and three-quarters, who is reported to be suffering from "smoker's heart" and whose case is to be investigated by the Oxfordshire Education Committee, is said to have been supplied with ten cigarettes a day and to have been exhibited at local shows. The story has not yet been proved.

OCTOBER 29, 1908

AIRSHIP FEAT: THE CHANNEL CROSSED

FRANCE TO ENGLAND IN HALF AN HOUR

THE FEAT OF flying across the English Channel in a heavier-than-air machine — a thing which had never before been done — was accomplished yesterday morning by M. Louis Bleriot, in a monoplane of his own construction. It was done, moreover, in the short period of 33

minutes, the start being made at 4.35 a.m. and the descent at 5.08 a.m. The distance traversed was 26 miles or more, the bee-line distance being 22 miles, whilst parallel run along the coast from St Margaret's to Dover, would be four to five miles.

It was nearly half-past four yesterday morning when the news reached Dover that M. Bleriot contemplated making the flight, and a few minutes later came a wireless message stating that he was actually on his way across the French coast, having ascended at Baraques, a village two miles to the west of Calais. The monoplane travelled with great rapidity, and its motor made such a din that it was heard when it must have been six or seven miles from Dover, and nothing could be seen there. Dover had intended making a suitable demonstration when the Channel was first crossed on a flying machine, but as events turned out there was no time to do anything whatever. M. Bleriot's great bird-like machine was first sighted over the Channel to the eastward of Dover, heading for St Margaret's Bay, a little resort about five miles along the cliffs between Dover and Deal. When off St Margaret's it suddenly came round with a fine sweep to the westward, still at a high rate of speed. Strange as it may seem, the monoplane, now that it was heading westward, was travelling against a fresh south-west twenty-mile-an-hour breeze, but this appeared to cause no diminution in the surprising rate of travel.

JULY 26, 1909

STRAUSS'S "SALOME"

STRAUSS'S OPERA "SALOME", which the English journalists were privileged to see in Dresden, impressed them more than it did their German colleagues. Curiously enough, the Germans were cold and critical, while the Englishmen fell completely under the spell. Certainly the opera owes little of its fascination to the "book". Wilde's play, on which it is founded, is a singularly frigid piece of work, for all its violence of language. The passion of Salome for John is cold and mechanical; its very perversity becomes dull and platitudinous; her passionate declarations of love have no dramatic force, but are comparable rather in their effect to some lurid decorative frieze in a dark and gloomy chamber. Everything else is abstract, mechanical, symmetrically perverse. The play could thrill no one, but the opera is a succession of "thrills". The grinning skeletons start into life, and we get the impression that we are witnessing the play of human passion. It is an amazing transformation.

JUNE 17, 1907

NEAR EAST CRISIS ENDS

THE DEFINITIVE STAGE of the Austro-Servian crisis was reached yesterday; when, in consideration of the acceptance by the British Foreign Office of the Austrian amendments of the formula which the Powers are to propose to Servia, the Austro-Hungarian Government, "appreciating the sentiments of conciliation of which Great Britain has given proof," decided not to insist on demanding from the Powers recognition of the annexation of Bosnia-Herzegovina before a settlement has been reached between Austria-Hungary and Servia. Today the formula as amended by Austria will be communicated by the representatives of the Powers to the Belgrade Government, which has already intimated its acquiescence beforehand, and has, in fact, begun to disarm. Friendly negotiations will follow between Austria-Hungary and Servia, and as soon as an agreement has been come to the Powers will spontaneously give their adhesion to the annexation of Bosnia-Herzegovina as an accomplished fact.

MARCH 29, 1909

The light that flees ... an artist's impression of Halley's comet

HALLEY'S COMET

BY OUR MANCHESTER STAFF

LAST NIGHT THE long-looked-for comet was visible at last to us in the north. In Manchester itself the haze which the smoke-stacks of industry gather over the city hid it from view, but out in the country parts of Lancashire and Cheshire the sky was beautiful and clear, and the brilliance of a moon reaching its full was not enough to blot it from sight. From the rising of the stars it hung there (so those who saw it tell us), just clear of the mists on the fields, pallid and strangely blurred beside the shining definiteness of Castor and Pollux to the right of it and the great constellation of Leo sprawling over its head. Its unfamiliarity made it easy for the eye to light upon it, but it was very dim and distant, and there was nothing but a faint luminosity about the edge to suggest to the naked eye the tail through which our planet had gone swimming in the past week. But because its fires glow pale and faint to us here we are not to think that two thousand years (so far we can trace back its appearances in history) have burnt it out. In America and other parts of the globe it has shone with all its former brilliance, accompanied by the same strange rout of terrestrial ecstasy and panic as it had in days gone by. When the time comes no doubt each country will fit its appearance to their special catastrophes, and in history books centuries after this Frenchmen will read that its coming was heralded by the flooding of their capital, and Englishmen will say that it killed a king. And last night returning Whit-week travellers peered at it from railway carriage windows and joked about the length of its tail.

MAY 24, 1910

THE CRUELTY OF THE STAG HUNT

UNIVERSITY SADISTS

UNFORTUNATELY (THOUGH THERE is still a chance of the matter being reopened before the High Court) the difficulty of a legal definition of "captivity" prevented the shocking cruelty of the Cambridge Stag Hunt being properly brought home to its perpetrators by the local magistrates last Saturday. The case was notable because of the readiness

Unsporting behavoiur . . . hunters pursue their prey

with which the Bench decided that when hunting-crops and clothes-poles were being used to slash and prod a stag in a small enclosed yard the "hunt" was still going on, and by the apparent refusal of the defendant to recognise any cruelty in his action at all. Some public contrition for what on the best possible construction was thoughtless cruelty might have been expected; instead, the reiterated declaration that the animal was "sulky" and would not allow itself to be hunted with sufficient goodwill was all that this "sporting" member of the University cared to say in explanation. This shocking case, coming after an equally disgraceful one at Surbiton some months ago, should rouse public opinion to put down the hunting of carted stags altogether.

SEPTEMBER 8, 1909

MYSTERIOUS LIGHTS IN THE SKY

REPORTED VISITS OF GERMAN AIRSHIPS

DURING THE PAST week scores of persons in various parts of England have convinced themselves that they have seen an airship in the night sky. Most of the reports agree that two bright lights appeared close together, hovered in the air for a time, and then rapidly disappeared. Some of the observers add that they heard the droning of an engine. The reports come from several places on the east coast and also Portsmouth. Based on these facts suggestions are now being made in many quarters and positive assertions in others that German airships have travelled each night over England.

For many reasons such a conclusion should be regarded with grave suspicion. First there is no satisfactory evidence that an airship has been seen. Four years ago several English newspapers spent many days working up an airship scare which in the end feebly frittered out. At that time the evidence was as good as the evidence advanced today.

No doubt the observers who report the lights act in good faith, but even an expert would find considerable difficulty in making sure of the presence of a dirigible at night. And the observers have not been experts. Moreover, a vessel paying a secret and unwelcome visit to England would have every reason for hiding her lights, which she could easily do. An interesting fact bearing on this point is that the lights have usually been seen in the western sky about the time when the planet Venus, now very bright, is sinking towards that horizon.

FEBRUARY 11, 1913

THE ATMOSPHERE OF MARS

IT IS ANNOUNCED that observations made by Professor Percival Lowell indicate the presence of oxygen in the atmosphere of Mars. Following statements made a day or two ago that indubitable evidence has been obtained of the presence of aqueous vapour around the planet, Professor Lowell's latest discovery has aroused renewed interest in his theory that life as it is known upon earth is possible in Mars.

FEBRUARY 11, 1913

THE DERBY AND THE SUFFRAGETTE

DEATH OF MISS DAVISON

"THEY HAD JUST got round the Corner, and all had passed but the King's horse, when a woman squeezed through the railings and ran out onto the course. She made straight for Anmer, and made a sort of leap for the reins. I think she got hold of them, but it was impossible to say. Anyway the horse knocked her over, and then they all came down in a bunch. They were all rolling together on the ground. The jockey fell with the horse, and struck the ground with one foot in the stirrup, but he rolled free. Those fellows know how to tumble. The horse fell on the woman and kicked out furiously, and it was sickening to see his hoofs strike her repeatedly. It all happened in a flash. Before we had time to realise it was over. The horse struggled to its feet — I don't think it was hurt — but the jockey and the woman lay on the ground.

FLAG TIED ROUND HER BODY

The ambulance men came running up, put them on stretchers, and carried them away. Most of the other jockeys saw nothing of it. They were far ahead. It was a terrible thing."

This was an account given to me (writes a representative of the *Manchester Guardian*) by a man who was standing behind the rails quite near to the place where the woman rushed out.

The jockey, said one man, "flew from the horse's back like a stone from a sling," and it was doubtless only owing to his jockey's skill in knowing just how to fall that he was not far more seriously injured.

The woman was far more seriously hurt, and the first report that spread about the course was that she was killed. She turned out to be one of the best known of the militant suffragists, Miss Emily Wilding Davison. It is said that underneath her jacket was found a suffragette flag tied round her body. A house surgeon at the Epsom Cottage Hospital a couple of hours after the accident reported that she was suffering from severe concussion of the brain. "She has lain unconscious since the time of her admission," he said, "and it is impossible to say for a few hours whether her life will be saved."

JUNE 14, 1914

Emily Wilding Davison, the dead suffragette

THE SIEGE OF SIDNEY STREET

DESPERADOS PERISH IN BURNING BUILDING

BY OUR CORRESPONDENT

A RAID MADE by the London police early yesterday morning on a house in Stepney — 100, Sidney Street — in which two of the gang that murdered the three police officers in Houndsditch last month were believed to be hiding, developed into a pitched battle or siege. At the outset the police were received with pistol shots, and they summoned reinforcements. For several hours the police and a party of Scots Guards poured a heavy fire upon the windows of the desperadoes' refuge. The men within fired back with revolvers. Altogether one police officer was seriously wounded and several other persons, including some spectators, were slightly wounded. Soon after one o'clock the house was seen to be in flames, having been set on fire either by the fusillade or by the desperadoes themselves. The building was gutted. In the ruins were found the remains of two men, one of whom is believed to be "Fritz" and the other another member of the gang.

The police engaged were reinforced till they reached the number of at least fifteen hundred. The majority of these were employed in keeping well away from the firing the vast crowd which gathered in the neighbourhood, and which at one o'clock was estimated to number two or three hundred thousand. Mr Churchill, the Home Secretary, was on the spot for some hours.

While exploring the ruins of the burnt house, several firemen were injured by a fall of wreckage.

IN THE FIRING LINE

It was nearly noon when I pierced the police barrier at the end of one of the dingy little streets leading into Sidney Street. The little street was almost empty. Some women were hanging out of the open upper windows listening with dull faces to the sound of firing and looking towards it. As I went along there was a sharp cracking of revolver shots. At the top of the street, where it runs into Sidney Street, there were a knot of policemen and a few loungers. I went past them and was at once called back. "A man was shot there this morning," one said, and this was sufficiently startling, although the truth, as I learned afterwards, was that a journalist's walking-stick had been broken by a bullet.

Not a soul was to be seen along Sidney Street. At all the openings was an impassive line of police, and behind them a glimpse of scared faces. Nor was there at first anything to show where the duel was going on. Looking down the line of buildings I saw the tall, newish block of brick houses

with the surgery at the corner, and next to the surgery the windows of the assassins' fortress. As I watched there was a report, and a puff of smoke blew away from the first floor window, and then at once came a furious volley from the other side of the street. The duel was in full swing, and the policemen round me heard it and grinned — "That's a pretty one," they said.

THE SCENE FROM ABOVE

Just at the corner is the Rising Sun public house, its Sidney Street side about 40 yards away from the firing. I made my way through its tumultuous bar, where men were excitedly drinking, and out upon the roof, and there I found a score or so of pressmen looking down into that pit of death. This was a post of some danger, and if the murderers had cared to risk exposure they could have easily sent bullets amongst us. Bullets had been flying about the street all the morning, ricocheting off from the walls in a highly unpleasant manner.

Looking down obliquely through the chimney pots I could all but see into the ground-floor room of the murderers' house. The soldiers could not be seen; they were, we knew, lying flat in the shelter of the opposite windows pouring their lead into the house. There was dead silence but for the reports; everybody watched and waited leisurely. Away on the roof of a brewery at the other end of the street there was another small crowd, and it was a curious thing to see in the upstairs windows along the street itself men and women sitting with their children on their knees. With the whole area spread out below like a map one could see that the block of buildings where the murderers were is an island, and at the end of every opening there was the same police barrier and a grey wedge of people stretching away behind it. The stage was clear, and of the actors nothing could be seen.

THE HOME SECRETARY

The firing came in spurts. The murderers would shoot first from the ground floor, then from the window above, the shot sometimes followed by a tinkle of falling glass. Then there would be a barking of rifles in reply. Then again silence for minutes. Immediately below us in the street lay scattered the dirty newspaper boards on which the Guards had lain to fire earlier in the day.

At the further end of the block from us a group of officers sheltered. Now and then we saw someone in a tall hat and

Police take cover as Mr Churchill looks on

heavy coat come daringly out and take a look at the house. This was Mr Winston Churchill. "He's a cool one," someone said. But this was nothing to the risk he ran a little later on in the day. He seemed to be commanding all the operations.

THE BURNING OF THE TRAP

Close on one o'clock an especially sharp fusillade rattled like a growl of exasperation. In a few minutes some sharp-eyed watcher on our roof saw a little feather of smoke curling out of the window below the point of attack. We thought at first it was gun smoke, and then with a thrill we saw that the house was on fire. The smoke grew, and soon it was rolling thick out of the windows. "Now they are done for," we said, "this is the beginning of the end." But the soldiers had no mercy. They showered their lead into the smoke.

It was a strange sensation to be standing there and watching the fire eat up the house. A youth of the neighbourhood chuckled in unholy exultation. "They'll be fried like rats in an oven," he said. It was awful, but there was in that moment no thought of pity for the wretches about to give up their lives between the rifle muzzles and the flame. Slowly, very slowly the fire increased. Once we thought the murderers had put it out, but then it went with a rush, and soon the whole of the house above the ground floor was hidden in smoke. Through the broken windows at the bottom the air was fanning the fire. Suddenly a long tongue of flame

licked out from the second storey window, and then we knew, indeed, that all was up.

SHOTS BENEATH THE FLAMES

The men evidently had been driven down to the ground floor, for while the fire possessed all the rest of the house they kept up their smokeless volleys from below. They seemed terrible, inhuman. But we were all eyes for the flames that now burst out like a rosy fountain from both the upper windows, and wrapped themselves over the high-pitched roof. The alarm ran round that there would be an explosion. It was said that there would be a store of dynamite, and we trembled for the soldiers a few feet away. But there was no explosion, and we had to wait an intolerable hour until the fire had spread down into the bottom room. Shortly after two the ceiling evidently fell in, and now from pavement to roof the house was one furnace.

Before this we had heard the clanging of fire engine bells from somewhere beyond the crowd, and soon men in shining helmets were gathered at the corners of the streets waiting with the hose. That was perhaps the strangest incident of all — London firemen standing idle while a house burned itself out under their eyes.

Once in the thick smoke at an upper window something black was seen to stir, and we looked to see a man leap out. But it was only a blackened curtain. We watched the front door as a terrier watches a rat hole, half expecting to see some monstrous fellow rush out to die in the street under the rifles. None of these things happened. The fire pursued its orderly way, neatly avoiding the houses to either side. The crowd in the streets now found voice and seemed to be cheering.

A CAUTIOUS APPROACH

The next thing that happened was curious. From the group round Mr Winston Churchill a little man in dark clothes was seen stealing along the side of the building. He stuck close to the wall, a revolver in his hand. He was a detective officer, and he was the first man to approach the blazing house. When he got to the door he put out his arm and pushed it gingerly. Then he quickly retreated. Other men with revolvers were seen to creep round from the other side and go to the side exit from the buildings. They were there ready to meet a possible rushing out of the murderers.

Another interval, and then suddenly all the watchers seemed to take courage. We saw the Guards who had been firing into the house all day come out on the pavement and stand in a line pointing their rifles at the house. Then they moved the fire engine a bit nearer, and half a dozen firemen brought up a tall red ladder and placed it against the top window. Just about this time the roof fell in, and the street was strewn with burning timbers. A plucky fireman walked up to the gaping ground floor window and turned a stream of water into it. We half expected to see him drop, but as he did not everybody at last felt that there was no more danger, and people began to move up opposite the house. But Mr Churchill came near before anyone felt sure whether the murderers were dead or alive.

NOTHING TO AIM AT

Firemen broke down the door and went in, but it was too hot to stay in long. Others mounted the ladder and played into the bedrooms. They soon got the fire down, and all that was left to do was to explore for bodies. We saw firemen going in, but they carried nothing out, and the crowd, ready for a fresh sensation, fell to debating how the murderers died. Suicide was the popular theory. After two o'clock, when the fire was getting strong, one or two shots — the last — had been heard in the ground floor room, and these were said to mean suicide. Whether it was so or not we could not know, but to round the story off the news ran round that two bodies had been found in the kitchen behind the house. When all was over there was nothing to show but a line of blackened windows, marking the place where terrible passions had run to their end.

A mild-faced young policeman dandling a rifle stood outside receiving the congratulations of his friends. He had been one of the firing party in the bedroom. He said that they never saw anything to aim at — never a face, only now and then a hand. And it was curious proof of the deadly aim of the assassins that not one pane of glass was broken in the opposite windows; the bullets had all gone through the opening over the heads of the soldiers and policemen as they lay. A sash was broken and an ugly chip was taken out of the yellow brick wall.

JANUARY 4, 1911

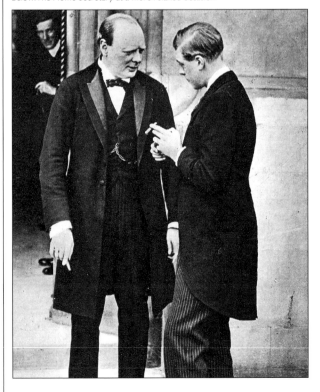

Above: Mr Churchill captures the camera's eye
Below: The Home Secretary at a more relaxed occasion

1914 | 1918

CONSCIENTIOUS OBJECTION

BERTRAND RUSSELL

THERE ARE NO doubt many kinds of reasons which lead men to become conscientious objectors, but I am convinced that the chief reason, and the most valid, is precisely that sense of "the solidarity of mankind" of "our membership with another," which "Artifex"* denies to us. It seems to me that when he wrote "mankind" he was thinking only of the Allies. But the Germans, too, are included among "mankind". The conscientious objector does not believe that violence can cure violence, or that militarism can exorcise the spirit of militarism. He persists in feeling "solidarity" with those who are called "enemies", and he believes that if this feeling were more widespread among us it would do more than armies and navies can ever do to prevent the growth of aggressive Imperialism, not only among ourselves, but also among potential enemies.

MARCH 19, 1917

*A Guardian columnist

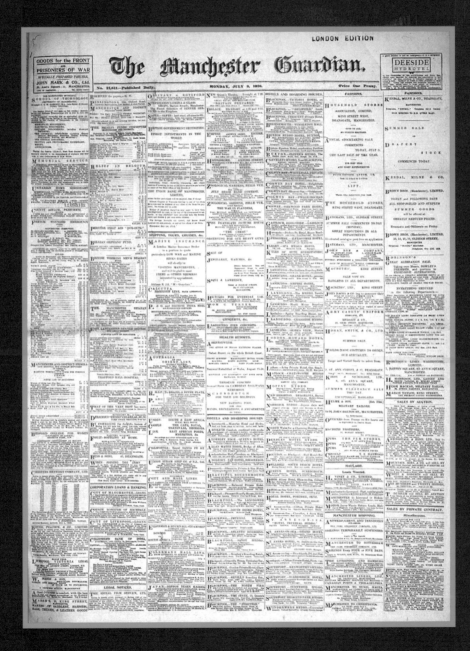

THE ARCHDUKE ASSASSINATED

THE ARCHDUKE FRANCIS Ferdinand of Austria, nephew of the aged Emperor and heir to the throne, was assassinated in the streets of Sarayevo, the Bosnian capital, yesterday afternoon. His wife, the Duchess of Hohenberg, was killed by the same assassin, a Serb student. Some reports say the Duchess was deliberately shielding her husband from the second shot when she was killed. One victim was struck in the body and the other in the face; the telegrams are contradictory about which wound the Archduke suffered and which his wife.

MAY 11, 1914

THE PICNIC BASKET

CATERING FOR A SUMMER OUTING

THE PROPER PACKING of the picnic basket is as essential as the provision of suitable viands, and the memory alone should not be regarded as sufficiently trustworthy when collecting the supply of eatables together. Make out a list of all that will be required, both table requisites and foods, then look over it and mentally sum up the accessories to meats and sweets and the number of knives, forks, and spoons required, also plates, allowing nothing superfluous but everything that makes for comfort. Do not forget the corkscrews and a tin-opener. Have a good supply of thick paper dishes, such as are used by fruiterers. They are easily packed and can be used for undressed salads, pastries, or bread; in fact, anything which is not moist. Paper serviettes are better than damask ones. Sandwiches should be packed in cardboard boxes in grease-proof paper, butter should be in a covered jar, cream should be taken in a bottle. Devonshire cream keeps better in a tin lined with grease-proof paper. Salt is better in sprinklers, no spoons then being required. Pepper will not be necessary if a small bottle of cayenne is taken. A jar of French mustard might well take the place of the mustard pot, which is liable to be broken or to allow the escape of the mustard.

MAY 11, 1914

NEW TERRACES AT THE LONDON ZOO

MOVING THE ANIMALS

THIS AFTERNOON AT the Zoo the keepers were persuading the haughty flamingoes to take up residence in their pond at the foot of the new Mappin terraces. All this week the animals will be walking two by two from their cages to the semi-liberty of the terraces. About a dozen bears are already there, sniffing about the concrete hillocks, but the bears in the rather dark and confined cages

under the old terrace walk have yet to be shifted. Their removal will be the toughest job, for the keepers tell you that you never know when you have a bear. The removal of the goats and other rock-climbing creatures that will inhabit the three mountains at the back will be easy.

Sam and Barbara, the two Polar bears, have been in their compartment since Christmas, and are as happy in it as if they had never lived anywhere else. They have never done anything so foolish as to try and cross the twelve-foot ditch that divides them from the gazers on the terrace. They have a good deep pond at the back, and behind the terraces there is a little window through which you can watch them actually swimming under water. It is a queer sensation to stand there and see Sam's eyes in the great white head gazing at you through the pane. Seen through the green water his body looks enormous as he slowly moves about. Sam can stop under water for three minutes, but Barbara beats him as a diver. One imagines that the concrete floor and walls must get unpleasantly hot in summer weather, but the keepers say this is not so. During the recent spell of heat the bears spent most of their time in the water, and rarely visited the cool caves constructed in the concrete at the back. The black Malaysian bears and the sloths were turned in a few days ago and are settling down happily.

MAY 26, 1914

THE CATASTROPHE APPROACHES

RUSSIA MOBILISES FORCES

EUROPE IS VERY near war. Last night even the firmest friends of peace were almost without hope.

Little doubt remains that all Russia's forces are being mobilised. In the House of Commons yesterday Mr Asquith, on the authority of Berlin, announced the extension of the partial Russian mobilisation reported several days ago. He understood that Germany would issue like orders.

Telegrams from St Petersburg do not conflict with the Prime Minister's statement. France is also making ready.

German news is equally grave. Official announcement is made of the suspension of the international train services into the Empire; telephone communication with Denmark and Belgium has been stopped.

Although the outer world still awaits the proclamation, the army is, it seems certain, being mobilised. A state of siege has been declared, and the country is under martial law. Germany is virtually cut off from other countries, except Austria, her ally.

AUGUST 1, 1914

ENGLAND DECLARES WAR ON GERMANY

KING HOLDS EMERGENCY COUNCIL

GREAT BRITAIN DECLARED war on Germany at eleven o'clock last night.

The Cabinet yesterday delivered an ultimatum to Germany. Announcing the fact to the House of Commons, the Prime Minister said: "We have repeated the request made last week to the German Government that they should give us the same assurance in regard to Belgian neutrality that was given to us and Belgium by France last week. We have asked that it should be given before midnight."

Last evening a reply was received from Germany. This being unsatisfactory the King held at once a Council which had been called for midnight. The declaration of war was then signed.

AUGUST 5, 1914

WITH THE GUNS

THE WAR OF MACHINES

BY DH LAWRENCE

THE RESERVISTS WERE leaving for London by the nine o'clock train. They were young men, some of them drunk. There was one bawling and brawling before the ticket window; there were two swaying on the steps of the subway shouting, and ending, "Let's go an' have another afore we go." There were a few women seeing off their sweethearts and brothers, but, on the whole, the reservist had been a lodger in the town and had only his own pals. One woman stood before the carriage window. She and her sweetheart were being very matter-of-fact, cheerful, and bumptious over the parting.

"Well, so-long!" she cried as the train began to move. "When you see 'em let 'em have it."

"Ay, no fear," shouted the man, and the train was gone, the man grinning.

I thought what it would really be like, "when he saw 'em".

LAST AUTUMN I followed the Bavarian army down the Isar valley and near the foot of the Alps. Then I could see what war would be like — an affair entirely of machines, with men attached to the machines as the subordinate part thereof, as the butt is the part of a rifle.

I remember standing on a little round hill one August afternoon. There was a beautiful blue sky, and white clouds from the mountains. Away on the right, amid woods and corn-clad hills, lay the big Starnberg lake. This is just a year ago, but it seems to belong to some period outside of time.

On the crown of the little hill were three quick-firing guns, with the gunners behind. At the side, perched up on a tiny platform at the top of a high pair of steps, was an officer looking through a fixed spy-glass. A little further behind, lower down the hill, was a group of horses and soldiers.

Every moment came the hard, tearing hideous voice of the German command from the officer perched aloft, giving the range to the guns; and then the sharp cry, "Fire!" There was a burst, something in the guns started back, the faintest breath of vapour disappeared. The shots had gone.

I watched, but I could not see where they had gone, nor what had been aimed at. Evidently they were directed against an enemy a mile and a half away, men unseen by any of the soldiers at the guns. Whether the shot they fired hit or missed, killed or did not touch, I and the gun-party did not know. Only the officer was shouting the range again, the guns were again starting back, we were again staring over the face of the green and dappled inscrutable country into which the missiles sped unseen.

What work was there to do? — only mechanically to adjust the guns and fire the shot. What was there to feel? — only the unnatural suspense and suppression of serving a machine which, for ought we knew, was killing our fellow men, whilst we stood there, blind, without knowledge or participation, subordinate to the cold machine. This was the glamour and the glory of the war: blue sky overhead and living green country all around, but we, amid it all, a part in some iron insensate will, our flesh and blood, our soul and intelligence shed away, and all that remained of us a cold, metallic adherence to an iron machine. There was neither ferocity nor joy nor exultation nor exhilaration nor even quick fear: only a mechanical, expressionless movement.

And this is how the gunner would "let 'em have it". He would mechanically move a certain apparatus when he heard a certain shout. Of the result he would see and know nothing. He had nothing to do with it.

Then I remember going at night down a road, whilst the sound of guns thudded continuously. And suddenly I started, seeing the bank of the road stir. It was a mass of scarcely visible forms, lying waiting for a rush. They were lying under fire, silent, scarcely stirring, a mass. If one of the shells that were supposed to be coming had dropped among them it would have burst a hole in the mass. Who would have been torn, killed, no one would have known. There would just have been a hole in the living shadowy mass; that was all. Who it was did not matter. There were no individuals, and every individual soldier knew it. He was a fragment of a mass, and as a fragment of a mass he must live and die or be torn. He had no rights, no self, no being. There was only the mass lying there, solid and obscure along the bank of the road in the night.

This was how the gunner "would let 'em have it". A shell would fall into this mass of vulnerable bodies, there would be a torn hole in the mass. This would be his "letting 'em have it".

And I remember a captain of the bersaglieri who talked to me in the train in Italy when he had come back from Tripoli. The Italian soldier, he said, was the finest soldier in the world at a rush. But — and he spoke with a certain horror that cramped his voice — when it came to lying there under the Snyder fire you had to stand behind them with a revolver. And I saw he could not get beyond the agony of this.

"Well," I said, "that is because they cannot feel themselves parts of a machine. They have all the old natural courage, when one rushes at one's enemy. But it is unnatural to them to lie

Previous page: Soldiers wait in line to be taken to the front   Above: "Better a bullet than the laceration of a shell ..."

still under machine-fire. It is unnatural to anybody. War with machines, and the machine predominant, is too unnatural for an Italian. It is a wicked thing a machine, and your Italians are too naturally good. They will do anything to get away from it. Let us see our enemy and go for him. But we cannot endure this taking death out of machines, and giving death out of machines, our blood cold, without any enemy to rise against."

I remember also standing on a little hill crowned by a white church. This hill was defended, surrounded by a trench halfway down. In this trench stood the soldiers side by side, down there in the earth, a great line of them.

The night came on. Suddenly, on the other side, high up in the darkness, burst a beautiful greenish globe of light, and then came into being a magic circle of country-side set in darkness, a greenish jewel of landscape, splen-did bulk of trees, a green meadow, vivid. The ball fell and it was dark, and in one's eye remained treasured the little vision that had appeared far off in the darkness. Then again a light ball burst and sloped down. There was the white farmhouse with the wooden, slanting roof, the green apple trees, the orchard paling, a jewel, a landscape set deep in the darkness. It was beautiful beyond belief.

Then it was dark. Then the searchlights suddenly sprang upon the countryside, revealing the magic, fingering every-thing with magic, pushing the darkness aside, showing the lovely hillsides, the bulks of trees, the pallor of corn. A searchlight was creeping at us. It slid up our hill. It was upon us; we turned out backs to it, it was unendurable. Then it was gone.

Then out of a little wood at the foot of the hill came the intolerable crackling and bursting of rifles. The men in the trenches returned fire. Nothing could be seen. I thought of the bullets that would find their marks. But whose bullets? And what mark? Why must I fire off my gun in the darkness towards a noise? Why must a bullet come out of the dark-ness, breaking a hole in me? But better a bullet than the lac-eration of a shell, if it came to dying. But what is it all about? I cannot understand; I am not to understand. My God, why am I a man at all, when this is all, this machinery piercing and tearing?

It is a war of artillery, a war of machines, and men no more than the subjective material of the machine. It is so unnatural as to be unthinkable. Yet we must think of it.

AUGUST 18, 1914

Deadly cargo ... German soldiers loading gas canisters

GERMAN GAS ENGINE IN ACTION

LARGELY BY THE use of a new and dangerous device the Germans obtained a considerable success on Thursday evening in an attack on a large scale on the French position north of Ypres in the direction of the Yser.

Late last night the following report from Sir John French was issued by the Press Bureau:

1. Yesterday evening the enemy developed an attack on the French troops on our left in the neighbourhood of Bixschoote and Langemarck on the north of the Ypres salient.

This attack was preceded by a heavy bombardment, the enemy at the same time making use of a large number of appliances for the production of asphyxiating gas.

The quantity produced indicates a long and deliberate preparation for the employment of devices contrary to the terms of the Hague Convention, to which the enemy subscribed.

The false statement made by the Germans a week ago to the effect that we were using such gases is now explained. It was obviously an effort to diminish neutral criticism in advance.

2. During the night the French had to retire from the gas zone. Overwhelmed by the fumes, they have fallen back to the canal in the neighbourhood of Boesinghe.

Our front remains intact except on the extreme left, where the troops have had to readjust their line in order to conform with the new French line. Two attacks were delivered during the night on our trenches east of Ypres and were repulsed.

3. Fighting still continues in the region north of Ypres.

4. This morning one of our aviators, during the course of a reconnaissance which he completed, successfully damaged a German aeroplane and forced it to descend. Our Flying Corps also brought down another German machine about Messines.

APRIL 24, 1915

A BRITISH OFFICER'S LETTER

FRIEND AND FOE AND THE DEAD

BY A SUBALTERN AT THE FRONT

A TRUCE HAD been arranged for the few hours of daylight for the burial of the dead on both sides who had been lying out in the open since the fierce night-fighting of a week earlier. When I got out I found a large crowd of officers and men, English and German, grouped around the bodies, which had already been gathered together and laid out in rows. I went along those dreadful ranks and scanned the faces, fearing at every step to recognise one I knew. It was a ghastly sight. They lay stiffly in contorted attitudes, dirty with frozen mud and powdered with rime. The digging parties were already busy on the two big common graves, but the ground was hard and the work slow and laborious.

In the intervals of superintending it we chatted with the Germans, most of whom were quite affable, if one could not exactly call them friendly, which, indeed, was neither to be expected nor desired. We exchanged confidences about the weather and the diametrically opposite news from East Prussia. The way they maintained the truth of their marvellous victories because they were official (with bated breath) was positively pathetic. They had no doubt of the issue in the east, and professed to regard the position in the west as a definite stalemate.

It was most amusing to observe the bland innocence with which they put questions, a truthful answer to which might have had unexpected consequences in the future. One charming lieutenant of artillery was most anxious to know just where my dug-out, *The Cormorants*, was situated. No doubt he wanted to shoot his card, tied to a "Whistling Willie". I waved my hand airily over the next company's line, giving him the choice of various mangle-heaps in the rear.

They spoke of a bottle of champagne. We raised our wistful eyes in hopeless longing. They expressed astonishment, and said how pleased they would have been, had they only known, to have sent to Lille for some. "A charming town, Lille. Do you know it?" "Not yet," we assured them. Their laughter was quite frank that time.

Meanwhile time drew on, and it was obvious that the burying would not be half finished with the expiration of the armistice agreed upon, so we decided to renew it the following morning. They left us alone that night to enjoy a peaceful Christmas. I forgot to say that the previous night (Christmas Eve) their trenches were a blaze of Christmas trees, and our sentries were regaled for hours with the traditional Christmas songs of the Fatherland. Their officers even expressed annoyance the next day that some of these trees had been fired on, insisting that they were part almost of a sacred rite.

DECEMBER 30, 1915

A PROFESSOR IN THE RANKS

BRIEF ARMISTICE FOR BURIALS

ON BOXING DAY at the agreed hour, on a pre-arranged signal being given, we turned out again. The output of officers of higher rank on their side was more marked, and the proceedings were more formal in consequence. But while the gruesome business of burying went forward there was still a certain interchange of pleasantries.

The German soldiers seemed a good-tempered, amiable lot, mostly peasants from the look of them. One remarkable exception, who wore the Iron Cross and addressed us in slow but faultless English, told us he was Professor of German and English dialects at a Westphalian university. He had a wonderfully fine head. They distributed cigars and cigarettes freely among our digging party, who were much impressed by the cigars. I hope they were not disillusioned when they came to smoke them. Meanwhile the officers were amusing themselves by taking photographs of mixed groups. The Germans brought us copies to send to the English illustrated papers, as they received them regularly.

FORMAL SALUTES

The digging completed, the shallow graves were filled in, and the German officers remained to pay their tribute of respect while our chaplain read a short service. It was one of the most impressive things I have ever witnessed. Friend and foe stood side by side, bare-headed, watching the tall, grave figure of the padre outlined against the frosty landscape as he blessed the poor broken bodies at his feet. Then, with more formal salutes, we turned and made our way back to our respective ruts.

FOOTBALL MATCH

Elsewhere along the line I hear our fellows played the Germans at football on Christmas Day. Our own pet enemies remarked that they would like a game, but as the ground in our part is all root crops and much cut up by ditches, and as, moreover, we had not got a football, we had to call it off.

JANUARY 1, 1916

SINN FEIN OUTBREAK IN DUBLIN

THE EASTER RISING

A VERY SERIOUS outbreak organised by Sinn Feiners occurred in Dublin on Monday. A large body of men, mostly armed, seized St Stephen's Green and the Post Office, and also occupied houses in St Stephen's Green, Sackville Street (where the Post Office is situated), the adjacent Abbey Street, and on the quays along the Liffey. The telegraph and telephone lines were cut.

The rebels opened fire on soldiers and police killing about a dozen and wounding about eighteen. The casualties suffered by the Sinn Feiners are not exactly known.

It is worthy of note that two of the men killed by the rebels and six of the wounded were National Volunteers. The force organised by the Irish Nationalist party in the months immediately preceding the outbreak of the war evidently played an important and courageous part in grappling with the outbreak.

APRIL 24, 1916

THE HANGING OF ROGER CASEMENT

LETTER TO THE EDITOR

BY GEORGE BERNARD SHAW

I PRESUME I may count on a general agreement that Casement's treatment* should not be exceptional. This is important, because it happen that his case is not an isolated one just now. There are several traitors in the public eye at present. At the head of them stands Christain De Wet. If De Wet is spared and Casement is hanged, the unavoidable conclusion will be that Casement will be hanged, not because he is a traitor, but because he is an Irishman ... The reasonable conclusion is that Casement should be treated as a prisoner of war ... In Ireland he will regarded as a national hero if he is executed, and quite possibly a spy if he is not.

[On the eve of the Easter Rising, Casement, knighted for his exposure of atrocities in the Congo, landed in Ireland from a German submarine, for which he was sentenced to death.]

JULY 22, 1916

A BOOK THAT STOPPED A BULLET

SAVED BY LITERATURE

OF THE ASSAULT on Montauban, a wounded sergeant back in England (who had a marvellous escape from a bullet through the heart) gives the following picture:

"We went over in grand style and found nothing much in the way till we got into Montauban. Here the place was in an awful mess. Most of the houses had been knocked head over heels. The only ones I saw standing were a couple of cafés. As we came on we saw lots of Germans running out of the back of the village, but when we got into the streets there were plenty of them monkeying about the ruins. We had divided the company up into groups of six, but as we neared the village we all joined up again. My five pals were five of the best, and we kept well together. We saw some Huns in a ground-floor room, so we dropped a Mills bomb through the window and didn't wait for an answer."

GERMAN MACHINE-GUN

"As we turned the corner we saw a German lying round the end of a wall. He'd got a machine-gun, and had made a little emplacement with bricks. He turned this thing on me and got me in the foot. It didn't stop me though, and when I was getting near him I felt two kicks over the heart. I did not wait to see what had happened, but simply went at him and bayonetted him. I couldn't go on much further, so I sat down to see what was the damage."

BULLETS LODGED IN BOOK

"My foot was pretty bad, but when I looked at my left-hand breast pocket I saw two holes in it. I opened my pocket and found two bullets had gone through my metal shaving mirror, through my pocket book case, and had nosed their way into a book I was carrying. Funnily enough, earlier in the morning my officer gave me the book and said I could read it when I got into the German trenches. So I put it in my pocket, little thinking that I should be able to read a bit of it on hospital ship coming back."

JULY 8, 1916

BOOKS IN WARTIME

A REVIEW OF "THE TITANS"

BY T S ELIOT

Charles Doughty ... one cannot blame him for writing an epic

THIS IS AN epic dealing with the creation of the world, the battle of Titans against gods, their defeat and their final subjugation in the service of man. One does not find fault with Mr Doughty for writing an epic. No literary genre, once established, is ever outworn. But mythology is dangerous literary material. It should either be a mythology in which the author more or less believes or a mythology in which some people once believed. A mythology cannot be created for literary purposes out of whole cloth; it must be the work of a race. Mr Doughty's mythology is neither Greek nor Hebraic nor Scandinavian; hence it lacks outline, it lacks tradition, and it lacks concreteness.

The theme suggests Milton and Keats. But Milton and Keats at their best communicate a feeling, the one of titanic revolt, the other of titanic silence and despondency. When they fail they suggest Mr Doughty. Mr Doughty's Titans have bulk without meaning. When Dante says "*Mi parve veder molte alte torre*" an image arises; one feels the reality of immense bodies with something like human spirits in them. The Titans of this poem have violence, but no passions.

> Leaned to time-fretted cliffs
> Is entered weariness, in each marble corse.

In Hyperion the weariness is made actual; here it is stated. One does not know quite why such creatures should be weary at all, unless from the boredom of their inactivity. One cannot understand them. Not being human, they have not even the reality of definite abstractions. Bios and Kratos in Prometheus Bound succeed because they are boldly and intentionally abstract, and as such produce their effect by contrast with a passionate suffering human being. Aeschylus was a master of effects of abstract and concrete; he never fell into the error of the vague.

As for Mr Doughty's style, one is puzzled; one wonders whether he was himself quite sure what he wanted to do. He aims at the ruggedness of the Saxon tongue. If he were thoroughly and consistently Anglo-Saxon he might arrive at giving a total impression; even employing, as he does, many words of which one does not know the meaning. But there are heavy Latinisms too. One turns from the harsh

> From the mount's knees, up to his frozen breast:
> Eotons and rime-giants strive mainly and sweat

to

> the adamantine Elements
> Couched indivisible particles...
> Shall his mathesis, through unerring thought,
> Discern ...

with a touch of Browning at the end.

One can enjoy a style of excess — Sir Thomas Browne, or Lyly, or Mr Wyndham Lewis, or Browning — if it is excess in a peculiar and exclusive direction. Mr Doughty's style is not archaic; it is not the style of any time or the style of any intelligible pose; it is eccentric, but not personal. Thus it recalls several writers without being imitative of them. It recalls especially Blake; not the Blake of extraordinary creations of phrase springing at a leap from the unconscious, but the Blake of such verse as America.

JULY 24, 1916

ARMOURED CARS IN ACTION

ENEMY TERRIFIED BY "IRONBOXES"

BY OUR CORRESPONDENT

THE BRITISH ARMY has struck the enemy another heavy blow north of the Somme. Attacking shortly after dawn yesterday morning on a front of more than six miles northeast from Combles, it now occupies a new strip of reconquered territory including three fortified villages behind the German third line and many local positions of great strength.

Armoured cars working with the infantry were the great surprise of this attack. Sinister, formidable, and industrious, these novel machines pushed boldly into "No Man's Land", astonishing our soldiers no less than they frightened the enemy. Presently I shall relate some strange incidents of their first grand tour in Picardy, of Bavarians bolting before them like rabbits and others surrendering in picturesque attitudes of terror, and the delightful story of the Bavarian colonel who was carted about for hours in the belly of one of them like Jonah in the whale, while his captors slew the men of his broken division.

It is too soon yet to advertise their best points to an interested world. The entire army nevertheless is talking about them, and you might imagine that yesterday's operation was altogether a battle of armed chauffeurs if you listened to the stories of some of the spectators. They inspired confidence and laughter. No other incident of the war has created such amusement in the face of death as their debut before the trenches of Martinpuich and Flers. Their quaintness and seeming air of profound intelligence commended them to a critical audience. It was as though one of Mr Heath Robinson's jokes had been utilised for a deadly purpose, and one laughed even before the dire effect on the enemy was observed.

STROLLING DOWN THE HIGH STREET

"Walking wounded" grinned through their bandages and grime as they talked of these extraordinary beasts while waiting their turn at the advanced dressing stations. Even the stretcher cases chuckled as they lay in the ambulances. I heard the fragment of one conversation as a grievously wounded man was lifted out at a casualty clearing station: "And he says, 'Lord, there was one of them iron boxes strolling down the high street of Flers like it was Sunday afternoon.'" The man who invented these new and efficient machines of destruction deserves much of the army, if for no more than that he has made it laugh as it fought, not the laughter of ridicule but of admiration.

SEPTEMBER 18, 1916

AN HEROIC ADVANCE

OUR DEAD SOLDIERS' VALIANT STORY

BY OUR CORRESPONDENT

IF YOU WOULD know what a man the British soldier is, read today the writing embossed over the gentle undulations of ground that lead along the river to Beaucourt. A soldier lies at one spot tightly gripping a German with both hands. The two are joined just as they fell, both, it is probable, shot by a German machine-gun. For hereabouts the machine-gun was very busy. You could race the full course of its discharge by many signs.

Everyone who has walked across the field of battle comes away with an admiration that is indeed reverence for the men who slowly, steadfastly walked that autumn morning one hundred yards after another over fields deadly with the enemy's devices. Wire caught and tripped them and tangled them, but they stumbled on. It was cut and tumbled everywhere by artillery work of the highest accuracy, but wire, especially German wire, is indestructible as material, and no acres along the front have been so roofed with it. Men were shot as they disentangled themselves coolly as you would dislodge a bramble, and if a wounded man who had already fallen attempted to shift his position he was a dead man, for in all the fighting in this area since July the Germans, by deliberate policy, have watered the ground with bullets after an attack, and have appointed special snipers to fire at any moving object.

In the gloom and fog of this autumn morning the attack somewhat lost evenness and cohesion — or so the writing suggests — and the groups missed the encouragement of an even charge, when every man has companions to follow and feels himself part of a machine. In this advance one group after another relied wholly on itself, and its reliance was not misplaced. Every man, every little assembly of men, went forward in spite of a hundred barriers that would have plausibly held up platoons or battalions less game than these. They were out to win their spurs. He who runs might read the story — yesterday. After a famous victory such as this the dead lie on the field of their fame as they fell for a day — it may be for several days. Then, with quick care and stern reverence, the last rites are paid.

We have had many great fights — none finer than this. It was heroic in every turn and phase. And the heroism was nowhere vain. Everywhere it won its end — yea, and more than its end. Nor was its cost beyond measure as figures go. It is only that every fibre of feeling is touched to see one good man fallen before he reached the end. To see him there, said one who returned, was to swear an immortal oath that his sacrifice should not fail of its end — the freedom of his children from the threat of war and the unstained liberty of his nation.

Tomorrow I may be able to name the unit to whom the glory of this part of the field peculiarly belongs.

NOVEMBER 22, 1916

VENEREAL DISEASE

WHEN THE QUESTION was raised yesterday at the annual meeting in London of the Association of Poor Law Unions as to the source of venereal infections, it was stated that it was well known that Germans were very amenable to the disease by the looseness of their moral code.

Germans had, it was argued, a high scientific process to deal with contagion, but, said the Revd RT Tacon, "they do not apply that in the channel which is the most important. I have four sons in the army, and I don't want them to be contaminated: I would rather that we could infect the German with good, healthy English blood."

The meeting decided that it would be no harm to have detention of infected cases, but that the natural disinclination of affected persons to declare their disease rendered the notification condition a negation of the good object in view.

The discussion arose out of a letter from the Salford Board of Guardians calling for the internment of all Germans as a source of infection. Approving the idea, the conference instructed the Executive Council to take all the necessary steps to give effect to this view.

NOVEMBER 25, 1916

FEAR OF PROHIBITION

GLASGOW'S GREAT RUSH FOR WHISKY

YESTERDAY THE PEOPLE of Glasgow manifested their belief that there will be prohibition by an extraordinary rush to obtain supplies of whisky. As soon as the premises of the wholesale and retail wine merchants were opened they were rushed by waiting queues, and large travelling hampers were used in which to take away numerous bottles. The merchants state that the rush was unparalleled. Many shops were cleared of their stocks soon after midday.

The rush for supplies is said to be due to the Clyde shipbuilders' pronouncement that there must be prohibition if they are to execute the mercantile tonnage on hand.

DECEMBER 19, 1916

A BARRAGE BALLOON AT PASSCHENDAELE

QUEER BEAST OF THE BATTLEFIELD

WHAT IS PASSCHENDAELE? As I saw it this morning through the smoke of gunfire and a wet mist it was less than I had seen before a week or two ago, with just one ruin there — the ruin of its church — and a black mass of slaughtered masonry and nothing else, not a house left standing, not a huddle of brick on that shell-swept height. But because of its position at the crown of the ridge, that crest has seemed to many men like a

prize for which all these battles of Flanders have been fought, and to get to this place and the slopes and ridges on the way to it great numbers of our most gallant men have given their blood, and thousands — scores of thousands — of British soldiers of our own home stock and from overseas have gone through fire and water — the fire of frightful bombardments, the water of the swamps, of the "beeks" and shell holes, in which they have plunged and waded and stuck and sometimes drowned.

UP TO THE FRONT

There was a wet smell in the wind which told one that the prophets were not wrong about the coming of rain. But the duck-boards were still dry, and it made walking easier, though any false step would drop one into the shell crater filled to the brim with water of vivid metallic colours or into broad-stretching bogs churned up by shells that flung up waterspouts after their pitch into the mud. The German long-range guns were scattering shells about with blind eyes, doing guesswork at the whereabouts of our batteries, or perhaps firing from aeroplane photographs to wipe out the windings of

our duck-board tracks and railway lines. For miles around and along the same track where I walked single files of men were plodding along, their grey figures silhouetted where they tramped along the skyline with their capes blowing and their steel hats shining. Every few minutes a big shell burst near one of these files. Always when the smoke cleared the line of men seemed unbroken, and they did not halt on their way.

AEROPLANES TAKE FLIGHT

The wind was blowing gustily, but all this grey sky overhead was threaded with aeroplanes — our birds — going out to the battle. They flew high in flights or singly at a swift pace, and beneath their planes our shells were in flight from heavy howitzers and long-muzzled guns whose fire swept one with blasts of air and smashed against one's ears with hammer strokes.

Out of the wide wild desert of these battlefields there rose a queer beast, monstrous and ungainly as a mammoth in the beginning of the world's slime. It was one of our sausage balloons getting up for the morning's work. Its big air-pockets flapped like ears, and as it rose its body heaved and swelled.

NOVEMBER 7, 1917

REFORM BILL PASSED

WOMEN'S VOTE WON

THE REPRESENTATION OF the People Bill, which doubles the electorate, giving the Parliamentary vote to about six million women and placing soldiers and sailors over 19 on the register (with a proxy vote for those on service abroad), simplifies the registration system, greatly reduces the cost of elections, and provides that they shall all take place on one day, and by a redistribution of seats tends to give a vote the same value everywhere, passed both Houses yesterday and received the Royal assent.

FEBRUARY 29, 1918

AUTOMATIC TELEPHONES

NEW EXCHANGE OPENED IN LEEDS

BY OUR CORRESPONDENT

A NEW AUTOMATIC telephone exchange was opened by the Postmaster General (Mr Alfred Illingworth) in Basinghall Street, Leeds, this afternoon. The new exchange is the largest automatic one in Europe, having 6,800 subscribers.

The Postmaster General expressed the great pleasure which it gave him to take part in the inauguration of the new system. The system was another illustration of what they had seen during the war — the transference from dependence upon the individual to reliance upon mechanical and automatic means. Telephone subscribers would now be put in connection with each other without the intervention of the manual worker, and if anything went wrong with the machine the short-tempered subscriber would not get any help or satisfaction by cursing the machine. During the war most people had been more or less "nervy", and he was afraid that often language had been used to the operators which was not justifiable in any circumstances.

Sir William Sligo, the engineer-in-chief at the General Post Office, said that for many years they had been struggling hard to get the automatic principle recognised. Automatic machinery must replace human effort in telephoning as in most other branches of industry. Nothing could stop it, and the sooner the country recognised the fact the better it would be. The longer the development was delayed the greater would be the amount of capital that would have to be sunk and of machinery and material that would have to be scrapped. They were hoping that the experience of Leeds would be such as to induce subscribers in other large cities to agitate for similar installations. The manual instruments displaced at Leeds would be sent at once for service at the front.

HOW CALLS ARE EFFECTED

The proceedings on Saturday included a tour through the buildings, and an explanation of the new apparatus. Some 50 per cent of the operators at the manual machines will be displaced, but work has been offered to them in other departments of the postal service. The automatic service is only for Leeds, and it is of course impossible to dispense entirely with a manual telephone service for the city, as connections have to be established with subscribers in other places. One of the special features of the new process is the automatic instruments with their dial-calling devices.

The first thing to be done in making a call, it was explained, was to lift the receiver from the rest. Next a fingertip has to be placed in the hole of the dial opposite the first figure of the number of the subscriber required, and the dialling wheel pulled round as far as it will go and then released. The process is repeated for the following figures. When the full number has been fashioned a bell rings at the telephone of the subscriber called for, or if he is engaged "an intermittent buzzing noise" is heard in the receiver by the caller. Should a mistake be made in the process of dialling a number the fault can be remedied and a new start made by at once replacing the receiver on the hook. This severs all connections so far established.

Putting you through ... the old system of manual operators

Many advantages are claimed for the automatic system. The time occupied in calling is reduced to a minimum. Prompter attention is given to calls by the subscriber called on, as the bell keeps ringing. Instantaneous disconnection takes place on the replacement of the receiver, and this makes the number immediately available for another call. Constant service is given throughout the day and night without the attendance of operators.

MAY 20, 1918

A GIGANTIC "BEANFEAST" OF PRISONERS

THOUSANDS PACKED IN CAGES

BY OUR CORRESPONDENT

THERE IS SO much to tell that one can only touch on the more salient incidents. The whole German front opposite the British army, from the Somme by Peronne to the Messines Ridge in Flanders, is in a state of flux, and it is difficult to say that the enemy is holding firmly anywhere, though everywhere he is doing his best to cover his retreat with rearguard actions.

How real is the defeat the Germans have suffered in the Drocourt–Queant line south of the Scarpe is perhaps best shown by the fact that the official report has told that we took ten thousand prisoners yesterday. That was mostly on a narrow front of not more than 11,000 yards, which would be evidence enough that the ground was strongly held. But here these troops were holding and were definitely put in to hold what the Germans no less than we have recognised as one of the strongest complications of defensive positions devised since trench warfare was

Tired and hungry . . . German prisoners of war packed behind barriers

invented. In a few short hours we had shattered all his defences and captured an enormous number of prisoners.

MORE THAN TEN THOUSAND MEN

When all are counted it will be found that there were more than ten thousand. I saw a vast crowd of something like seven thousand massed this morning. It was at the First Army cage, where already within the barriers (though parties had been drafted out as fast as possible) there were over four thousand men, making one huge, solid block of blue-grey against the yellow dun of the stubble and dry grass of the upland plain. It was like Epsom Downs, as dense and immobile. While I was there another column, numbering over 2,200, marched up in a column of fours — a great blue-grey snake trailing its length farther than the eye could see.

The officers were drafted into their special compartments first, and one saw the nonchalant way in which Thomas Atkins checked off Prussian officers like sacks of coal. When all the officers were in the tally was found correct at 62. Then the turn of non-commissioned officers came.

There were all sorts of men, some very young, some ripe and stalwart, and some more than middle-aged. Many were good and many obviously unfit for service in the front line. Prussians, Bavarians, Saxons, Guards, infantrymen and gunners, and all sorts of miscellaneous units. Five out of every six had his shoulder-straps cut off before capture to avoid identification. Quite a number wore ribbons and Iron Crosses.

As newcomers arrived they were greeted with shouts of laughter and welcome by comrades already within the wires, and greetings and badinage and names were called back and forth. Those inside were mostly eating, and held up bully beef tins and biscuits for the new arrivals to see, and the latter cheered responsively, for many of them are very hungry when we catch them, not having had regular rations in some cases for three or four days. Many were evidently very tired, but the whole scene suggested a trainload of revellers at some annual beanfeast being welcomed by fellow holiday-makers.

Today's captures, however, can only number hundreds where yesterday's numbered thousands, because the Germans in this section have everywhere flown, all having apparently got behind the line of the Nord Canal and the valley of the Agache towards Douai and Cambrai.

SEPTEMBER 4, 1918

THE END OF THE WAR

BY LEONARD HOBHOUSE

THE WAR IS over, and in a million households fathers and mothers, wives and sisters, will breathe freely, relieved at length of all dread of that curt message which has shattered the hope and joy of so many. The war is over. The drama is played out. After years of tedium there opened on March 21 a short and sharp fifth act of swift and surprising changes. Our language misses that single word applied by the Greeks to those sudden and complete changes of fortune which they regarded as appropriate to the final act of a tragic drama. No historic change of fortune so swift, so pulverising to the loser has occurred since Napoleon's retreat from Moscow as the reversal that began on July 18. And since July 18 blow has followed blow with a rapidity which, if it has almost bewildered the victors, must have stupefied the enemy.

But it is not of the drama that we would think mainly for the moment, nor even of the problem that the war has opened. For, if peace between the nations has returned, within each nation there is open or suppressed ferment. The old order in Europe has perished. The new is hardly born, and no one knows what its lineaments will be. Tomorrow we shall be brought up against the hard immediate problems of re-establishment. Before we grapple with these, let us give a moment to the review of the position gained and try our best to sum up the result of four tremendous years as it may be measured by the historian.

From Waterloo to Mons there elapsed almost a hundred years. The first part of this period was one of peace and progress, industry and optimism. Below the surface were seething forces of democracy and nationalism, and soon these began to break forth to disturb the complacency of statesmen. But for the thinker these forces were full of hope, and the men of the mid-nineteenth century foresaw a better order, a civilised humanity, a race dedicated to the works of peace and the cultivation of a gentler and yet a nobler life. Towards the end of the century their optimism gave way to a gloomier view. Unrest and anxiety took hold of the more thoughtful minds. Democracy had everywhere progressed but had not brought healing. The burden of armaments lay heavy on the nations, and the war cloud lowered dark on the horizon. The main cause of this change was the success of the Prussian system under Bismarck. The year 1870 divides the period of which we have spoken into two nearly equal halves, of progress and hope on the one side, and reaction and apprehension on the other. The union of Germany was, indeed, accepted, even welcomed, by liberally minded men as the overdue consummation of a long and unhappy political travail, but the mode in which it was accomplished turned out to be more fateful to Germany and the world than the achievement itself.

From 1870 men began to accept the doctrine of blood and iron. Ideas, arguments, appeals to right and justice took a lower place. Force and fraud seemed to make their way, if only men would be thorough in the use of them. The Prussian idea enjoyed all the prestige of immense success, and the pre-eminence of Germany in many fields of learning, backed with this prestige, won its way in the regions of the mind. The idea of humanity receded in favour of the State, freedom gave way to discipline and organisation, right to the strong hand, reason to passion, and self-restraint to ambition. Meanwhile in one country after another there arose the sense of instability. It began to be felt that things could not last as they were. The piled-up armaments were like vast electric accumulators awaiting their discharge.

In England these influences penetrated more slowly, but from the time when Germany set out seriously to become a great naval Power we felt that we, too, were being drawn in. For long years, even to the last, many of us hoped that ours might be the balancing power, so exerted as to deter either side in the great Continental combinations from a fatal plunge. But it was not to be. The Prussian idea swept Germany out of itself and gave to the world the final demonstration of naked deformity. The circumstances of the war were such that, a very few individuals apart, it united all the humanitarian enthusiasm, all the political love of liberty, which nowadays go to the support of peace, in favour of a stern resistance, carried through, at whatever cost, to indubitable victory. The defeat of Prussianism was rightly stated by Mr Asquith at the outset as the object which

Overwhelming joy ... crowds gather in the streets to celebrate

included all others. Prussianism — an idea, a system, not a nation or an army — is hopelessly defeated today. It is defeated more completely by internal disruption than by any blow in the field. Its hold on the world's future is gone, and the human mind is empty, swept and garnished, of its worst idol. That is the real and decisive victory in the war.

Into the mind that is swept and garnished the parable tells us that other devils might enter. In fact anarchy — which is disorganised in place of organised force — seems waiting at the door. But anarchy is never more than a transitory evil. When all is cleared up we believe it will be seen that by the final test as between the doctrines of might and right the foundations of a new world-order have been laid. The old sovereign nation State has destroyed itself, as the feudal nobility destroyed itself in the Wars of the Roses. As that spectacle of prolonged and senseless anarchy made men turn with relief to the order secured by the absolute monarchy, so the anarchy of the international world has forced upon people for the first time as a serious practical proposal the political organisation of civilised mankind. It is felt to be a choice between the continued risk of mutual destruction in wars which must grow ever more deadly on the one side, and some organised form of international co-operation on the other.

The world has once sacrificed its soul in hecatombs, in masses the mere figures of which will appal future eyes. It is a thing not to be done again without sapping the very vitals of human feeling. As it is, the loss of capacity in the extinction of the most promising men of a generation is a catastrophe only to be compared with some of the great historic pestilences. We were caught up in the vortex and could not escape. We had to go through it, whatever the sacrifice of life. But if, after this experience, we allow such a thing to recur, we ill repay those who have died for us in the hope of a better order. If, on the other hand, we buckle to our task we can found a nobler State than any that have gained glory in former wars, a kingdom or, say rather, a commonwealth of man, in which all the great nations that have played their part in this tragedy will have their share. In this we are achieving, not anything out of keeping with human nature, but rather the natural culmination of historic development which is, stage by stage, a movement towards more complete political organisation, of larger scope and powers, on the whole founded more broadly upon right and leaning less upon force. The nineteenth century had already built up a higher order than any that its predecessors achieved. The democratic State on the national scale, with its deepened sense of public responsibility, still conserving regard for personal freedom, was the highest political organisation yet known to the world, and the war has proved it tougher and firmer than its autocratic rival. But the States, considered together, were an arch without a keystone, and they fell to pieces. We have now to rebuild them into a world-order, and in doing so, in dispelling fear and hostility between nations, we shall remove the main obstacles to the growth of equal freedom and brotherly comradeship within.

By the hundred thousand young men have died for the hope of a better world. They have opened for us the way. If, as a people, we can be wise and tolerant and just in peace as we have been resolute in war, we shall build them the memorial that they have earned in the form of a world set free from military force, national tyrannies, and class oppressions, for the pursuit of a wider justice in the spirit of a deeper and more human religion.

DECEMBER 12, 1918

1918 | 1939

IRELAND

MICHAEL COLLINS

IRELAND HAS NEVER been a British colony. She has been a separate nation, kept subject by a more powerful neighbour for that neighbour's own advantage, but she has never ceased to fight for her freedom, and now, after centuries of political struggle and armed conflict, she was won independence. The British people hardly realise the change which has come and the nature of the new era which is dawning, not only for the two islands but for the whole world. All former phases of the Anglo-Irish struggle . . . all these are now seen to have been but incidents in the English claim to dominate Ireland and to control Irish destinies in English interests. England has now in substance renounced that claim, and the business of the Irish Conference is to shape the form of the partnership or alliance in which two peoples of equal nationhood may be associated for the future benefit of both.

DECEMBER 7, 1921

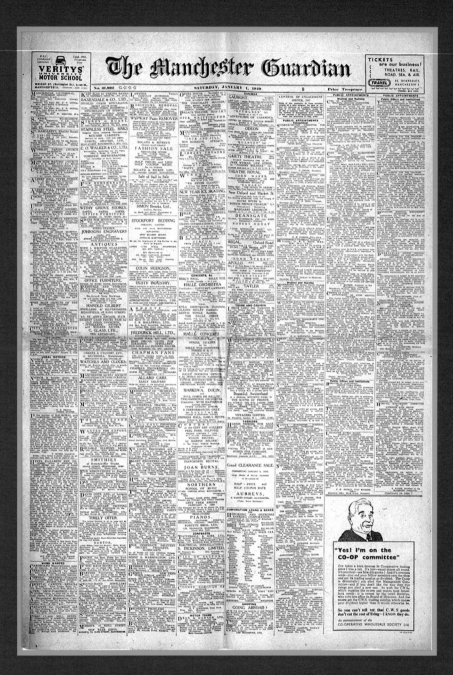

AN INTERVIEW WITH LENIN

HIS CLEAR, COLD BRAIN

BY WT GOODE

THE INTERVIEW WITH Lenin had been a matter of some difficulty to arrange; not because he is unapproachable — he goes about with as little external trappings or precautions as myself — but because his time is so precious. He, even more than the other Commissaries, is continuously at work. But at last I had secured a free moment and drove from my room, across the city, to one of the gates of the Kremlin.

A small wooden office beyond the bridge, where a civilian grants passes, and a few soldiers, ordinary Russian soldiers, one of whom receives and verifies the pass, were all there was to be seen at this entrance. It is always being said that Lenin is guarded by Chinese. There were no Chinese here.

I hung up my hat and coat in the ante-chamber, passed through a room, in which clerks were at work and entered the room in which the Executive Committee of the Council of People's Commissaries holds its meetings. I had kept my appointment strictly to time, and my companion passed on to let Lenin know that I had arrived. I then followed into the room in which Lenin works and waited a minute for his coming.

Lenin entered the room. He is a man of middle height, about fifty years old, active, and well proportioned. His hair and pointed beard have a ruddy brown tinge. The head is well domed, and his brow broad and well raised. He has a pleasant expression in talking, and indeed his manner can be described as distinctly prepossessing. He speaks clearly in a well-modulated voice, and throughout the interview he never hesitated or betrayed the slightest confusion. Indeed, the one clearly cut impression he left on me was that here was a clear, cold brain, a man absolutely master of himself and of his subject, expressing himself with a lucidity that was as startling as it was refreshing . . . .

I took up the thread by asking what was the attitude of the Soviet Republic to the small nations who had split off the Russian Empire and had proclaimed their independence.

He replied that Finland's independence had been recognised in November 1917 . . . that the Soviet Republic had announced some time previously that no soldiers of the Soviet Republic would cross the frontier with arms in their hands. . . .

For the third time I took up the questioning asking what guarantees could be offered against official propaganda among the Western peoples, if by any chance relations with the Soviet Republic were opened. His reply was that they had declared . . . that they were ready to sign an agreement not to make official propaganda.

I asked if he had any general statement to make, upon which he replied that the most important thing for him to say was that the Soviet system is the best, and that English workers and agricultural labourers would accept it if they knew it.

OCTOBER 21, 1919

FAMINE ON THE VOLGA

EATING HORSEDUNG

BY ARTHUR RANSOME

WE WENT DOWN to the shore of the Volga, down a rough broken street, past booths where you could buy white bread, and, not a hundred yards away, found an old woman cooking horsedung in a broken saucepan. Within sight of the market was a mass of refugees, men, women, and children, with such belongings as they had retained in their flight from starvation, still starving, listlessly waiting for the waggons to move them away to more fortunate districts. Some of them are sheltered from the rain that is coming now, too late, by the roofs of open-sided sheds. Others are sitting hopelessly in the open, not attempting to move, not even begging. I shall never forget the wizened dead face, pale green, of a silently weeping little girl, whose feet were simply bones over which was stretched dry skin that looked like blue-black leather. And she was one of hundreds.

CROWD WAIT FOR VACCINATION

A little crowd was gathered beside a couple of wooden huts in the middle of the camp. I went up there and found that it was a medical station where a couple of doctors and two heroic women lived in the camp itself fighting cholera and typhus. The crowd I had noticed were waiting their turns for vaccination. At first the people had been afraid of it, but already there was no sort of difficulty in persuading them to take at least this precaution, though seemingly nothing will ever teach them to keep clean. The two women brought out a little table covered with a cloth and the usual instruments, and the crowd already forming into a line pressed forward. I called to Ercole and he set up his camera.

There were old men and women, girls and little ragged children. Shirt after shirt came off, showing ghastly bags of bones, spotted all over with bites and the loathsome scars of disease. And, dreadful as their condition was, almost all showed an interest in the camera, while I could not help reflecting that before the pictures are produced some at least of them will have left the camp and made their last journey into the cemetery over the way, the earth of which, as far as you could see, was raw with new-made graves.

In the siding beyond the camp was a refugee train, a sort of rolling village, inhabited by people who were for the most part in slightly better condition than the peasants flying at random from the famine. These were part of the returning wave of that flood of miserable folk who fled eastwards before the retreating army in 1915 and 1916, and are now uprooted again and flying westwards again with the whip of hunger behind them. To understand the full difficulty of Samara's problem it is necessary to remember the existence of these people who are now being sent back to the districts or the new States to which they belong. They have prior right to transport, and, in the present condition of Russian transport, the steady shifting of these people westwards still further lessens the means available for moving the immediate victims of the drought. I walked from one end of the train to the other. It was made up of cattle trucks, but these trucks were almost like huts on wheels, for in each one was a definite group of refugees and a sort of family life. These folks had with them their belongings, beds, bedding, chests of drawers, rusty sewing machines, rag dolls. I mention just a few of the things I happened to see.

Families that had lost all else retained their samovar, the central symbol of the home, the hearth of these nomads; and I saw people lying on the platform with samovars boiling away beside them that must have come from West of Warsaw and travelled to Siberia and back. In the doorway of one truck I found a little boy, thinner than any child in England shall ever be, I hope, and in his hand was a wooden cage, and in the cage a white mouse, fat, sleek, contented, better off than any other living thing in all that train. There were a man and his wife on the platform outside. I asked them where they were going. "To Minsk," said the man, "those of us who live; the children are dying every day." I looked back at the little boy, warming his mouse in the sun. The mouse, at least, would be alive at the journey's end.

OCTOBER 11, 1921

MICHAEL COLLINS KILLED IN AMBUSH

"BURY ME IN GLASNEVIN"

BY OUR IRISH CORRESPONDENT

MICHAEL COLLINS, Commander-in-Chief of the Irish army, was killed in an ambush near Bandon, county Cork, within a few miles of his birthplace, on Tuesday night.

ACCOMPANIED BY BODYGUARD

Accompanied by several leading Free State officers, he was visiting the National Army's posts in South Cork and was returning to Cork City by byroads owing to obstacles on the main road. He was accompanied by an armoured car and a bodyguard. There were about twenty men altogether in the party.

Michael Collins (left)

The Irregulars, who are said to have numbered about two hundred, had been almost beaten off when Collins was shot in the head. It was clear from the first that the wound was fatal, but he went on firing. His last words were "Forgive them. Bury me in Glasnevin with the boys."

AUGUST 24, 1922

TUTANKHAMEN'S TOMB

A NEW PAGE OF HISTORY UNSEALED

BY A STUDENT OF EGYPTOLOGY

THE DISCOVERIES OF Mr Howard Carter at Thebes, reported by the Cairo correspondent of *The Times*, are likely to be of high importance to the student of comparative religion as well as to the Egyptologist. The cache unearthed in the Valley of the Kings by Mr Howard Carter, who for sixteen years has been assisting Lord Carnarvon in excavations on the site of ancient Thebes, contains the funeral furnishings of King Tutankhamen. He was one of the Heretic Kings of the Eighteenth Dynasty, and it was he who reverted to the traditional polytheistic worship of the Egyptians which his father-in-law, Akhenaton, had exchanged for a more enlightened monotheism.

Three sealed chambers have been discovered, and one of the three has not yet been opened. Its door is guarded by two life-sized bitumenised statues of Tutankhamen, with delicately carved features, hands, and feet, and headdresses richly studded with gems. From their presence it appears possible that the unopened chamber may be the tomb of Tutankhamen. The outer chamber in which these statues stood was crammed with a medley of treasures. There were three magnificent state couches, exquisitely carved, supporting beds ornamented with carving, gilt, and inlaid ivory and semi-precious stones. Beneath one of the couches was the state throne of Tutankhamen, which *The Times* correspondent describes as "probably one of the most beautiful objects of art ever discovered."

A heavily gilt chair was adorned with portraits of the king and queen and encrusted with gems. Four chariots were in the chamber, their sides encrusted with semi-precious stones and richly decorated with gold, and a charioteer's apron of leopard-skin hung over the seat of each. Other objects in the same chamber were a stool of ebony inlaid with ivory, boxes of exquisite workmanship, one of them containing royal robes, handsomely embroidered, a throne-stool with Asiatics carved upon it, bronze-gilt musical instruments, alabaster vases of intricate and unknown design, wreaths still looking evergreen, and large quantities of provisions for the dead, such as trussed ducks and haunches of venison, all packed in boxes. There was also a box containing rolls of *papyri*, and these, it is expected, will add considerably to our knowledge of the period.

DECEMBER 1, 1922

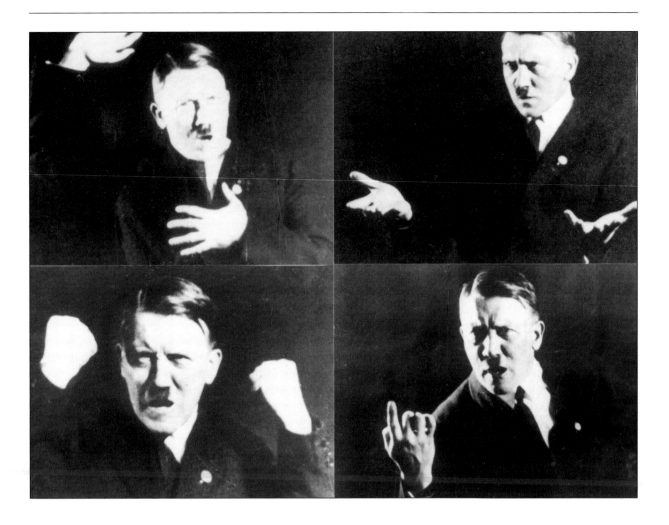

HITLER STORMS THE BEER HALL

A CLOCKWORK FIGURE

BY OUR CORRESPONDENT

THE NATIONALIST DEMONSTRATION held in the Bürgerbräu Keller (Beer Hall) yesterday was of a highly dramatic character. Dr von Kahr had been speaking for about three-quarters of an hour when a commotion was noticed in the entrance hall, and Herr Hitler, escorted by two heavily armed National Socialists, was seen forcing his way in.

Von Kahr was about halfway through his speech when the fateful moment arrived. Hitler burst into the beer restaurant, his face glowing with emotion, his eyes fixed and brilliant. He waved a Mauser pistol in one hand. He was followed by an armed bodyguard. The street outside was crowded with armed men, who shouted "Long live Hitler!"

He strode up to the platform from which Von Kahr, who is a short, fat man, was peering with startled eyes that could only just overlook the reading desk on which he had his manuscript. Hitler moved his arms with rapid, angular gestures as though he were clockwork or a figure in some weird expressionist drama. He raised his Mauser and fired a shot into the ceiling, to the great consternation of Von Kahr and those present. Then he shouted, "The National Republic is proclaimed."

NOVEMBER 10, 1923

WOMEN AS NEWS

MISS ROSE MACAULAY ON A NUISANCE

MISS ROSE MACAULAY, lecturing on "Women as news" at the meeting of the Six-Point Group this evening, said that in this aspect women were becoming a great and increasing nuisance. People were always discussing such subjects as: Do women understand art? Have women any sense of honour? or Should clever women marry?

"I am always being rung up or written to by some newspaper and asked what my opinion is, but I do not believe men novelists are ever asked 'Should clever men marry?'"

An enormous number of books were written about "women", and as for the press, she thought sometimes that if a future chronicler were to study the files of our newspapers he would get the impression that there had appeared at this time a strange new creature called woman who was receiving great attention from the public. If a speaker made an unimportant reference to women that small part of his speech had special prominence. If a scientist in a lecture remarked that women were not as strong as men one might suppose that the obvious truth would pass unnoticed, but the newspapers would jump at it and discuss it eagerly. As a topic woman was hardly annual or, it might be said, a hardy daily.

Men insisted on generalising about women. Instead of regarding them as so many millions of individuals with separate temperaments and outlooks, all they saw was an odd, conglomerate being which they called women. "How will the women vote!" they ask before elections. "Of course you can generalise to a certain extent," said Miss Macaulay. "I should say that women have on the whole less brain power than men, less initiative and courage, and more highly strung nervous development and weaker sex emotions. That is fairly obvious, but as you realise the many exceptions all you can safely say is that most women on the whole have certain qualities in a rather greater or rather less degree than men."

Miss Macaulay amused her audience very much by reading from some magazine an article about women in which the writer described the qualities that pleased or displeased men. She had altered this slightly and read it as if all the inane hints applied to men. "Let us give women a rest," said Miss Macaulay, "and write articles on men, their temperament, qualities and habits."

NOVEMBER 13, 1925

THE INFANT POOR

BY RH TAWNEY

LIFE IN THE twentieth century for the children of the poor is still a dangerous business: how dangerous the figures of child mortality and, still more, of child sickness reveal. Now, up to six, in colliery village and factory town, in overcrowded tenement and foetid slum, they are to scramble along unaided . . . Swift once suggested killing babies and tanning their skins, which, he shrewdly observed, would make excellent leather, and could be sold by business men at a profit. Is it much more humane to "save" money by reducing height, weight, vitality, and mental development of children between 5 and 14?

[From a response to the Geddes Report, which recommended raising the age of school admission and reducing expenditure on medical and other provisions.]

FEBRUARY 21, 1922

GENERAL STRIKE DISTURBANCES

5000 STRIKERS CONFLICT WITH POLICE

UGLY SCENES WERE witnessed in the chief thoroughfares of Leeds about noon today.

The trouble began when several thousand strikers attacked one of the emergency tramcars with lumps of coal taken from a passing lorry, a number of windows in the tramcar being smashed and passengers having narrow escapes. The strikers rushed towards another tramcar a moment later, but were held back for a time by a strong body of police. Amid loud cries of "down with the police," the strikers rushed on to them. The police backed to a narrower thoroughfare, where they defended themselves with their batons.

Several windows in the main part of Briggate were smashed by the strikers. A man was arrested, and the police managed to get him into a side street.

About five thousand strong, the strikers dashed round another street, but the police, who had been reinforced, managed to keep them clear by their truncheons.

About ten minutes later the windows of two more tramcars were smashed and several passengers were cut on the face.

MAY 6, 1926

Burnt-out bus damaged by strikers

THE WEEK ON THE SCREEN

IN TELLING YOU that *Ben Hur*, which goes to the Piccadilly today for a run of four weeks, is a film poor in thought, acting, and direction I am quite aware that, for the sake of a critical scruple, I am wasting your time and mine. You will have to see *Ben Hur*, just as I have, to write about it. The thing has become too big for us — we are irresistibly drawn to try our own judgements on a film that has towered above so many conversations, lined up queues for so many London theatres, occupied so much

space in the British and American press. The important fact about *Ben Hur* is, not that it is such a poor film, but that, being so poor, it has achieved such a fabulous reputation. Few picture-goers can be incurious enough not to want to see for themselves how it was done.

My own opinion of it is that the producers succeeded, not through any knowledge of the nature of a film, but through an implicit knowledge of the nature of the public. *Ben Hur* is not a film — it is not a formal unit of any kind. It is the cunning

assemblage on a screen of all the subjects that provoke the most pleasant emotions in the watcher — the great shop-window display of passion and sentiment.

When you have paid your money to see *Ben Hur* you will find yourself able to sample, one after another, the cinema's most popular lines in emotional wares. Under that fine drawing title, which catches you by all the happy associations of your young reading days, you will find love and danger, jealousy, tenderness, mobility, excitement, comfortable religion, and nebulous

patriotism spread out, ticketed and priced in dollars before your eyes. Some one of the samples will surely take your fancy — the fire of Ramon Navarro's Ben Hur, the modesty of May MacAvoy's Esther, the scope and eagerness of the early scenes in Bethlehem, the tumult of the chariot races, the measure of the galley's movement, the horror of the valley of lepers, the sheer weight and volume of crowds. Each article is a striking example of its kind. Together they dazzle you from the dark setting of the screen surround; the first as good as the last, the last as the first, without sequence, connection, or formal hierarchy.

When *Ben Hur* was first shown in England, at the Tivoli, the manager and press agent, knowing very well the importance to a film of the mental attitude created by its original run, were careful to emphasise the shop-window aspect. They never presented *Ben Hur* as a unity. Outside the theatre were big programme-sheets, giving to the minute the time of every spectacular incident in the film, as if each were a separate item in the theatre's bill of fare. Checking the time-sheet with our watches, we could pick and choose whether we should go in for the sea fight or the quadriga race, the processions of triumph through the streets of Jerusalem, the mutiny in the galleys, the quarrel with the Roman Messala, or the miraculous healing of the mother and sister of Ben Hur. We could turn over the goods and make our own selections. Thus suggestion of freedom in this idea was completely and ridiculously compelling.

By cunning exhibition methods designed to show up the commercial highlights of the film, by a skilful inducement of society to lead the way into the shop window to look at the goods — for who can resist buying entertainment elbow to elbow with a real princess? — *Ben Hur* has had the benefit of its innate showman's qualities at the Tivoli, where it broke all records, and more recently at a score of theatres in the outer London area. Otherwise intelligent men and women talk about it in hushed voices. I have been asked whether I was not proud to have the honour of reviewing it. Certain acquaintances of mine are rumoured to have seen it forty-nine times. And I do not doubt that its four weeks in Manchester and its booking at good, bad, and indifferent picture-houses all over the country will only confirm the conclusions of its London run — that *Ben Hur*, with its excellent window display, invites the public to participate in what is probably the best and biggest sale that the movies have ever made.

NOVEMBER 19, 1927

ASBESTOS
A REAL ASSET

ITS HOUSEHOLD USES

ASBESTOS HAS BECOME a very real asset in the home. Although it is originally a mineral substance, it is nevertheless of a fibrous nature, and can, therefore, be woven into fabrics and formed into boards. Its greatest virtue lies in the fact that it is fireproof, and, as it is a bad conductor of heat, it has great value in many household uses.

Asbestos cord bound round the handles of kettles, saucepans, and irons, will prevent burnt fingers. Asbestos mats placed on the stove make a safe surface for casseroles and other fireproof ware during the cooking of the food in them. Asbestos table mats are also very popular as a means of preventing hot plates and dishes from marking the table surface where a tablecloth is not used. These asbestos mats can be obtained with charming embroidered, or otherwise decorated, slip covers. Asbestos tiles, such as are used for roofing purposes, are exceptionally useful in the kitchen, as a hot dish or saucepan can be placed on them without the fear of marking or burning the table. When the weather is frosty the tragedy of frozen pipes can be avoided by binding the exposed parts with asbestos cord. This prevents the heat from escaping, and equally prevents the frost from affecting the pipes.

An asbestos device of great utility is the fire-blower. This is just a sheet of asbestos mounted on a wire, in which a detachable cane rod is fastened. The blower can be placed in front of a fire which refuses to burn up and, as it is fireproof, can be safely left in position until a cheerful blaze has appeared. It is a good plan to have a sheet of asbestos in the house as a safeguard against fire. If it is spread across the hearth, flying sparks cannot ignite the carpet or rug. If a spark does at any time start a fire it can be prevented from spreading by throwing the asbestos cloth on the burning material.

Asbestos can also be bought in the loose fibrous form, and is excellent for temporarily repairing leaking gas and water pipes. For this purpose the asbestos fibres should be mixed to a thick paste with water-glass, spread over the hole or weak spot in the pipe and bound over with cloth.

NOVEMBER 21, 1927

BILLION DOLLAR CRASH ON
NEW YORK EXCHANGE

WILD SELLING IN RECORD SHARE TURNOVER

THE HEAVY BREAK on the New York Stock Exchange, which began on Saturday and has been increased on each succeeding day except Tuesday, when there was a slight recovery, reached catastrophic proportions yesterday with a crash described as the worst in the history of the Exchange.

The floor of the Exchange was a scene of the wildest excitement, and the shouts of the brokers seeking to unload their stocks at any price could be heard in the streets. It is estimated that $1,000,000,000 in paper values had been swept away by the close of the market.

The day's sales were 12,895,000 shares, against the previous highest number of 8,240,000 on March 26. The tape machine records of prices finished nearly three hours behind the market.

The fall at the opening of the market was so rapid that a conference of leading bankers was hastily called and a reassuring statement issued. This had a temporary rallying effect in certain sections, but the liquidation was continued elsewhere.

OCTOBER 25, 1929

RUSSIAN CINEMA

EISENSTEIN'S POTEMKIN

EVERYBODY HAS HEARD of this film. Few people in England have seen it, and when it came on the screen at the Film Society's show last Sunday the audience found they were watching the most famous of all Soviet films, familiar by hearsay, many of its scenes well known through reproduction of isolated stills and notorious from frequent bannings.

They found that they had to merge all the facts they knew into witnessing the picture as a whole; they had to see the famous scenes, such as the flight down the steps and the piece of bad meat, in relation to the whole, whilst at the same time recognising these scenes and finding others that they did not know were equally beautiful and just as effective. And they had to forget that the film was censored if they were to see it for what it was.

It is curious, but perhaps natural, that though *Potemkin* was for long the only Russian picture about which anything was generally known, little was said about its importance as sheer cinema. There was no idea of what it stood for, of the picture as a whole. It was known to be Soviet propaganda. Various scenes had acquired a disproportionate significance; and so it is quite conceivable that many people, reacting against the vivid experience technically dragged out of them, should think that all they had actually seen was a story in which the population of a town, welcoming a mutinous ship, were ruthlessly shot down and should take comfort in knowing that, historically, it was not true to facts.

But *Potemkin* has more than this. It is important, not for being Soviet propaganda, but for being Soviet cinema. While bans exist propaganda is bound to have a distorted significance, but the thing that matters is that Soviet cinema, while being propagandist, contains a use of all the different branches of film-making which is recognised and practised in no other country.

NOVEMBER 16, 1929

MR CP SCOTT

TRIBUTE TO HIS EDITORSHIP

BY THE NEW YORK HERALD TRIBUNE

THE MANCHESTER GUARDIAN was founded by John Edward Taylor in 1821, and for fifty-seven of the intervening 108 years Taylor's nephew, Mr C. P. Scott, has been its editor. Now Mr CP Scott's son, Mr Edward Taylor Scott, succeeds to one of the most distinguished posts in newspaperdom. The *Manchester Guardian* was a great paper before young CP Scott, 25 years old and just three years out of Oxford, became its editor in 1872, but in the intervening decades it has achieved much higher distinction. All over the world when men speak of standards in journalism they must take the *Manchester Guardian* into consideration.

Although he has had as collaborators some of the foremost names in British journalism, the *Guardian* has been CP Scott and Scott the *Guardian*. He has written day after day the *Guardian*'s leaders. He read every proof, and when "or" was used for "nor" or "nor" for "or" he scribbled a note to the sub-editor. Foreign correspondents, accustomed to the neglect of home offices, were for half a century frequently startled by little handwritten notes of appreciation or suggestion from the chief in Manchester. When the paper was put to bed at midnight Mr Scott, until he was well past seventy-five, mounted his bicycle and rode five miles home.

But Mr Scott is far more than an interesting human being. He has character in the richest sense. "Character," as he himself once said, "is a subtle affair, and has many shades and sides to it. It is not a thing to be much talked about, but rather to be felt. It is the slow deposit of past actions and ideals. It is for each man his most precious possession, and so it is for that growth of time the newspaper. Fundamentally it implies honesty, clearness, courage, fairness, a sense of duty to the reader and the community."

Those are terms which have peculiar fitness as applied to CP Scott. No one has ever dreamed of questioning his honesty, and the *Guardian* is one of the cleanest newspapers in England. Since 1873 it has published none of the racing tips which every English newspaperman knows are circulation-makers in that land of horse-racing. Scott showed his courage when he boldly defied his Government and denounced its course throughout the Boer War, so that police had to mount guard at his office and his home. Fairness he has in a rare degree. And no newspaper in the world has manifested a prouder sense of duty to its city and its nation.

CP Scott has retired at the ripe age of eighty-three. But those who have worked with him will not soon forget his example, and the character of his newspaper is an inspiration in newspaper offices throughout the English-speaking world.

JULY 5, **1929**

HUGE INCREASE IN UNEMPLOYMENT

RISE OF 343,000 IN TWO WEEKS

BY OUR LABOUR CORRESPONDENT

THE UNEMPLOYED TOTAL on Monday, December 29 — 2,643,127 — was the highest recorded since the unemployment insurance statistics began in 1921. It is a higher figure than was reached during the worst months of 1921, when the trade slump was aggravated by the coal stoppage.

It is not, however, likely that the figure will continue at quite this level, as the rise is to a large extent owing to the temporary closing down of works for extended holiday stoppages. Of the fortnight's increase 63,446 is among the "wholly unemployed" and 277,822 among the "temporarily stopped", the number of whom has risen from 494,798 to 774,620.

A large increase in the "temporarily stopped" always occurs in the last week of the year, and a temporary rise of a quarter of a million is not unusual. This year the rise has been far greater than usual, and probably a considerable part of it will remain and be carried forward.

JANUARY 7, 1931

No job to go to . . . an unemployed man stands with his children

BURGLAR ON HIS PROFESSION

PRISONER INTERJECTS IN COURT

WHEN ALBERT LAND Guthrie (26), of no fixed address, pleaded guilty at Barnsley today to charges of burglary at the Girls' High School and the Grammar School, Mr Herbert Smith, the Yorkshire miners' president, who was the presiding magistrate, addressing the prisoner, said, "You have already been convicted on ten charges, and there are three today and eight more to be taken into consideration." Mr Smith was proceeding to say, "You seem to be determined to carry on this business," when Guthrie interjected, "Yes, sir. It is my profession." He was committed for trial at the Quarter Sessions.

Henry John Biggs, a miner, of Summer Lane, Barnsley, who was charged with receiving a number of the articles stolen, was sent to prison for six months. Biggs told the magistrates he merely hid the articles for Guthrie.

JULY 11, 1930

DOCTRINES OF DEATH

SOVIET PEASANTRY

BY MALCOLM MUGGERIDGE

LIVING IN MOSCOW and listening always to statements of docttrine and policy, you forget that Moscow is the centre of a country stretching over a sixth of the world's surface and that the lives of a hundred and sixty millions of people, mostly peasants, are profoundly affected by discussions and resolutions that seem, when you hear them or read of them in the press, as abstract as the proceedings of a provincial debating society. "We must collectivise agriculture", or "We must root out kulaks" (the rich peasants). How simple it sounds! How logical. But what is going on in the remote villages, in the small households of the peasants? What does collectivisation of agriculture mean in practice in the lives of the peasantry? What truth, if any, is there in the gloomy reports that have been reaching Moscow?

MARCH 25, 1933

GANDHI'S MARCH TO THE SEA

PROTESTING WITH SALT

AT SIX O'CLOCK yesterday morning "Mahatma" Gandhi left Ahmedabad on foot at the head of a band of civil resistance volunteers on a hundred-mile march to the sea at Jalalpur, on the Gulf of Cambay. He thus signalled the beginning of civil disobedience or non-violent defiance of the British administration, and brought into action the new

Congress policy of Purna Swaraj, or complete independence.

For a fortnight Gandhi's march is intended to be only a demonstration. Then, when he expects to be at the sea, he will begin to produce salt from brine, and so infringe the Government salt monopoly, defying the Government to arrest and punish him. At the same time his supporters everywhere have been incited by him to refuse to pay local taxes.

There were sympathetic demonstrations yesterday in various parts of India, but apparently little excitement, and no reported incident of serious disorder. Gandhi, of course, represents a section of India only. His campaign has found no support in the National Assembly, while the Moslems are definitely opposed to it.

MARCH 13, 1930

YOUTH BURNED ON ALCOHOL TINS

US BOOTLEGGERS SUSPECTED

REUTER'S

A MESSAGE FROM Stegeer, Illinois, says that the body of a youth was found by the police on a pile of flaming alcohol tins in a car near here yesterday. The police believe that the lad was killed for encroaching on the preserve of a gang of bootleggers.

JULY 11, 1930

PROHIBITION OVER

"GREAT EXPERIMENT" ENDS

SHORTLY AFTER TEN o'clock (Greenwich time) tonight Utah — the Mormon State — became the thirty-sixth State to ratify the repeal of Prohibition and thus brought the "great experiment" to an end.

Confusion was caused in the United States today when it became known that Utah had decided to postpone her ratification from three o'clock this afternoon until this evening. The United States had been expecting the end of Prohibition to come in good time for dinner tonight, and Utah's postponement meant legally a postponement of the celebrations.

END TO SPEAKEASIES

But the United States was determined to celebrate, even if it was with illegal liquor. Consequently speakeasy owners who last night said farewell to old and valued clients over a last drink were in happier mood today when they learned that Utah had given them another day's grace.

By eight o'clock in the evening noisy sightseers, undeterred by drizzling rain, had completely jammed the traffic in the Broadway district. The nine hundred policemen on duty were rendered virtually helpless.

When the news became known the lunching of "Old Man Prohibition" in Broadway was the signal for general rejoicing. The effigy was cut down from a flagpole and dragged in a coffin through Broadway by a camel. The most popular of the many new drinks was a "New Deal" cocktail.

The news from Utah was flashed all over the country by telegraph and wireless, while the delivery vans of newspapers waited ready to speed away with special editions.

At hotels, restaurants, and cafés portable bars were used because of the State regulation against drinking at bars.

Celebrations were arranged in Greenwich Village — the Chelsea of New York — and in Harlem.

Import restrictions have delayed ships with liquor cargoes, but the Majestic and the Scythia, due yesterday, brought the first "wet" cargoes.

DECEMBER 6, 1933

COMMUNISTS TO BE INTERNED

FIRST CAMP IN BAVARIA TO HOLD 5000 MEN

THE PRESIDENT OF the Munich police has informed the press that the first concentration camp holding five thousand political prisoners is to be organised within the next few days near the town of Dachau in Bavaria.

Here, he said, Communists, "Marxists", and Reichsbanner leaders who endangered the security of the State would be kept in custody. It was impossible to find room for them all in the State prisons, nor was it possible to release them. Experience had shown, he said, that the moment they were released they

always started their agitation again. If the safety and order of the State were to be guaranteed such measures were inevitable, and they would be carried out without any petty considerations.

This is the first clear statement hitherto made regarding concentration camps. The extent of the terror may be measured from the size of this Bavarian camp — which, one may gather, will be only one of many.

The Munich police president's statement leaves no more doubt whatever that the Socialists and Republicans will be given exactly the same sort of "civic education" as the Communists. It is widely held that the drive against the Socialists will reach its height after the adjournment of the Reichstag next week.

MARCH 21, 1933

ANTI-SEMITISM IN BERLIN

STORM TROOPS PICKET SHOPS

DEMONSTRATIONS AGAINST THE big stores in Berlin today developed later in the evening into an active outbreak of anti-Semitism. In several parts of Berlin a large number of people, most of whom appeared to be Jews, were openly attacked in the streets and knocked down. Some of them were seriously injured. The police could do no more than pick up the injured and take them off to hospital.

Today Herr Goering, the Prussian Commissioner for the Ministry of the Interior, issued an order to the Storm

Troops calling for stricter discipline, and asking them to refrain from acts of violence, but the order does not yet appear to have had the desired effect.

During the busiest shopping hour this evening the following scene could be witnessed outside the Kadewe, the largest department store of the West End. A detachment of Storm Troops marched up to the shop, formed a cordon in front of the entrance, and put up a large notice, "Germans! Don't buy from Jews." The people inside the shop left hurriedly and no others were allowed to go in. The police looked on with apparent indifference. Many people who had assembled outside seemed to be favourably impressed by this demonstration, and talked cheerfully to the Storm Troopers, who assured them that "they would put an end to the Jewish shops."

MARCH 10, 1933

LETTERS TO THE EDITOR

GERMANY UNDER THE NAZIS

SIR — FOR MANY years I have been a reader of the *Manchester Guardian* and have always liked its objectivity. But I am sorry to tell you that, during the last few weeks, its reports regarding present events in Germany are untrue and more than offending for this country.

In my opinion all these lies are dictated by the infernal hatred which the German Jewish press has against all that is national in Germany — lies which are the attempts of the Jewish adder to take revenge for the collapse of the old Socialist regime of corruption, a period of lucrative business for blackguards like ——,——, and many, many others. Of course there is no planing without chips! But tell me, please, of a single Jew maltreated without being guilty of having supported the Socialists and Communists for the purpose of gaining a powerful influence upon political and administrative State affairs. There is not one. No, our national revolution is the most un-bloody revolution the world has ever seen.

Abroad, however, one need not wonder that our national Government protects the regained order and honour of Germany from its enemies by conveying them to concentration camps where, at length, they will have leisure enough to reflect upon all the dreadful dissaster their "red" regime brought and still was to bring to a nation broken down and in despair, to a nation ruined by taxes and unemployment, the consequences of the tactics of parties apparently enjoying the *Manchester Guardian*'s full sympathy.

—Yours, &c., HEINZ BARTSCH
Bahnholstr.
35, Stolp in Pommern

APRIL 1, 1933

NAZI TERROR

STORM TROOPS (Hitlers followers) are arresting Communists in their homes or on the streets. They take them into their Nazi barracks in order to torture them, as is being told us by eye-witnesses. In the Nazi barracks they whip the Communists and break their fingers in order to get from them confessions and addresses.

MARCH 16, 1933

STERILISATION OF THE UNFIT — NAZI LEGISLATION

"HEALTH COURTS" TO BE SET UP

A LAW FOR the sterilisation of the unfit and those afflicted with hereditary diseases has been drafted and will shortly receive the sanction of the Cabinet. It provides that persons such as hereditary and incurable drunkards, sexual criminals, lunatics, and those suffering from an incurable disease which would be passed on to their offspring are to be operated upon and rendered sterile even against their will if a college of doctors decides by a majority of votes that such an operation is necessary for the welfare of the nation.

A voluntary application for a sterilisation operation can also be made by any man or woman afflicted with hereditary disease. The health court to be formed would decide by a majority vote for the acceptance or rejection of the application.

As the final court of appeal on questions of voluntary or compulsory sterilisation, an upper court of health is to be constituted.

JULY 26, 1933

NAZIS PROHIBIT CHAPLIN FILM

"COMMUNIST TENDENCY"

CHARLIE CHAPLIN'S NEW film *Modern Times* has been prohibited in Germany. Reuter was informed at the Propaganda Ministry this afternoon that there was at present no prospect that the picture would be shown in this country. Another Nazi spokesman said that reports from abroad had indicated that the picture had a "Communist tendency" and that this was no doubt the reason why the picture was unacceptable.

In recent months Charlie Chaplin's films . . . have vanished from the screen on account, it has been presumed, of doubts existing here as to the Aryan purity of the comedian's ancestry. Picture postcards of Chaplin, which used to be displayed in show-windows all over Berlin, have now vanished, and it is understood that by official order no more are now being issued.

FEBRUARY 18, 1936

SHIRLEY TEMPLE

CURLY TOP

SHIRLEY TEMPLE, THAT exceptional child whom everyone seems to believe should be both seen and heard, appears in *Curly Top* at the Gaumont this week. She must have gained the crown of "world's sweetheart" by this time, for here she is cast in a story similar to one of Mary Pickford's, that of the orphanage girl who won the love of a trustee. Shirley is too young to marry yet, so in *Curly Top* she is content to win the heart of Edward Morgan (John Boles) and let her

sister (Rochelle Hudson) do the marrying. This film begins in the vein of a musical extravaganza, with Shirley taking a live pony to bed in the dormitory and then performing a song and dance for the orphanage children, but it soon resolves itself into a straightforward love story, with Shirley providing the bond.

It is all highly artificial and sentimental and should be avoided by some film-goers. There is no doubt, however, that the instinct of the masses is sound in its choice of Shirley Temple as a favourite. She possesses the most adorable characteristics of little girls and it is pleasant to note where they emerge from beneath layers of vulgar direction. Sometimes she conveys a rare impression that this film-making is all a delightful game. That is the sugar and the spice.

JANUARY 7, 1936

THE OLYMPIC GAMES

BERLIN'S CEREMONY

THE OPENING CEREMONY of the eleventh Olympic Games took place here this afternoon in the Stadium at the Reich Sports Field, and the athletic competitions will begin to-morrow morning. It was probably the longest ritual that has ever heralded the opening of these Games. It was arranged and carried out with mathematical exactitude by the German Organising Committee, and in the course of it there were moments of beauty and significance which one will remember.

GERMAN NATIONAL FEELING

There were others — not many of them — when one felt that the strength of German national feeling had a little outgrown discretion, but it was a memorable ceremony, immensely enhanced by the nobility of the great Stadium in which it was carried out. . . .

OLYMPIC BELL TOLLS

The flags of the competing nations were hoisted and unfurled themselves lightly against the sky, and the Olympic bell was tolled in deep booming notes. The Games were open . . .

The German team gave their national salute; there followed a speech by the president of the German Olympic Committee; Herr Hitler declared the games open and then the Olympic flag was hoisted; the artillery fired a salute and thousands of pigeons were released to flutter from the track like grey snowflakes blown in a gale.

THE OLYMPIC FLAME ARRIVES

Richard Strauss's Olympic Hymn was played, and then all eyes were turned to the eastern gates. On the top of the long steps a runner in white was standing with a lighted torch in his hand. He was the last of a long line that has brought the Olympic flame three thousand miles across Europe. He ran lightly and beautifully down the steps and along the track carrying the torch aloft, ran up the opposite flight of steps and lit the Olympic fire between the towers of the Marathon Gate. As the fire gushed upwards the huge crowd broke into a roar of cheers.

AUGUST 3, 1936

TOWN OF TEN THOUSAND IN RUINS

THREE HOUR MASSACRE FROM THE AIR

BY OUR CORRESPONDENT

GUERNICA, A TOWN of some ten thousand inhabitants, was yesterday reduced to a mass of burning ruins by countless numbers of German planes which kept up a continuous bombing for three and a half hours.

The full story of yesterday's massacre is not yet known, but what details there are are horrible enough. It is now disclosed that the rebel planes bombed and set fire to isolated farmhouses for a distance of five miles around Guernica. Even flocks of sheep were machine-gunned.

THE DEAD UNKNOWN

In Guernica itself it is not known how many hundreds of people — men, women, and children — have been killed; it may indeed never be known. The town is in ruins. The buildings left standing can be counted almost on the fingers of one hand. Among them is, remarkably enough, the Basque Parliament building, with its famous oak tree.

The church of St John was destroyed, but the principal church, St Mary's, is almost intact, except for the chapterhouse and part of the tower. The convent of Santa Clara, which was being used as a hospital, was destroyed, with many of its inmates. Another small hospital, with 42 beds, was completely wiped out together with its 42 wounded occupants. Yet a third hospital was wrecked with many victims.

MARKET DAY

The raid occurred on market day when the town was full of peasants who had come into sell their produce. The bombers, all of them said to be German, came over in waves of seven at a time. Many of the people who raced desperately for the open fields were systematically pursued and machine-gunned from the air by swooping fighters.

The survivors spent a night of horror sleeping where and if they could, awaiting with resignation their evacuation today. Since early this morning the roads leading to the rear have been thronged with long streams of peasants whose whole remaining possessions are dumped on ox-carts.

Today I visited what remains of the town. I was taken to the entrance of a street like a furnace which no one had been able to approach since the raid. I was shown a bomb shelter in which over fifty women and children were trapped and burned alive. Everywhere is a chaos of charred beams, twisted girders, broken masonry, and smouldering ashes, with forlorn groups of inhabitants wandering in search of missing relatives.

I picked up an incendiary shell which failed to explode. It was made of aluminium, weighed nearly two pounds, and was liberally stamped with German eagles.

STREETS IMPASSABLE

When I visited the town again this afternoon it was still burning. Most of the streets in the centre were impassable, so that it is still unknown how many victims there are. In the ruins the fires have been so extensive that many bodies will never be recovered. I confirmed the death of Father Aronategi, an aged priest, who perished while trying to rescue children from a burning building. The bodies of the few dead yet recovered are horribly mutilated.

Thousands of homeless people have been evacuated with efficiency by the Basque authorities and are now at Bilbao. Their arrival may increase the difficulties of food supply in this city. Some of the refugees related that German aeroplanes machine-gunned women working in the fields.

Guernica, like the other Basque country towns, was absolutely defenceless, and was provided with neither anti-aircraft guns nor planes.

APRIL 28, 1937

Pablo Picasso's response to Guernica

MASS OBSERVATION

RECORDS OF CONTEMPORARY LIFE

MASS OBSERVATION IS the name of a movement which was started about a year ago by a group of people interested in providing the historian of the future with a true documentation of contemporary life. If was felt that social surveys, such as the brilliant "Middletown" relied too much on reported as opposed to observed fact, that too little opportunity was given for those actually living in certain surroundings to describe them.

A letter in the weekly press asking for helpers drew replies from about fifty people. As a form of training in observation these volunteers were asked to supply the following information:-

(a) A short report on themselves.
(b) A description of their environment.
(c) A list of objects on their mantelpieces.
(d) A day survey: an account of all that they saw and heard on the twelfth day of the month.

Six months after the first meeting Mass Observation was able to organise a national survey of Britain on Coronation Day. A team of fifteen reported on the actual procession, while from provincial towns and villages reports came in on local celebrations. From these "mass observations" the first full-length book has been compiled, shortly to be published.

There are now about fifteen hundred active observers who are periodically sending in to not only day surveys but replies to questionnaires on such subjects as class distinctions, behaviour at mealtimes, reading habits. This national network, which is still increasing, works from the individual observer outwards, one task of Mass Observation being to see how the individual is linked up with society and its institutions. Direct observation of the masses is also being done by a group of full-time research workers in an industrial town. Their method is to start from the outside and to work inwards, getting into the society and so coming to the individual. Their methods differ from those of most sociologists, mainly in the degree of scepticism with which they approach their problem. The manner of approach is rather that of anthropologists, studying the beliefs and the behaviour of an unknown people.

SEPTEMBER 14, 1937

RETURN FROM MUNICH

MR CHAMBERLAIN'S PIECE OF PAPER

NO STRANGER EXPERIENCE can have happened to Mr Chamberlain during the past month of adventures than his reception back home in London. He drove from Heston to Buckingham Palace, where the crowd clamoured for him, and within five minutes of his arrival he was standing on the balcony of the Palace with the King and Queen and Mrs Chamberlain.

The cries were all for "Neville", and he stood there blinking in the light of a powerful arc-lamp and waving his hand and smiling. For three minutes this demonstration lasted. Another welcome awaited the Premier in Downing Street, which he reached fifteen minutes later. With difficulty his car moved forward from Whitehall to Number 10. Mounted policemen rode fore and aft and a constable kept guard on the running board of the car.

Every window on the three floors of Number 10 and Number 11 was open and filled with faces. The windows of the Foreign Office across the way were equally full — all except one, which was made up with sandbags. Everywhere were people cheering. One of the women there found no other words to express her feelings but these, "The man who gave me back my son."

Mr and Mrs Chamberlain stood for a few moments on the doorstep acknowledging the greeting. Then Mr Chamberlain went to a first-floor window and leaned forward happily smiling on the people. "My good friends," he said — it took some time to still the clamour so that he might be heard — "this is the second time in our history that there has come back from Germany 'peace with honour'. I believe it is peace for our time."

OCTOBER 1, 1938

1939 | 1945

"HOT MUSIC"

REPORT OF A SPEECH BY SIR SAMUEL HOARE

"LET THE WORLD ponder upon these things and particularly let those ponder on them who say that we [British] have grown weary with age and feeble in power. So they thought in 1914. They had a rude awakening . . . I am told that in the United States there is a class of people who sit listening in hysterical excitement to what is called "hot music" and waiting for the final crash. Americans in their forcible language call them "jitterbugs". There are many people in Europe today who seem to be behaving in much the same way. They sit listening to all the hot music of the scares and alarms, waiting helplessly for the crash that, according to them, will destroy us all."

JANUARY 27, 1939

FINNEGANS WAKE

JAMES JOYCE

BY B IFOR EVANS

MR JOYCE'S *Finnegans Wake*, (Faber, 25s.), parts of which have been published as "Work in Progress" does not admit of review. In twenty years' time, with sufficient study and with the aid of the commentary that will doubtless arise, one might be ready for an attempt to appraise it. The work is not written in English, or in any other language, as language is commonly known. I can detect words made up out of some eight or nine languages, but this must be only a part of the equipment employed. This polyglot element is only a minor difficulty, for Mr Joyce is using language in a new way. A random example will illustrate:

> Margaritomancy! Hyacinthous pervinciveness! Flowers. A cloud. But Bruto and Cassio are ware only of trifid tongues the whispered wilfulness ('tis demonal!) and shadows shadows multiplicating (*il folsoletto nel falsoletto col fazzolotto dal fuzzolezzo*), totients quotients, they tackle their quarrel.

The easiest way to deal with the book would be to become "clever" and satirical or to write off Mr Joyce's latest volume as the work of a charlatan. But the author of *Dubliners*, *A Portrait of an Artist*, and *Ulysses* is obviously not a charlatan, but an artist of very considerable proportions. I prefer to suspend judgement. If I had had to review Blake's *Prophetic Books* when they first appeared I would have been forced to a similar decision. What he is attempting, I imagine, is to employ language as a new medium, breaking down all grammatical usages, all time space values, all ordinary conceptions of context. Compared with this, *Ulysses* is a first-form primer. For *Ulysses* had a theme which could be described, as the story of the Homeric "Ulysses" can be described, in a few words. In this volume the theme is the language and the language the theme, and a language where every association of sound and free association is exploited. In one of the more lucid passages Mr Joyce appears to be discussing language:

> Has any usual sort of ornery josser, flat-chested, fortyish, faintly flatulent and given to ratiocination . . . ever looked sufficiently longly at a quite everyday looking stamped addressed envelope? Yet to concentrate solely on the literal sense of even the psychological content of any document to the sore neglect of the enveloping facts themselves circumstantiating it is as hurtful to sound sense (and let it be added to the truest taste) as . . .

But I must leave the sentence there, for the comparison would fill a quarter of a column.

What, it may be asked, is the book about? That, I imagine, is a question which Mr Joyce would not admit. This book is nothing apart from its form, and one might as easily describe in words the theme of a Beethoven symphony. Those who have been privileged to discuss the work with Mr Joyce suggest that he has been influenced by the proposal in Vico's *Scienza Nuova* to write an ideal and timeless history into which all ordinary histories are embodied. The clearest object in time in the book is the Liffey, Anna Livia, Dublin's legendary stream, and the most continuous character is HC Earwicker, "Here Comes Everybody": the Liffey as the moment in time and space, and everything, everybody, all time as the terms of reference, back to Adam or Humpty Dumpty, but never away from Dublin. This seems the suggestion of the musical half-sentence with which the work begins:

> Riverrun, past Eve and Adam's, from swerve of shore to bend of bay, brings us by a commodious vicus of recirculation back to Howth Castle and Environs.

Who, it may be asked, was Finnegan? Again, I should have been unable to tell, unaided, from Mr Joyce's book. But I gather that there is an Irish story of a contractor who fell and was stretched out for dead. When his friends toasted him he rose at the word "whiskey" and drank with them. In a book where all is considered, this legend, too, has its relevance.

One concluding note. Mr Joyce in a parody of Jung and Freud ("Tung-Toyd") mentioned "Schizophrenia". One might imagine that Mr Joyce had used his great powers deliberately to show the language of a schizophrenic mind, and then he alone could explain his book and, I suppose, he alone review it.

MAY 12, 1939

AT WAR

WE ARE NOW at war and there is no further room for argument. Quiet living has ended; we are plunged into a new world of desperate hopes and fears. Yet for the last act none of us can have any regrets. There was no other way. Conciliation was open to the end. Hitler would have none of it. The British Government held its hand for a day and a half after its warning. The French Government gave even longer time for a final gesture from Germany. Italy played a part (not yet known in detail) in trying to secure a cessation of hostilities. It was all to no effect. The German Government let the sands run out. It had counted the risks and it took them. It deliberately chose to bring calamity on Europe. And now the darkness of war falls on us, broken only by occasional flashes of vital news, a darkness in which our part is to work with patience, trust, and energy.

The British people have never been so united in accepting a challenge as they are today in determining to resist the tyranny with which all free peoples are threatened. Never indeed have safety and honour been so indissolubly linked together. It has at times been argued that the British Empire could stand aloof from the Continent of Europe, nursing its strength and pursuing its own special interests in the world. The hard facts have destroyed this illusion. While Great Britain was still an island her statesmen and strategists held that the preservation of the integrity and independence of the Low Countries was vital to her safety. It is true that at the Peace of Amiens Great Britain was obliged to leave France in possession of Belgium, but that very fact stamped the peace with the character of a truce.

The great historian Sorel pointed out that the neutralisation of Belgium was really essential to peace in Western Europe. But once it was granted that Great Britain would be in danger if the Low Countries passed under the control of powerful and ambitious Governments, it became clear that Britain's interest in the state of the Continent went far beyond this. Any State that threatened to become the master of the Continent threatened Great Britain, for, on the narrowest view, it was of supreme importance to her what happened in the Low Countries. The isolation school was therefore on weak ground even in the days, those days to which we look wistfully back today, when we were still an island on the edge of a continent and not part of that continent itself. Today we are no longer an island. It is easier for Germany's airmen to attack us than it is for our airmen to attack Germany.

The case for isolation thus breaks down if we are merely looking to our safety. But of course the question is much larger than this. The future of the world is at stake, and for one of the great leading Powers of Europe to leave the world to its fate would be an act of abdication deadly to its good name and to its spirit and its character. Particularly would this be true of Great Britain. For there is no nation that has gained so much in wealth, in power, in reputation, and in the experience on which political wisdom is nurtured from contact with other peoples and other continents. Can you say of a people that has spread its name and its institutions all over the globe, that has brought across every sea the treasures of distant lands, that has used its power in three continents to guide the destinies of strange peoples, that has built up its economic strength by riches gained in many cases by the lawless methods of the lawless centuries — can you say of such a people that it owes nothing to mankind and that its only duties are to itself? If we had accepted Hitler's invitation to share power with him and leave him to make Eastern Europe his vassal, we should have betrayed every moral principle in politics. Only a few months ago we were proclaiming that the defence of the League of Nations was our first principle in politics. If we had accepted Hitler's invitation we should have been guilty of one of the most cynical treasons in history.

Few people who have lived through the last two years can be in any doubt of the importance of the issue. Europe and the world cannot live and develop their ideas, their capacities, and their virtues in the strident and brutal anarchy into which they have been thrown by the gangster methods. What is to become of religion, of culture, of beauty and happiness, of the merest decencies, of the settled habits and purpose in daily life if men and women are to remain under the shadow of perpetual war, and war infinitely more barbarous than that of the ages we call savage? For the most ruthless warfare of all is the warfare that combines the unchecked violence of uncivilised man with the weapons and resources of the civilised.

This is the process that we have to arrest. And of all the peoples of the world there is not one of whom it is more important that this attack on civilised custom should be overpowered. Democracy is the basis of our life and our society. In fighting the cause of the freedom of Europe we are fighting the cause of freedom in these islands and in all the societies that make up the British Commonwealth. War, it is said, will not solve our problems. That is true. They demand, as we have often said in these columns, constructive and imaginative statesmanship. But it is only by war, alas! at this hour that we can obtain for the world the opportunity for statesmanship. If Hitler overruns Europe, the constructive task will fall on him, and we have only to look at Germany, Austria, and Czecho-Slovakia to see what he will make of it. Today we have to exert the whole strength of the British people to avert that catastrophe. Democracy, said Fox, gives a power of which no other form of government is capable. That power and the intense passion with which men love liberty are our chief hope and comfort as we enter on the night which begins to darken upon the world.

SEPTEMBER 4, 1939

DR SIGMUND FREUD

PROFESSOR SIGMUND FREUD, the distinguished psychologist and originator of psychoanalysis was born in Freiberg, Moravia, and educated at Vienna and Paris. He was of Jewish extraction and fled from Austria — he was then eighty-two years of age — on the Nazi invasion of the country, and had since found asylum in England.

Freud's attitude towards psychoanalysis cannot be understood until his two fundamental beliefs are appreciated. The first is that every event in the mind can be described and explained in mental terms; the other, loaded as it is with complex philosophical implications, can only be mentioned. It is that determinism applies as rigidly to the mind as to the body. For Freud the word chance had no meaning, except in the scientist's sense. In his view, the wildest dreams, the most obscure delusions, the most trivial forgetting or mislaying are as much a matter of cause and effect as an eclipse of the sun. Whatever the verdict upon Freud's contributions to science may be in another hundred years, it is certain that he will be known as the man who forced thinkers to take dreams seriously. For the blended flippancy and boredom which characterised the writers on dreams before 1900 Freud has substituted deadly earnestness.

He believed that the dream was the functional nervous disorder in miniature, that in it indirect satisfaction was obtained during sleep for mental trends which in waking life were unsatisfied or repressed. But the system of analysis or dissection of dreams which Freud created must be carefully distinguished (and it seldom is) from the interpretation of dreams which he proposed. If a complicated piece of machinery were discovered in a new country it might be possible for several engineers to agree perfectly concerning its constituent parts while dissenting violently from each other as to its probable function. So it is with the dream. By reminding us that so-called free association is not free at all but is ruled by laws, however numerous and complicated they may be and however little we may know about them, Freud again contributed to knowledge.

For Freud the dominant factor in human life was the sex

Father of psychoanalysis . . . Sigmund Freud

instinct. It is true that he meant by the word sexuality very much more than the narrow meaning often put upon it. But in fairness it should be recorded that he probably meant something much more related to our popular conception of it than some of his apologists would have us believe. His belief that the dominant factor in the psychoneuroses was some disturbance of the love life was put to a vast test on the outbreak of the Great War. Many who did not accept, or even violently opposed, some of his fundamental theories regarded his conception of repression as one of first-rate importance. In fact, there are critics who think that if Freud had broadened the basis of his theory to include the repression of what might be called the danger instincts and the self-preservation instincts, it covers very well the neuroses of war.

In the second period of Freud's constructive thinking he showed increasing awareness that to describe repression was not enough. To discover the nature of the mental forces which brought about the repression was just as important. He then produced his picturesque, attractive, baffling concept of the super-ego, the integration of the moral elements in oneself. Though it has much in common with familiar concepts of conscience it cannot be equated with them. Particularly penetrating was his suggestion that the neurotic's symptoms are often self-punishments, and that an almost-healthy person's super-ego may oppress his life with undue severity, causing him to be austere towards himself and cruel to others, all with a moral or quasi-moral motive or excuse. In a person placed in authority such a state of mind may cause agony to millions of innocent people.

Freud often seemed to be on the verge of giving substantial help to the psychology of society. But he was perhaps too closely confined to his own "culture pattern", even to his consulting-room. His ideas have permeated psychological writings so thoroughly that it is difficult to criticise him without using his own language. And the applications of those ideas have led many patients from suffering to serenity.

SEPTEMBER 25, 1939

GOODBYE TO BERLIN

CHRISTOPHER ISHERWOOD

BY THOMAS MOULT

MR CHRISTOPHER ISHERWOOD, whose collaboration with Mr Auden in several volumes suggests that he is a poet by nature even if his work so far is in prose, and drama, has collected a group of his sketches about pre-Nazi Germany and, to leave them less inconclusive than they might have been in their fragmentary state, also about the same country since Hitler. The main impression left by *Goodbye to Berlin* (Hogarth Press, 7s. 6d.) is one of smouldering indignation that is only kept from blazing up by an artistically

Sketches and poems ... Isherwood and Auden

assumed detachment. Judged solely as art, though, the six pieces, including fragments of a diary, are vague and uneven, and as personal impressions they are overegoistic and too lacking in the saving grace of humour. But, like his generation, Mr Isherwood has a horror of what they call sentimentality, and this is a pity, because the meatless bones at the other literary extreme are no more attractive. The story of Sally Bowles, for instance, is so dry and tasteless that we speculate as we read it — and it comes early in the book — where Mr Isherwood's virtue lies as artist. Fortunately before the end there is a study of Jewish family life entitled The Landaeurs and this is Mr Isherwood as we expected him. Almost with a stroke of the pen he makes the outpourings of the Nazi fanatics seem not only mean but pygmy.

MARCH 24, 1939

FIRST BEF CASUALTIES IN ACTION

MEN ON NIGHT PATROL WORK

THE FIRST CASUALTIES suffered by men of the British Expeditionary Force in action on the Western Front are reported today. The numbers of dead and wounded are not announced, but the total is understood to be very small.

DANGER FROM MINES

The men killed and wounded were on night patrol work in front of that part of the Maginot Line which is now held by British troops under French command. Patrol units are in constant danger from small mines laid in the wooded country between the two front lines.

A message received at British GHQ from French headquarters says, "The British now have their wounded and even their dead on French soil once again."

DECEMBER 18, 1939

THE END OF THE GRAF SPEE

SCUTTLED BY HER CREW

THE GERMAN "POCKET battleship" *Admiral Graf Spee* scuttled herself at 10.55 British time last night. She had lifted anchor at 8.45 p.m, and at 9.30 p.m. — the limit of the time set by the Uruguayan Government for her stay at Montevideo — she set sail.

Three miles from shore the remnant of the crew who had remained on board were loaded on to two tugs and a barge, which pulled away from the battleship. Then there were three explosions and she went down.

HITLER GAVE ORDER

The German News Agency reported early this morning that Hitler gave the order for the scuttling of the ship.

Thus the seal was set on the British victory of Wednesday, when the light cruisers, the *Achilles*, the *Ajax*, and the *Exeter*, crippled the powerful battleship and forced her into the temporary refuge of the neutral harbour.

DECEMBER 18, 1939

MR CHURCHILL TAKES OFFICE

BLOOD, TOIL, TEARS, SWEAT

MR CHURCHILL'S WORDS yesterday were sombre but heartening. We have before us, as he said, "many, many long months of struggle and of suffering." Our lot is "blood and toil and tears and sweat." But the greater and the closer the danger the better the heart in which we go forward. We at last, even the most

careless of us, see that everything we value in life is in jeopardy. Mr Churchill put the truth in a phrase: "If you ask what is our policy, I will say it is to wage war, war by air, land, and sea; war with all our might and with all the strength that God can give us." To that everything is subordinate.

MAY 14, 1940

FASHIONS FOR THE BLACK-OUT

WHITE GLOVES, WHITE Lancaster cloth large pockette, button-hole of luminous discs with felt leaves. Plastrons of white Lancaster cloth worn both back and front. White shiny armlets and gas mask case. And a less obvious effect — white fur, gloves, and bag.

SEPTEMBER 30, 1939

THE HOMECOMING FROM DUNKIRK

MIRACLE OF THE BEF'S RETURN

BY EA MONTAGUE

IN THE GREY chill of dawn today in a south-eastern port, war correspondents watched with incredulous joy the happening of a miracle. By every canon of military science the BEF has been doomed for the last four or five days. Completely out-numbered, out-gunned, out-planed, all but surrounded, it had seemed certain to be cut off from its last channel of escape. Yet for several hours this morning we saw ship after ship come into harbour and discharge thousands of British soldiers safe and sound on British soil.

We went down to our reception port last night by a train which took more than twice the usual time to cover the distance. The reason was easy to see. Again and again we stopped outside a station while the dim shape of a troop train shot past us northward bound.

As the rising sun was turning the grey clouds to burnished copper the first destroyer of the day slid swiftly into the harbour, its silhouette bristling with the heads of the men who stood packed shoulder to shoulder on its decks. As it slowed down and drifted towards the dock side the soldiers on board shouted cheerful ribaldries to us who stood watching them with a mixture of pride and pity. They at any rate did not

Soldiers march ashore

regard themselves as the central figures of tragic drama. The gangways were in position in no time — on these ships all ceremony had been waived for the time being — and the unconscious heroes began to clamber upwards to the soil of England.

One watched them with a pride that became almost pain as one cheerful, patient figure succeeded another. They had passed through nights and days of hunger, weariness, and fear, but nearly every man still had his rifle and a clip or two of ammunition: nearly all had brought away their full kit with them — and what an agony its weight must have been at times; most of them had shaved, and quite a number were carrying the extra burden of a Lewis gun or a Bren gun. Their eyes were red with weariness above dark bags of tired skin, but they were still soldiers and still in good heart.

The wonder of their self-discipline became all the greater when one heard their stories. They were of all units and ranks. Some were in the position of the gunners whose battery had been shelled out of existence near Oudenarde, because our overworked fighter planes had had no time to deal with the German reconnaissance planes. Their battery

Above and overleaf: soldiers on their way home

commander had told them to do the best they could for themselves now that their usefulness had gone, and they had walked thirty miles to Dunkirk, there to take their chance on the Dunkirk beach, which will become as famous in history as the beaches of Gallipoli.

It is a stretch of level sand backed by dunes. The sea in front of it is shallow for some way out, so that ships cannot come close in, and successive sand-banks parallel to the shore catch at the keels of rowing-boats which come in at low tide.

Many of the men have spent two or three or four days on this beach, hiding in hollows scratched in the sand or in communal dug-outs in the dunes from the German planes which have scourged them with bomb and machine-gun. Their nights have been sleepless, and they have lived only on biscuits and water. Yet even here discipline holds. Units had been told off to look after "beach organisation" and to detail men for embarkation whenever one of the gallant destroyers moors beside the jetty.

At other times the various craft, which are risking their lives to rescue the soldiers, cannot come near the shore. When that happens the men must row themselves out in small boats or swim to the waiting ships. I met a Staff officer today who had spent the last twelve hours before his embarkation in the sea, continuously in water up to his waist, helping to push off the boats which had grounded on the sand-banks. For a large part of the time he was under fire.

Even when the men have embarked their danger is not over. Every now and then among the men who climb the gangplank into England one sees stretcher-bearers carrying a still form, its face bloodless and remote in some dream of pain, its bandages white and brilliantly stained. It is a man who has been hit by one of the shells from the German shore batteries, or by a bomb from the planes which on occasion have pursued the ships to within a few miles of the British coast. Yet they survive in their tens of thousands and are able to joke and sing as they march ashore.

Their condition is astonishingly good. Perhaps one man in a thousand is shaking with nerves and obviously fit for nothing but hospital. The rest are clearly tired, hungry, and in most cases footsore. They walk stiffly, and some of them obviously find it painful to walk at all.

The long string of steel-helmeted men passes steadily but swiftly up the gang-plank and away into the station, where they will be put into trains, fed, and dispatched to depots, where they can be reorganised and rested. A few stretcher cases are hoisted out of the ship in slings, the litter of forgotten kit is cleared away into sorting sheds, and in no time the ship is ready to return to Dunkirk.

But long before it is ready another has drawn up alongside, and as often as not the men on the second ship are being unloaded across the decks of the first.

British ships and French and Dutch, warships, drifters, trawlers, yachts, barges, they bring their loads across the hostile Channel and then go back undaunted into the inferno, where Navy and Air Force and Army are fighting furiously to keep open the last loophole of escape for our men. All the selfless courage of two nations is being thrown into the resistance at Dunkirk, and it looks as if it will not be spent in vain.

JUNE 1, 1940

SMOKING

3

Services continue in the burnt-out shell of Coventry Cathedral

COVENTRY'S ORDEAL

RUTHLESS BOMBING

THE SPIRE OF Coventry Cathedral today stood as a sentinel over the grim scene of destruction below following a dusk-to-dawn raid on the town which the Nazis claimed was the biggest attack in the history of air war. Casualties are officially estimated as being in the region of one thousand.

Some fires were still alight when, with the coming of dawn, the German bombers flew off to terminate a night of merciless, indiscriminate bombing. The Luftwaffe, carrying through the raid (which Berlin, claiming that five hundred planes took part, described as reprisal for the RAF attack on Munich), used terror-bombing tactics. From dusk to dawn there was seldom a period of more than two minutes when a bomb could not be heard falling. The centre of the city bears witness to the savagery of their attack.

In the first six hours of the attack wave upon wave of 25 or more bombers in quick succession scattered hundreds of bombs of all types over a wide area. Brilliant moonlight was not sufficient for the German airmen, who dropped flares and incendiary bombs to light up the scene soon to be bathed in a great red glow.

The barrage from the ground defences never slackened and for most of the night the raiders were kept at a great height from which accurate bombing was impossible.

The famous Cathedral is little more than a skeleton, masses of rubble forming huge mounds within its bare walls, while other targets included two hospitals, two churches, hotels, clubs, cinemas, public-shelters, public baths, police stations, and post offices.

The Provost (the Very Revd RT Howard) and a party of cathedral watchers attempted to deal with twelve incendiary bombs. They tackled them with sand and attempted to smother them, until a shower of other incendiaries, accompanied this time by high explosives, rendered impossible their efforts to save the cathedral, only the tower and steeple of which remain. "The cathedral," said the Provost, "will rise again, will be rebuilt, and it will be as great a pride to future generations as it has been to generations in the past."

Tonight the Cathedral was a reeking shell. Blackened arches and window faces of fretted stone, still stately for all their disfigurement, framed a picture of hideous destruction. Blocks of masonry, heavy pieces of church furniture, and plaques commemorating famous men were merged into a common dust.

NOVEMBER 16, 1940

Dive bombed ... Pearl Harbour under attack from the Japanese air force

JAPAN DECLARES WAR ON UNITED STATES AND BRITAIN

HEAVY RAID ON PEARL HARBOUR

THE JAPANESE, WITHOUT any warning, yesterday afternoon began war on the United States with air attacks on the naval base at Pearl Harbour, Hawaii, and the adjacent city of Honolulu. The White House also announced an air attack on Manila, in the Philippines, but it could not confirm the report.

Imperial Headquarters in Tokyo later announced that Japan had entered into a state of war with Britain and the United States in the Western Pacific from 6 a.m. today.

President Roosevelt has mobilised the Army and ordered all the armed forces to take up their war stations, and imposed a censorship.

As more than 150 planes took part in the attacks on Pearl Harbour and Honolulu, it is thought that there must

be at least three Japanese aircraft-carriers, and probably more, engaged. Several planes were shot down.

Considerable damage was done at Pearl Harbour and there were numerous casualties. It is officially announced that the Army casualties were 104 killed and 300 wounded. It is thought that these occurred when the airfield was hit. The civilian casualties are unknown.

The White House also announces that an Army transport carrying lumber has been torpedoed 1,300 miles west of San Francisco.

The Japanese yesterday took complete control at Shanghai, sank with all hands one of our small river gunboats, the *Petrel*, and seized an American gunboat.

DECEMBER 8, 1941

ROMMEL IN FULL RETREAT

ROMMEL'S DESERT ARMY is in full retreat and his "disordered columns" are being relentlessly attacked by Allied land and air forces.

This great news was given late last night in a special communique from British GHQ in Egypt.

The Axis forces in the Western Desert, after twelve days and nights of ceaseless attacks by our land and air forces, are now in full retreat.

Their disordered columns are being relentlessly attacked by our land forces and by the Allied Air Forces by day and night.

General von Stumme, a senior general who is said to have been in command

during Rommel's absence in Germany, is known to have been killed.

So far we have captured over nine thousand prisoners, including General Ritter von Thoma, Commander of the German Afrika Korps, and a number of senior German and Italian officers.

It is known that the enemy's losses in killed and wounded have been exceptionally high.

Up to date we have destroyed more than 260 German and Italian tanks and captured or destroyed at least 270 guns. The full toll of the booty cannot be assessed at this stage of the operation.

In the course of these operations our air forces, whose losses have been light, have destroyed and damaged in air combat over three hundred aircraft and have destroyed or put out of action a like number on the ground.

NOVEMBER 5, 1942

SOCIAL SECURITY

THE BEVERIDGE "PLAN for Social Security" will stir up more controversy — and raise more hopes — than any project for social change since Mr Lloyd George's National Health Insurance Bill of 1911. The controversy is inevitable; "vested interests", private and bureaucratic, are challenged in a hundred ways. But while many will find room to criticise, it cannot be too urgently pleaded that judgement should not be hasty.

"FREEDOM FROM WANT"

And those who resist change should also reflect that this is a very different England from that of thirty years ago. It is an England that cannot be frightened by the bogey of State action; it has seen too many ways of life altered to be sensitive to sectional claims if it can be convinced that they stand in the way of the general good. The Beveridge plan is a big and fine thing. It is not only the welding into an administrative unity of our splendid but untidy and wasteful social services, but the charting of a great piece of national reconstruction. If it is carried through by the Government, as in all its essentials it surely must be, it will be the redemption, on a large section of the home front, of the promises of the Atlantic Charter. It will go far towards securing for the British people "freedom from want" and, completed by a really national health service and by determined attempts to prevent cyclical mass unemployment, it will greatly strengthen our democracy by raising the happiness and well-being of "the common man".

POLITICAL CONSEQUENCES

The report is now open for discussion and action. It will rouse keen hopes and expectations not only among the British people here and in the forces but among our allies. The Government and Parliament have an opportunity which they will neglect at their peril and ours. For if we do not get something like the "Plan for Social Security" into being before the war is over the political consequences will be serious. Instead of victory we shall have suffered defeat.

DECEMBER 2, 1942

VILLAGE EVACUATED TO MAKE US TRAINING GROUND

FARMERS, LANDOWNERS, SHOPKEEPERS, and other members of the community of a village in the south-west of England met in the small church there yesterday to discuss their enforced departure from the area. It is to become the training-ground of part of the United States Army. The Lord Lieutenant of the county, the Regional Commissioner, Government experts, members of the War Agricultural

Committee, the WVS and billeting officials were also present, and the proceedings opened with prayers. From the chancel screen hung a map of the area to be evacuated.

The Lord Lieutenant and the Regional Commissioner were sympathetic but pointed out the necessity for uprooting the community. It was the decision of the War Cabinet. A military representative added: "This war isn't going to be on for ever. When it is over come back to this land." The villagers were told that assurance had been given by the Americans that as little damage as possible would be done.

Evacuation is to be completed by December 20 and Service men and Land Army girls are to be drafted into the area at once to help the farmers to lift their crops. Every effort is to be made to place agricultural labourers and others in work.

FEBRUARY 1, 1943

D-DAY

BY DAVID WOODWARD

A BRITISH PARACHUTE unit formed part of the Allied air-borne force which was the spearhead of the Second Front. It was landed behind the German lines, seized vital positions, and then linked up with the Allied forces which had landed on the beaches.

I watched the unit go to war at dusk on D-1 (the day before D-Day), parading with everybody, from its brigadier downwards, in blackened faces and wearing the camouflage smocks and rimless steel helmets of the air-borne forces. Each of the black-faced men appeared nearly as broad and as thick as he was tall by reason of the colossal amount of equipment which the parachutist carries with him.

The brigadier and the lieutenant colonel made brief speeches. "We are history," said the colonel. There were three cheers, a short prayer, and in the gathering darkness they drove off to the aerodromes with the men in the first lorry singing, incredible as it seems, the notes of the Horst Wessel song at the tops of their voices. The words were not German.

It was nearly dark when they formed up to enter the planes, and by torchlight the officers read to their men the messages of good wishes from General Eisenhower and General Montgomery.

Parachutes fill the skies

Then from this aerodrome and from aerodromes all over the country an armada of troop-carrying planes protected by fighters and followed by more troops aboard gliders took the air.

The weather was not ideal for an air-borne operation, but it was nevertheless decided to carry it out. The Germans would be less likely to be on their guard on a night when the weather was unfavourable for an attack.

First came parachutists, whose duty it was to destroy as far as possible the enemy's defences against an air landing. Then came the gliders with the troops to seize various points, and finally more gliders carrying equipment and weapons of all kinds. Out of the entire force of planes which took the unit into action only one tug and one glider were shot down.

By the time the glider on board which I was had landed it was very nearly daylight, and the dawn sky was shot with the brilliant yellows, reds, and greens from the explosions caused by the huge forces of Allied bombers covering the sea-borne attack, which was about to begin. A force of Lancasters led by Wing Commander Gibson, VC, of Mohne Dam fame, put out of action a German battery which otherwise would have made the landing of troops on that beach impossible.

Meanwhile the parachutists had been busy, and the inhabitants of the little French villages near where the landings took place awoke to find themselves free again. In little knots they gathered at windows and at street corners and watched us. They were a little shy and a little reserved for the most part, probably because they remembered Mr Churchill's statement that feint landings would take place, and they reflected that if what they were watching was a feint then the withdrawal of the British troops would mean that they would be responsible once again for their actions to Himmler and Laval.

These considerations did not affect some of them, however. One elderly Frenchman walked into a cemetery where British wounded were being collected amongst grotesque examples of French funerary art and laid upon the stretcher of one of the most seriously wounded men a huge bunch of red roses — an unwittingly appropriate tribute to the wounded men.

Other paratroops told me that as they marched through a small village which had just been devastated by Allied air bombardment they were cheered by French men and women standing among the still smoking ruins of their homes. As D-Day went on it was possible for us, studying the maps at the headquarters of the air-borne division, to see the very high degree of successful surprise which the unit had achieved. German officers were captured in their beds in several places, and it became clear that the anti-air landing precautions were not nearly as thorough as the Germans had been trying to make out for the past two years.

German prisoners proved a very mixed bag. The Reichsdeutsche was usually either a boy in his teens or an elderly veteran of the last war. There were some units of Volksdeutsche who had had German nationality forced upon them after the Hitlerian conquests of Poland and Czechoslovakia, as well as a number of Italians. The generally poor quality of these troops was not unexpected, and it was realised that behind them lay some of the best units of the German Army ready to counter-attack.

As our men prepared to meet these counter-attacks they were continually harried by snipers, who fought with great resolution until they were killed or until their ammunition was exhausted.

Later German tanks and Panzer Grenadiers in armoured lorries began their attack. In theory paratroops, because of their lack of heavy equipment, are considered light-weights for this kind of work, but these men stood up to the Germans just the same. When the fighting was at its most critical a large force of gliders carrying reinforcements flew right into the battle zone and, circling round, landed their cargoes in spite of continued German shelling of the landing zone.

These gliders turned the tide, and next morning it was an easy matter for us to drive in a captured car from the positions held by the air-borne forces to the beachhead formed by the troops from the sea. The countryside looked empty, but it still looked like posters advertising summer holidays in Normandy.

Small bodies of British troops moved along under cover of woods and hedges. Here and there were the discarded parachutes of our troops. Scattered over the ground were the black shapes of our gliders, most of which had been damaged in one way or another in their landings, with wings or tails sticking up at odd angles.

We could see where the beachhead was long before we got there by the clumps of barrage balloons flying over the

Above and overleaf: Allied troops on the beaches

ships which lay off the shore. Material already landed was being moved forward in ducks or lorries, or concentrated where it would be best hidden from the air. Mine-clearing operations were going on through the streets of a typical small French seaside resort, with occasional actions between our patrols and German snipers. In one corner of the village lay several German miniature tanks, all put out of action.

Down on the narrow beach transport moved over wire netting, shifting the stores, and on huts and tents the usual rash of British military initials had already broken out. Up to their chests in the surf troops were wading ashore from the landing craft. Out in the middle distance were supply ships and destroyers, while the background of the picture was provided by two big battleships slowly, purposefully shelling German positions with their heavy guns.

These guns had already supported the air-borne landings far inland and had badly damaged the local section of the "Atlantic Wall", which consisted at this place of medium-sized concrete blockhouses and minefields. The Germans had left in such a hurry that they had not removed the mine warnings which they had put up for their own troops so that our work was made simpler by our having the minefields clearly labelled.

A beach dressing station was full of men, British and Germans, mostly lightly wounded. In one corner there I saw a German NCO showing to three British soldiers a set of picture postcards he had bought in Paris representing the principal buildings of the town.

The pilots of the gliders which had done so well the day before were embarking in an infantry landing-craft for England to get more gliders to bring over. Having become a casualty, I travelled with them across the Channel, which in places seemed literally crowded with ships making their way along the swept channels through the German minefields.

The glider pilots landed this morning at one of the ports used to receive men during the evacuation from Dunkirk. One of the glider lieutenants told me he had been brought there at that time. "The people cheered us then," he said, "and now they just watch us go by. Do you suppose the English ever cheer their victories?"

FRIDAY JUNE 9, 1944

ALLIES INSIDE PARIS

JOY AND TUMULT

BY ROBERT REUBEN

PARIS TODAY IS a city of wild tumult and celebration. The tumult is the battle. It is not yet over, for the Germans still remain in control of key sections.

I slept in an hotel near Paris last night, but all night long Parisians and French troops hunted the Germans with a ferocity harsher than anything yet seen in France, while all night long guns fired in the battle.

French people walking from the central sector of Paris, which is reported to be still controlled by nine thousand German troops, said that fighting was still continuing. Allied tanks are pouring into the city,

and the French and American troops are receiving a riotous welcome.

The reported armistice was never definite and was not observed by the Germans.

SLAUGHTER ON A BRIDGE

One Seine bridge was littered with dead Germans this morning. Piling into cars, they tried to break through our tank guard on the bridge to reach safety. Their vehicles form a long line of still burning wreckage.

In a park near by small groups of beleaguered Germans chose to fight it out rather than surrender. Today they are dead. So confused are the Germans that once a German officer and two soldiers approached our tanks to ask questions before they realised that they were not German tanks.

The Americans are barricading themselves around the Majestic Hotel, digging in on the Longchamps Racecourse, and even digging trenches in the city streets.

Despite the food shortage, the Parisians gave their dwindling supply of pears to the troops. This liberation of Paris will live long as one of the great military spectacles of history. An elderly woman said to me in broken English, through her tears, "My stomach is empty, but my heart is breaking with happiness."

DANCING AMID BATTLE

[Another correspondent adds:] Under a vivid blue sky and hot August sun, Allied armour fought its way into Paris today. Paris is liberated after four long years — but Paris is not free of war.

German artillery is at present ensconced on the far side of the French capital, laying down shells and blanketing our advancing column. Bursts of shrapnel and shooting flames are everywhere. But, unmindful of all of it, the French, who have stayed up all night to greet the liberators, joyously dance amid the actual fighting at the risk of their lives.

One Allied tank blew up from a direct hit by the Germans, and ammunition stores inside continued to explode for several minutes, much to the hazard of civilians rushing out hysterically to greet the soldiers. One war photographer, who was risking his life to secure actual pictures of the troops fighting their way into Paris, said in a disgruntled tone: "This is a fine show. Even if I get out alive with the pictures, they will look phoney because of these crazy civilians running about as if the tanks were not firing."

AUGUST 26, 1944

TRIPLE RAID ON DRESDEN

3,600 PLANES TAKE PART

DRESDEN AND CHEMNITZ, both lying in the direct path of the advancing Russian armies, and Magdeburg, about seventy miles south-west of Berlin, were the main targets for devastating blows by the RAF on Tuesday night and the Eighth United States Air Force in daylight yesterday. Altogether over 3,600 planes took part. Raid warnings broadcast by the Germans last night showed that the assault was being continued. Gorlitz reported "strong air formations between Leipzig and Dresden flying east" at 12.40 this morning.

The city of Dresden had not previously suffered a major raid and huge fires started by the RAF on Tuesday night were still burning when the Americans arrived at midday yesterday.

Fortresses and Liberators from Italy attacked oil targets and communications in Vienna, while other formations of heavy bombers pounded the Maribor railway yards in Yugoslavia for the second consecutive day.

FEBRUARY 15, 1945

CONCENTRATION CAMP: RECORDS DISCOVERED

WHAT AMERICANS FOUND AT BUCHENWALD

BY OUR SPECIAL CORRESPONDENT

RECORDS KEPT BY the SS Oberfuhrer in charge shows the deaths at the Buchenwald concentration camp near Weimar in all numbered 6,477 in January, 5,614 in February, 5,479 in March, and 915 in April. The April toll was only up to the 10th of the month. The next day the American Third Army overran the area and brought release to the 21,000 inmates at this resort of starvation, torture, hangings, and shootings.

Mostly the inmates were pitiful wrecks in consequence of the lack of food, hard work, and the ever present fear of beatings or violent death. At one time up to eighty thousand people from a score of nations were here made to work long hours on the production of bombs.

GUARDS OVERPOWERED

When the sound of gunfire from the approaching Americans was heard thousands of the inmates were marched off by six hundred SS Guards to an unknown destination. Then the camp underground acted, overpowered the remaining guards, locked them up in small cells, and ran the camp themselves till the Americans arrived.

In spite of the cruel vigilance of the guards the prisoners maintained an active underground and even listened to broadcasts by means of a concealed radio. Inevitably, almost among so many thousands, the SS found some morally weaker or more brutalised whom they were able to use for their own purpose. Such were used for spying and to cause dissension.

There were mass exterminations of 12,500 Jews in May and June, 1938. After the Nazi occupation of Austria a great influx of political prisoners and Jews took place. Among the sudden deaths was that of the Austrian Minister of Justice, Winterstein. With the outbreak of war several thousand Vienna and Polish Jews were slaughtered. One hundred and four Polish snipers taken prisoner were left foodless until they died. After the Munich beer-cellar bomb incident in 1939 twenty-one Jews were shot at random and the remainder forbidden food for five days.

In July, 1941, two truckloads of prisoners taken to Pirna died under poison-gas experiments. In March, 1942, four truckloads of ninety Jews each were taken to Bernburg experimental laboratory and died there. In October, 1941, about seven thousand Russian prisoners of war were shot in the stables at Buchenwald, the usual scene of the shootings.

According to prisoners the outstanding place of extermination in the world was Auschwitz, near Cracow, where they said 4,000,000 Jewish, Polish and Russian men, women, and children have been liquidated. Buchenwald evidence repeatedly writes off hundreds as transported to Auschwitz.

BRITONS ESCAPE

A few days before the Americans arrived a Londoner accused of espionage was hanged. This prompted three other Britons, knowing that the Americans were drawing near, to hide under the floor of their hut, where they remained for some days till the Third Army arrived. The Britons were well but undernourished. They told of Gestapo interrogations accompanied by beating and worse. One method was to make a man stand with his toes and forehead touching the wall, pull him back by the hair and then crash his face against the wall. For the least offence the meagre diet was withdrawn completely for days, and, suspended in narrow punishment cells with their hands tied behind their backs, men would be lashed till unconscious.

Some sixty thousand to seventy-five opponents of Hitlerism have perished at Buchenwald either from violence or harsh conditions.

EXPERIMENTAL LABORATORY

Set apart from the main camp was an enclosure for women, where forty thousand lived at one time, it is said, and two thousand still remained. Till a few days ago Leon Blum and his wife and Daladier, the former French Premier, were in a specially guarded sector of this camp. Among those still here is a former Lord Mayor of Prague.

Here over these acres of suffering and misery enclosed by a 10 ft. high electrically charged fencing of barbed wire is the stark gruesome reality of Fascism, with cells, a crematorium in the ovens of which still lay charred skeletons and piles of ashes, and among which still lay burned bones, a gallows, an experimental laboratory in which serums were tried on the prisoners, and a cellar store in which normally five hundred bodies awaited transfer to the busy crematorium. Hangings were carried out in a cellar from which an electric lift carried the bodies to the incinerators above. The usual method was slow killing by hanging.

APRIL 18, 1945

Above: The remains of exterminated Jews. Previous page: Prisoners at the Buchenwald SS death camp

THE LIGHTS THAT HERALD VICTORY

LAST NIGHT'S SCENE IN LONDON

FROM THIS ROOF it looks much the same as it did on a medium bad blitz night. The difference is that the dial on the Big Ben tower is shining bright and a great illuminated Union Jack sways over the Cable and Wireless office on the London Embankment.

The tugs and barges on the river are rejoicing in lugubrious moanings. But it is the red glows that bring it all back, and the searchlights and rockets. Some of the glows are on the old places, near Elephant and Castle and out Kennington way. And the bonfire on the north might be on the burnt-out site of the rocket landing that killed so many in Farringdon Market.

There are bonfires on the Surrey hills; one must be near where the Crystal palace once raised its glass and towers.

Shouts and cries come up from the streets. The celebrations are gathering way. Someone arrives with stories of Piccadilly doings. Norwegian sailors climbing lamp-posts, American soldiers singing "Over there," Poles dancing, British commenting on the distance they are from Tipperary.

It is the red glares that ring London, however, that hold the roof watchers. But they look up no more, only out and down. The long, long fight is over and won, and it is time to rest.

MAY 7, 1945

DEATH OF HITLER IN THE BERLIN CHANCERY

DONITZ HIS SUCCESSOR

HITLER HAS DIED in Berlin. This was announced on the German radio last night by Admiral Donitz, who has been appointed his successor. The news was given to the German people in the following terms:

"From the Fuhrer's headquarters it is announced that our Fuhrer, Adolf Hitler, this afternoon at his command post in the Reich Chancellery, fighting till his last breath against Bolshevism, fell for Germany. On April 30 the Fuhrer appointed Admiral of the Fleet Donitz his successor. The Admiral and successor of the Fuhrer will now speak to the German people."

In his speech Admiral Donitz said: "German men and women, soldiers of the German Wehrmacht, our Fuhrer, Adolf Hitler, has fallen. In deepest sorrow and reverence the German people bows. He recognised the terrible danger of Bolshevism at an early date and dedicated his existence to this struggle. The end of this, his struggle, and of his unswerving straight path of life, is marked by his heroic death in the capital of the Reich."

NEWS SHOUTED ON RADIO

The announcement of Hitler's death was preceded by three volleys of drums. It was read by an announcer who sounded like a newcomer and was so nervous that he shouted the news. After Donitz's broadcast there were again volleys of drums followed by an announcement that the German radio would keep a three-minute broadcasting silence. The radio then resumed Wagnerian and similar music.

MAY 2, 1945

CONDOLENCES

MR DE VALERA, Eire's Prime Minister and Minister for External Affairs, accompanied by Mr JP Walshe, Secretary to the Department of External Affairs, yesterday called on the German Minister in Dublin, Dr Eduard Hempel, to express his condolence on the death of Hitler.

MAY 3, 1945

ATOMIC BOMB USED ON JAPAN

THE MOST DEADLY WEAPON

THE FIRST ATOMIC bomb has been dropped on Japan. It has two thousand times the blast-power of the RAF's ten-tonner, which was previously the most powerful bomb in use. Thus British and American scientists have achieved what the Germans were unable to do and have won the "greatest scientific gamble in history".

The announcement was made yesterday by President Truman, who said: "We are now prepared to obliterate more rapidly and completely every productive enterprise the Japanese have above ground in any city . . . If they do not now accept our terms they may accept a rain of ruin from the air the like of which has never been seen on this earth."

The first bomb was dropped on a port serving as one of the Army's main supply bases. An impenetrable cloud of dust and smoke covered the town, so that the results could not be observed at the time.

AUGUST 7, 1945

MUSSOLINI'S BODY EXHIBITED

THE THIRST FOR VENGEANCE

THE ITALIAN PARTISANS have carried out swift justice on Mussolini and other Fascist leaders. They have been shot and their bodies have been exhibited in public squares in Como and Milan.

Milan radio comments: "From the entrance of the Piazza it is impossible to move because the crowd is so great. It is interesting to see the hate, the fury of those around Mussolini. People spit upon the body, but that is only a continuation of the justice he should have suffered. He died too quickly.

"One woman shot five times into the body saying: 'Five shots for my five assassinated sons.' All approve and want more. They want the bodies to stay there for six months, and that is not enough. Never has so much hate, rancour, and thirst for vengeance been seen. This is justice. This is a good example and it will be followed by others."

APRIL 30, 1945

THE ATOMIC BOMB

MAN IS AT last well on the way to mastery of the means of destroying himself utterly. All future international relations will be influenced for good or ill by the existence of the atomic bomb, whose discovery and use was revealed for the first time yesterday by the President of the United States. It is in its infancy, but it has begun with a destructiveness two thousand times greater than that of the largest bomb used against Germany. "Forthcoming improvements," Mr Stimson added to the President's statement, will "increase several-fold its present effectiveness." In spite of the horror that must be kindled in all hearts by the very thought of such a weapon being turned against the human species, its use against the Japanese is entirely legitimate. It is illogical to judge the morality of bombing by the size of the bomb used. If the RAF since the beginning of its campaign against Cologne to the end of the war has dropped on that city only the equivalent of one and a half atomic bombs we have done enough to create a precedent for their use. Perhaps the figures for Cologne drive home the character of the new bomb most effectively, for our efforts against that city are still in our minds with the many raids and the great number of planes and men used. Cologne had nearly 32,000 tons; the new bomb, a small thing itself, equals 20,000 tons.

Germany was racing the Anglo-American scientists for the discovery of this fearful weapon; some have estimated that she would have been ready to use it during this month. No race was ever more worth winning, and the wisdom of Mr Churchill and Mr Roosevelt in acting on the advice of their scientific advisers and fostering this weapon's early promise, in spite of so many other claims on our war research, is something to be ever remembered with gratitude by this country and the United States, and, indeed, by the world.

Naturally the first thought in most people's minds will be of how this weapon, so perilous to the world should it fall into the wrong hands, may be controlled. President Truman said yesterday: "I have asked Congress to consider promptly the establishment of an appropriate commission to control the production and use of atomic power within the United States. I shall give further consideration and make a further recommendation to Congress as to how atomic power can become a powerful and forceful influence towards the maintenance of world peace.

"At the moment one may assume, though one cannot be sure, that the secret of the bomb's production lies only in the hands of Britain and the United States. The two plants making it are in America.

The forward march of science, however, can never be hemmed in by one or two national frontiers. We know that German science had advanced nearly as far in this direction as we had ourselves, and her scientists, many of them, are still alive. To show how nearly matched the leading nations are we have only to look back to an earlier discovery which must have powerfully stimulated the research leading to this bomb — the discovery of how to disintegrate the atom artificially by electric discharge. This was made at Cambridge under Rutherford's guidance, but the Cambridge team was only just ahead of another in Germany and another in America. We have no guarantee that only Britain, America, and Germany were in the race for the atomic bomb and that some other nation's scientists will not in their turn pass the winning-post — possibly without saying anything about it to the rest of the world."

The President stated that the technical processes of the bomb's production would not be divulged for the present, which may cause heart-burning in some quarters. One would feel more secure, however, if the essential ore used — uranium — were found only in certain limited and controllable territories. Unhappily the black pitchblende mineral from which uranium derives is scattered fairly widely through the world — from Cornwall to Norway and from North America to Russia and the Belgian Congo. There are even some famous sources in Saxony and Austria. Clearly the future control of Germany will have to take the new potentialities of this mineral into account. By the numbers of men employed in the manufacture of these bombs in America one would say that their production could hardly ever be a small and easily hidden business. But we are only at the beginning and German revengefulness might well drive her scientists on to the discovery of new processes which it might be easier to hide. Clearly the ideal keeper of this weapon and of all means or producing it would be an international organisation charged with the maintenance of peace. On the other hand, it would be foolish to imagine ourselves yet particularly skilled in the administration of international possessions of this kind. What would be made of it, for instance, by the Security Council of the United Nations Organisation as at present devised? But if anything could knock sense into the national Governments it is surely the existence of this weapon. Lasting agreement between great States is difficult to gain and to keep, but it is a preferable alternative to the annihilation which the atomic bomb would bring to all slow starters in any future war.

AUGUST 7, 1945

1945 | 1950

THE LOST GENERATIONS

ARTHUR KOESTLER

EACH WAR AND revolution produces its lost generation. Israel's lost generation are the middle-aged, those who came here at a time of their life which still allows them to remember Europe. Not the fleshpots of Europe; for most of them lived in penury. Not the safety of Europe; for they were persecuted. They do not plan or even yearn to go back, for their bridges have been burnt — either by their own free will or by the torches of their persecutors. They know that for them, as for the whole nation, there is no turning back.

NOVEMBER 19, 1948

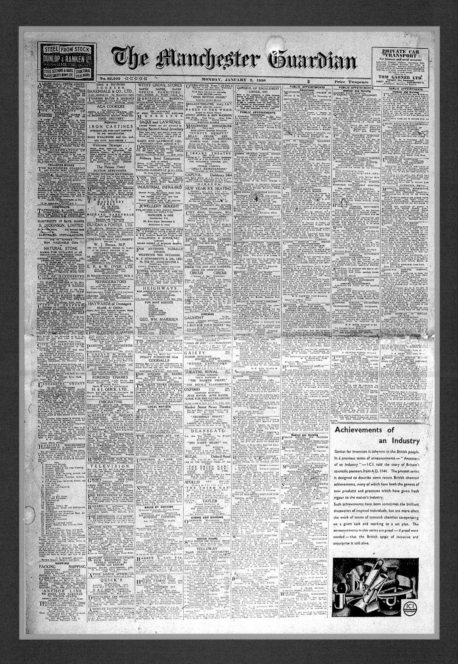

DICKENS ON FILM

GREAT EXPECTATIONS

FILMING DICKENS ALWAYS brings up the same problems — how to preserve something of the original descriptive gusto and the charm of the narrative style; above all, how to cope with the thick-crowding minor characters, all really indispensable, but so numerous and often so much larger than life that they tend to upset the balance of any dramatised version. Purists will find some things to grumble about in *Great Expectations*. Many famous figures have disappeared and occasionally some famous repartee falls quite flat. For example, Joe Gargery's classic piece of self-effacement when asked if he would take tea or coffee ("Thank yee sir. I'll whichever is most agreeable to yourself.")

Curiously enough too, the film fails with Miss Havisham, though it generally excels in just such eerie matters, and (to mention all defects at once) some of the indoor scenes look a little overdressed.

But it must certainly be called the best Dickens film yet made. To an astonishing degree the director, David Lean, catches and communicates the humour, the sentiment, and the melodrama of the tale. The opening scenes on the marshes especially and later the episode of the attempted escape of Magwitch on the packet-boat are among the most vivid and authentic-looking that a British studio has given us. Here is that unstrained realism which also distinguished Mr Lean's *Brief Encounter*: we are miles away from the too common inspidities of the photographed costume piece.

The spirit of the original is very seldom lost and there are passages where it has been perfectly preserved — for instance, the scenes with Mr Jagger (Francis Sullivan). Pip and Estrella are perhaps more interesting as children than when they grow up (and turn into John Mills and Valerie Hobson), but that is as much Dickens's fault as anyone's. Mr Mills plays sympathetically, but he seems rather a pale hero among the many vivid small parts — two of which at least, Alec Guinness's Herbert Pocket and Finlay Currie's Magwitch, could hardly be better.

The film has an "A" certificate, but it is no more frightening than the book. Children, as well as adults, should enjoy greatly this notable product of a British studio.

DECEMBER 14, 1946

DELHI REJOICES AND MR GANDHI FASTS

INDIA WAKES TO LIFE AND FREEDOM

THE INDIAN CONSTITUENT Assembly met at midnight last night in New Delhi for its "independence meeting". Over two thousand members of the Assembly sat in the beflagged hall under the dazzle of arc lights. To a hushed House Mr Nehru, now Premier of India, said:

"Long years ago we made a tryst with destiny and now the time comes when we shall redeem our pledge not wholly or in full measure, but very substantially.

"At the stroke of midnight, the hour when the world sleeps, India will wake to life and freedom. We end today a period of ill-fortune and India discovers herself again.

"The ambition of Mr Gandhi, the greatest man of our generation, has been to wipe every tear from every eye. That may be beyond us, but so long as there are tears and suffering so long our work will not be over.

"Peace is said to be indivisible. So is freedom. So is prosperity now, and so also is disaster in this one world that can no longer be split into isolated fragments.

"Freedom and power bring responsibility. That responsibility rests upon this Assembly, a sovereign body representing the sovereign people of India. Before the birth of freedom we endured all the pains of labour and our hearts are heavy with the memory of this sorrow. Some of those pains continue even now. Nevertheless the past is over and it is the future that beckons to us now."

At the end of the meeting Mr Nehru and Mr Prasad, President of the Assembly, left to inform Lord Mountbatten that his appointment as Governor General had been endorsed.

CELEBRATIONS

Outside the Assembly the city was celebrating with guns, temple bells, fireworks, parades and just general rejoicing in the streets included the burning of an effigy of British Imperialism. Three hundred separate flag-raising ceremonies had been arranged by the authorities throughout the Dominion. All Hindu temples and Moslem mosques remained open for prayers.

In Bombay sirens of hundreds of mills and factories, the whistling of railway engines, and hooting from ships ushered in independence at midnight.

AUGUST 15, 1947

THE KON-TIKI EXPEDITION

4,000 MILES ON RAFT

A MESSAGE FROM the North American Newspaper Alliance published today in the *New York Times* says that the raft on which Mr Thor Heyerdahl and five other Norwegian scientists left Callao, Peru, on April 27 has ended its trip 4,000 miles away in the Tuamotu or Low Archipelago.

The purpose of the expedition was to test Mr Heyerdahl's theory that the Marquesas and other Pacific islands were settled by migrants from South America rather than by Asiatics. The raft, the *Kon-Tiki*, weighs 15 tons and measures 45 feet by 18 feet. It is built of balsawood and was designed to resemble as closely as possible the rafts of the Incas. The scientists determined to rely on ocean currents for propulsion, and only an oar was carried for steering.

The Tuamotu Archipelago is about 250 miles south of the Marquesas islands, which are 2,500 miles south of Hawaii. The newsagency message quoted Mr Heyerdahl as stating that the crew were safe. They had landed on an uninhabited island. The expedition was undertaken in conjunction with the United States Army Air Force, for whom the scientists have made oceanographic records.

A tenable theory about the origin of the Polynesians has hitherto been that they are descendants of a Caucasic group who migrated from the Asiatic mainland in the Neolithic age. There is no evidence of Sanskrit roots in their language, and a former theory that they were a branch of the Malays has been disproved.

AUGUST 12, 1947

ASSASSINATION OF GANDHI

BY OUR SPECIAL CORRESPONDENTS

MAHATMA GANDHI WAS shot and killed this evening by a Hindu fanatic. He was walking from Birla House to the lawn where his evening prayer meetings are held and was several minutes late for the meeting. He was as usual leaning on the shoulders of two grand-nieces, and when he approached the meeting a man dressed in a khaki bush jacket and blue trousers and standing within five feet of Gandhi greeted him with the customary Hindu salutation of namesteh — that is; with folded hands.

Flowers heaped on Gandhi's funeral pyre

Gandhi smiled at him, and, according to one version, spoke to him. The man then whipped out a pistol from inside his pocket and fired three times at point-blank range. The bullets lodged in Gandhi's chest, stomach and groin. He raised his hands above his head in the same salutation as he fell. He was carried into Birla House and died half an hour later, at about 5.40 p.m.

ASSASSIN BEATEN BY THE CROWD

The man, who gave his name as Nathuram, fired a fourth shot, apparently in an effort to kill himself, but a Royal Indian Air Force sergeant standing alongside jolted his arm and wrenched the pistol away. The sergeant wanted to shoot the man but was stopped by the police. An infuriated crowd fell upon the man and beat him with sticks, but he was apprehended by the police and taken to a police station.

Questioned by reporters, the man, who speaks English, said he was not sorry he had killed Gandhi but would explain his reasons in court. His origin is still obscure, but he is said to be a Brahmin, and according to one report, comes from Poona. The pistol he used was a 38 calibre Biretta of Italian manufacture; scores of these weapons were captured from the Italians in North Africa and smuggled back to India by Indian soldiers. The man is a fair-skinned individual of medium height and spare build aged about thirty.

News of Gandhi's death was announced by the All-India Radio at six o'clock and a crowd of several thousands immediately gathered at Birla House. The crowd was tense but subdued, and its mood appeared to be one of stunned sorrow. One man who asserted in a loud voice that the assassin was a Moslem was promptly arrested by the police. But in general the crowd was not communally minded.

Cabinet Ministers and political leaders, headed by the Prime Minister, Pandit Jawaharlal Nehru, and the Deputy Prime Minister, Sardar Vallabhbhai Patel, arrived at Birla House. Gandhi was reported to be conscious until shortly before he died, but it is not known whether he said anything. His body was wrapped in a shroud in orthodox Hindu fashion and his attendants recited gita (Hindu scriptures). Mr Nehru went out and addressed the crowd briefly in a voice broken with emotion and announced that the funeral would be at midday tomorrow.

Repercussions of the crime are certain to be widespread and intense throughout India and Pakistan. It may produce that change of heart for which Gandhi laboured and gave his life. On the other hand it may stimulate communal frenzy; the presence of 5,000,000 Hindu and Sikh refugees from Pakistan (of whom about 400,000 are in Delhi) has exacerbated public tempers and communal organisations such as the Hindu Mahasabha and Rashtriya Swayam Sewak Sangh have been active in preaching vengeance against Pakistan.

The position is heavy with ugly generalities and could easily get out of hand if political leaders do not give a firm and wise lead. Fortunately in Pandit Nehru India has a statesman of the highest calibre who has been consistently preaching moderation since August. He has shown great courage in challenging fanaticism and intolerance and there is no doubt that his life is also in danger.

WORLDWIDE MESSAGES OF GRIEF

The news of the assassination has had a profound effect throughout the world. Messages of sympathy have been sent by the King and the President of the United States and by many Premiers. The theme of all comment, whether by statesmen or by the common man, is the same — "a saint", "a giant among men", "irreplaceable".

JANUARY 31, 1948

WHY 492 WEST INDIANS CAME TO BRITAIN

BY IAIN HAMILTON

WHAT WERE THEY thinking, these 492 men from Jamaica and Trinidad, as the *Empire Windrush* slid upstream with the flood between the closing shores of Kent and Essex?

Standing by the rail this morning, high above the landing-stage at Tilbury, one of them looked over the unlovely town to the grey-green fields beyond and said, "If this is England I like it." A good omen, perhaps. May he and his friends suffer no sharp disappointment.

It was curiously touching to walk along the landing-stage in the grey light of early morning and see against the white walls of the ship row upon row of dark, pensive faces looking down upon England, most of them for the first time. Had they thought England a golden land in a golden age? Some had, with their quaint amalgam of American optimism and African innocence. But these had already been partially disillusioned by Flight Lieutenant JH Smythe, a native of Sierra Leone and now a member of the Colonial office Welfare Department. He travelled with them from the West Indies and towards the end had given them a little homily.

"I could not honestly paint you," he said to them, "a very rosy picture of your future in Britain." That was straightforward. Conditions were not so favourable as they thought. They would see the scars of war wounds that are still bleeding. Were they highly skilled? No — then it would not be easy to find a job.

"On the other hand," he went on, "if you are a serious-minded person and prepared to work hard in any vocation, you can make your way. It is left to you to win the respect of all those you come across and do your utmost to succeed in whatever sphere you may be placed."

Flight Lieutenant Smythe had arranged the immigrants into three groups during the voyage; those who had friends to go to, and some prospect of a job; those, ex-Service men all, who wished to rejoin the Army or the Air Force; and those with neither friends nor prospects.

The Colonial Office sent some welfare people. The Ministry of Labour sent a regional welfare officer and twenty assistants. There was no band, certainly, to greet the immigrants at Tilbury; but it was a welcome and, for officialdom, a warm welcome. The men seemed encouraged by it.

Mr Isaacs said in the House recently, "I consider that those who organised the movement of these people to this country did them a disservice in not letting us know." However, one could discover no evidence of "organisation". They had seen the advertisement of the shipping company in their local papers — a thousand berths on the troop decks vacant, £28 each — found the money, and in due time embarked with high hopes.

What manner of men are these the *Empire Windrush* has brought to Britain? This morning, on the decks, one spoke with the following: a builder, a carpenter, an apprentice accountant, a farm worker, a tailor, a welder, a spray-painter, a boxer, a musician, a mechanic, a valet, a calypso singer, and a law student. Or thus they described themselves.

And what has made them leave Jamaica? In most cases, lack of work. They spoke independently, but unanimously, of a blight that has come upon the West Indies since those who served America and Britain during the war returned home. The cost of living is high, wages are low. Many can earn no wages. Some had been unemployed for two years. One of them considered his chances in Britain (he was a builder), and said laconically, "If I survive — so good; if I don't survive — so good." Another,

lacking this philosophy, said with a bitterness unusual in the company, "When the situation is desperate you take a chance — you don't wait until you die."

This man has been idle two years. According to him, a working man in Jamaica, married and with a small family, must earn between £6 and £7 a week in order to live decently. But the average working-class family, where the father is lucky enough to be in work, gets between £4 and £5 a week.

Most of the married men have left their wives and children at home, and hope to send for them later. Only five complete families sailed. Two of the wives are Englishwomen who followed their husbands to Jamaica and now return with them to England.

They are, then, as heterodox a collection of humanity as one might find. Some will be good workers, some bad. Many are "serious-minded persons" anxious to succeed. No doubt the folk poets will find fit audiences somewhere. So will the complete dance-band which is journeying to Liverpool at this moment. And the boxer, who is going to meet his manager at Birkenhead, will surely find fights in plenty. Not all intend to settle in Britain; a 40-year-old tailor, for example, hopes to stay here for a year, and then go on and make his home in Liberia.

Their arrival has added to the worries of Mr Isaacs and the trade union leaders. But the more worldly wise among them are conscious of the deeper problem posed. Britain has welcomed displaced persons and has given employment to Poles who cannot go home. "This is right," said one of the immigrants. "Surely then, there is nothing against our coming, for we are British subjects. If there is — is it because we are coloured?"

JUNE 23, 1948

BERLIN GETS THOUSAND TONS OF FOOD

BY OUR SPECIAL CORRESPONDENTS

A THOUSAND TONS of food and 160 tons of general cargo reached Berlin by barge yesterday morning. This was the first bulk shipment of food to reach the city since the Soviet authorities closed the zonal frontier on the night of June 18. The ten barges which arrived yesterday left Hamburg on Monday, Tuesday and Wednesday last week. There is no news of their exact whereabouts, but this evening they had not yet reached Brandenburg, about fifty miles from Berlin by water.

Thirteen Dakotas of the RAF Transport Command, carrying forty tons of supplies, arrived at Gatow today, in addition to the normal RAF and commercial services. The Soviet authorities are also arranging for special imports from unusual sources. The stoppage of coal supplies from the West has compelled them to import coal from Poland and the first trainload of 1,000 tons arrived at the Klingenberg power station, in their sector, this afternoon.

REOPENING OF RAILWAY LINE

Persistent rumours have been current here in the last few days that the Berlin-Helmstedt railway line would be opened this evening. They were denied late this evening by a Russian official spokesman. He stated that the Soviet authorities had no knowledge of this reopening of the railway line beyond a message received from a London news agency. Nevertheless the transport authorities in Magdeburg recently announced that the line would be opened tomorrow. The Soviet authorities have also refused to grant visas to a number of Swedish citizens, until June 29. The situation remains obscure at the moment.

Inhabitants of the Western sectors were able to draw extra rations today in the form of prunes and Army "C" ration packs. These extra rations have been issued in accordance with a decision made earlier in the month by the food committee of the Allied Kommandatura.

The high prices still being paid for Deutschmarks are already beginning to drive them out of circulation. Wages in the Western sectors may soon be paid partly in Eastern marks. The shortage of Deutschmarks in the city is likely to compel the Western Allies to take this decision before long. Their financial experts are also considering the revision of the regulations covering payment for essential goods and services in the Western sectors.

The trade in Deutschmarks continues as briskly as ever, although the price has fallen slightly today. The Soviet

Berliners wait as RAF planes deliver supplies

authorities have now begun to carry out searches for Deutschmarks in their sector but seem to have made few actual arrests. An official Russian spokesman today refused to comment on reports that Deutschmarks were being bought by and on behalf of the Soviet authorities, but said that "speculation" in the new currencies was likely to continue for a fortnight or three weeks.

JUNE 29, 1948

YEATS GOES HOME TO SLIGO

BY GERARD FAY

HERE UNDER BARE Ben Bulben's mist-shrouded head, five miles outside Sligo, WB Yeats was buried in Drumcliffe Churchyard on a wet, Western day, after the long voyage from the South of France. Outside the church stood the ancient cross and the tree-screened ruined Round Tower; inside, lit only by oil lamps, was the tablet recording that his ancestor held the living early in the last century. Every detail, in fact, was exactly as Yeats himself had ordered it when he wrote his own epitaph:

> Under bare Ben Bulben's Head
> In Drumcliff churchyard Yeats is laid
> An ancestor was rector there
> Long years ago, a church stands near,
> By the road an ancient cross.
> No marble, no conventional phrase;
> On limestone quarried near the spot
> By his command these words are cut:
> Cast a cold eye
> On life, on death,
> Horseman, pass by!

Yeats died in January, 1939, at Cap Martin. Almost his last act was to dictate to his wife some corrections for a poem about Ben Bulben — the whale-headed mountain which was, like so much of County Sligo, almost an obsession with him. In September, 1939, his body was to have been brought from Roquebrune for reburial at Drumcliffe, but the war prevented it. So nine years after, he has had a second funeral in a solemn but not a mournful atmosphere, with every mark of national, municipal, and personal affection.

The coffin, landed from an Irish corvette at Galway in the early morning (to the dismay of local patriots in Sligo), was received at the borough boundary by the Mayor, Alderman Rooney; the Minister for External Affairs, Mr Sean MacBride, stood in the background, and a small "Who's Who" of Ireland's literature, drama, and art clustered round him. Behind the hearse were cars carrying Mrs Yeats, her son and daughter, Michael and Anne, Mr Jack B Yeats, and some close personal friends of the man called by TS Eliot "the greatest poet of our time — certainly the greatest in his language, and, so far as I can judge, in any language."

The Mayor's welcome was short and pleasingly unpompous. Then, behind an un-uniformed town band of wailing Irish pipes and shrouded thudding drums, the procession crawled into Sligo to the Town Hall. Here was the first sign of circumstance, when a military guard of honour filed out to surround the hearse and stand silent with arms reversed and heads bowed while a quiet crowd of townsmen huddled round, curious to see the coffin of the man for whom the tricolours were at half-mast, the shops closed, and the streets lined with policemen.

CROWD PAYS TRIBUTE

The coffin remained outside the Town Hall for over an hour, and the crowd stayed round it inspecting the few wreaths and seeking the autographs of the celebrities, Mr Lennox Robinson, Mr Michael MacLiammoir, and many another who had come from Dublin and other parts of Ireland and paid tribute in his own Sligo to their own Yeats. None was more appropriate to the occasion than Mr MacBride, son of the beautiful Maude Gonne, for whom Yeats wrote so many of his poems early and late, who was a symbol to all Irishmen of their country's struggle for freedom, and who at any time up to 1916 Yeats would so gladly have married.

After this pause the procession formed again, and again the Mayor escorted the hearse to another borough boundary on the road to Drumcliffe. The symbol-seeker might notice that the route lay along Markievicz Road, called after the Sligo girl of whom, when she was Constance Gore-Booth, Yeats wrote the lines beginning, "When long ago I saw her ride, Under Ben Bulben to the meet." And so to Drumcliffe, where the crowd pressed into the churchyard close to the grave to hear the unfamiliar Protestant Burial Service conducted by the Bishop of Kilmore, the responses muttered by the few who knew them. Here the dominant figure was Jack B. Yeats, standing tall, bare-headed, and taking in the picture with his artist's eye, which must have seen how the misty rain softened the graveyard scene and how the small birds darted among the trees, deputising for the hawks or eagles which might aptly have appeared for the last moments of his brother's burial.

Surely there was never such a crowd in this quiet country churchyard, and surely there was never such a day in this quiet country town. There might have been a time when Yeats's funeral would have been a less notable affair — for the good people of Sligo, and of Roman Catholic Ireland as a whole, have not always accepted him without question. It is firmly stated here that there was a time when he was thought to be a magician who could move himself five miles through the air in the twinkling of an eye; there was a time when his robust, scornful championing of Synge stamped him as an enemy of Ireland's faith; there was even a time when he was called pensioner of the hated British Crown.

But time has veiled these offences as the mists from the Atlantic veiled Ben Bulben today, and Ireland has given herself another place of pilgrimage. When Yeats's epitaph is cut in stone and placed on his grave Drumcliffe churchyard will certainly be a place for visitors to see, for whatever may become of Yeats the dramatist, Yeats the poet is clearly a growing force in a world which yearns for poets as wildly as it yearns for the peace they sometimes preach.

SEPTEMBER 18, 1948

A PRINCE IS BORN

CROWDS CALL FOR THE FATHER

BY OUR LONDON CORRESPONDENT

AT THREE MINUTES past eleven last night an official fixed on the main gate of Buckingham Palace a small gilt frame which contained a paper of official blue. On it was a handwritten message, but it was placed too high to be read in the rays of the lamps on the Victoria Memorial.

A student was given a leg up and then calling for silence he read the proclamation which told of the birth of a Prince and of the good health of mother and son. It was not news to the crowd. They had first learned of the birth from newspaper men but had refused to accept it.

But confirmation soon came, first from a man in evening dress who came from the Palace and was mistaken for the Duke of Edinburgh, then from a page in blue livery, a most important little fellow who marched across the courtyard and gave his message to a policeman, who passed it on to the crowd.

"WE WANT PHILIP"

And now people were appearing who had heard the broadcast announcement at 10.14 p.m. exactly an hour before.

"Philip, Philip, we want Philip," the crowd began to call and in between their demand they raised magnificent cheers that must have echoed, even if faintly, inside the Palace walls.

Servants, perhaps people of higher rank, could be seen looking out from the top windows, but who they were nobody could even guess. A policeman, a family man himself no doubt, appealed to the crowd to have a heart and make less noise. All he got was a cheer for himself and his solicitude and advice that if the Princess could hear it would only raise her spirits to know what people thought about it all.

The crowd was growing fast. All day there had been hundreds by the gates and on the memorial, and they had remained quiet and discreet. But now they felt it was time to rejoice. "We want Philip," they called. And then they sang "God bless the Prince of Wales," and "For he's a jolly good fellow."

Motorists and people in taxis who did not know the news stuck their heads out of the window. "Anything happened?" "It's a boy-ee!" they were told. They paid off their cabs or parked their cars and joined the throng.

NOVEMBER 15, 1948

LION ATTACKS TAMER

SCREAMS FROM THE audience helped to save the life of Swami, an Indian lion tamer, who was attacked by an African lion on the stage of the Grand Theatre, Bolton, last night.

The lion, Leo, was leaving the ring in the wake of two lionesses at the end of the first performance when it saw Swami slip and fall. It turned and leapt on to him. But when the audience, mostly of children, screamed and the curtain dropped the frightened lion ran back to join the lionesses. Clowns and equestrians ran into the stage to help the injured trainer.

A doctor dressed wounds to his shoulder, chest and arm but before he accepted this treatment Swami insisted on taking his bow before the curtain. He was taken to the Royal Infirmary but later returned to the theatre and would have appeared in the later show if he had been allowed.

DECEMBER 29, 1948

BOMBER FLIES NON-STOP ROUND THE WORLD

A SUPERFORTRESS BOMBER has made the first non-stop flight around the world, refuelling in mid-air on the way. It landed at Fort Worth, Texas, yesterday having covered the 23,000 miles in 94 hours and one minute, at an average speed of 244 miles an hour.

The comment made by Mr Stuart Symington, United States Secretary for Air, in Washington last night was: "It proves that, if necessary, the shadow of United States air power can be cast over any part of the world."

MARCH 3, 1949

POETRY AWARD FOR EZRA POUND

BY OUR CORRESPONDENT

EZRA POUND, THE American poet who was brought back from an American military prison in Italy to stand trial for treason and then was found to be insane and committed to a mental hospital near Washington, was last night awarded the Bollingen Prize for the best poetry by an American published in 1948. The prize was given for ten cantos (bringing his promised 100 up to 84) published last year as *Prison Cantos* and written while he was in prison. The award is made by the Fellows in American Letters, a board appointed by the librarian of Congress. This year's judges were TS Eliot, Conrad Aiken, WH Auden, Karl Shapiro, Allen Tate, Robert Lowell, Louise Brogan, Katherine Anne Porter, Willard Thorp, Paul Green, Robert Penn Warren, and the late Theodore Spencer.

The judges anticipated the stock response, which sure enough popped up today in a tabloid headline ("Poets honour Pound, held as a crazy traitor"), by putting out this statement.

"The Fellows are aware that objections may be made to awarding a prize to a man situated as is Mr Pound. In their view, however, the possibility of such objection did not alter the responsibility assumed by the jury of selection. This was to make a choice for the award among the eligible books, provided any one merited such recognition, according to the terms of the Bollingen Prize. To permit other considerations than that of poetic achievement to sway the decision would destroy the significance of the award and would in principle deny the validity of that objective perception of value on which any civilised society must rest."

Mr Pound was told about the award and "expressed gratification". He is now busy translating Confucius.

FEBRUARY 21, 1949

MR BOGART DEFENDED IN COURT

JUDGEMENT ON A NIGHTCLUB ROW

BY ALISTAIR COOKE

INTO A DINGEY midtown courtroom bristling with coatless vagrants, embattled landlords, and shuffling pedlars accused of selling fruit and vegetables without a licence walked today a familiar courtroom face and figure nicely done up in a smooth grey suit and a check bow tie. His identity was clinched when the judge heaved the shoulder of his gown and heard the marshal cry, "Humphrey Bogart on complaint of Robin Roberts."

For the first time in the dreary common round of this petty court, the swarthy Puerto Ricans forgot about their language troubles, the irate tenants about dead rats, and the bums about their discovered nests in empty warehouses.

MR BOGART AT REST

Mr Bogart, it appears, had been resting after his Hollywood labours in a merry session at a local night club in the early hours of last Sunday morning. His movie star wife, Lauren Bacall, was not with him, and by way of consolation and also as a fatherly tribute to his eight-month-old son, Mr Bogart bought from the cigarette girl a large panda, a doll, that is. Miss Roberts, a model wickedly accused by Mr Bogart's lawyer of having Hollywood aspirations, tapped over to his table and tried to take the panda from him. Knowing his rights under the penal laws, Mr Bogart held on to that which was his. In Miss Roberts's heartrending version this morning, he seized her wrist and before you could say, "Drop the gun, Louie" she had been hurled to the floor and suffered thereby grievous bodily harm, with three blue bruises on the chest and unmentionable hurt to the small of her back.

It probably did not help Miss Roberts's case that she had exhibited these wounds on the front page of a local afternoon paper in photographs taken by a studio which specialises in glamourising models with a hopeful eye on Hollywood contracts. Mr Bogart's lawyer brought all this out in a legal recital which had the judge nodding his big face in ominous agreement.

Asked to expatiate on his indignities, Miss Roberts flashed her black eyes and said she had gone after Mr Bogart's panda at the suggestion of the night club's publicity agent. Her lawyer backed this up with the remark that Mr Bogart had tangled once before with the night club's sense of decorum and been told, never to show his face there again.

This might have seemed to a bystanding peddler to be bad news for Mr Bogart. But the Judge did not think so. "You mean," he snapped, "that this night club did not want Mr Bogart there again and this publicity agent gets a girl to go and grab his property?" That was suddenly the way it looked.

The Judge inhaled triumphantly, while Mr Bogart flexed his jaw muscles and said nothing in his celebrated dead-pan way. His lawyer let slip the fact that Miss Roberts had discovered her bodily grief three days after the tussle happened. Whereupon the judge announced that according to the penal code any citizen had the right to protect his property and even to use force, but only, he cautioned, throwing up a fastidious index finger, "sufficient force to protect his property." He decided that there was a reasonable doubt that Mr Bogart, far from committing a third degree assault, was not actually upholding the relevant section of the penal code.

Accordingly he hardly waited for the defence lawyer to suggest that "this is a polite form of blackmail" before he waved a big arm and said there was not a court in the land that would prefer formal charges. The case was therefore dismissed, and Miss Roberts shook her raven hair and her blonde bosom-companion heaved her chest and rolled her big, big eyes.

A cheer went up from the assembled spectators, bobby-soxers, pedlars, and riff-raff. Mr Bogart nodded his expert appreciation of American court proceedings and the lawyers, the blondes, and brunettes swept out to the grinning crowd outside. There a swarm of photographers broke into frog-like stances at the foot of the steps. First came the Miss Roberts and her blonde helpmeet. They paused a moment at the top of the steps, took hands, and descended like models into a salon, with a one-two, hip-swinging rhythm. This earned them the raucous boos and cat-calls of the crowd.

THE TRAFFIC STOPS

Hardly a minute later and Bogart himself appeared, while the traffic stopped in its noonday swirl and a wave of cheers broke from the fans. The photographers begged him for a smile and a wave and urged the crowd to do likewise, which it did in ecstasy.

There was a rush for his waiting cab. Somebody stepped on an old lady's terrier and there was the unmistakable crunch of bones. At a rough estimate, there was about a score of delirious fans and loungers who suffered grievous bruises on the chest and the small of the back. Bogart was thrown into the cab. The traffic light at Madison Avenue turned from red to green and the cab roared away. Once again, justice had triumphed.

OCTOBER 1, 1949

MAKING THE BOMB

LEAVE IT TO THE US

BRITAIN NOW HAS the technical and scientific knowledge necessary to produce atomic bombs, participants in the recent American-British-Canadian atomic talks said today. But they added that the United States representatives had suggested Britain should not involve herself in the great capital investment and expense of building the plant and machinery to produce atomic bombs, but should instead rely on being able to use United States atomic-bomb facilities.

It is understood that the United States Defence Department also feels that with her present dollar shortage and economic difficulties Britain would find the manufacture of atomic bombs extremely expensive and would do much better to let the United States retain a monopoly of manufacture, Britain being allowed to use United States atomic bombs in the event of aggression. At the next Three-Power meeting Britain is likely to take the position that this is not the best solution.

Mr Alexander, the British Minister of Defence, said in May, 1948, that Britain was developing atomic weapons, and last March the Supply Ministry announced that Britain had produced plutonium — the fissile element required to create the atomic power in the bombs.

Officials were emphatic that the United States had made no effort to prevent Britain going ahead with bomb manufacture. The American proposal that it would be a pity to do so was related "only to the expense and capital investment involved."

DECEMBER 10, 1949

COMMUNISTS FOUND GUILTY

ELEVEN COMMUNIST LEADERS, members of the American party's Politbureau, were today found guilty of conspiring to advocate and teach the duty and necessity of overthrowing and destroying the United States Government by force. . . . five defence lawyers and one of the defendants, were convicted of contempt of court and sentenced to terms of imprisonment from one to six months.

OCTOBER 15, 1949

AN UPROAR IN NOTRE-DAME

FALSE FRIAR CHASED

HUNDREDS OF ASTOUNDED foreign tourists, including many British, today heard a false Dominican friar denounce the Roman Catholic Church from the pulpit at Notre-Dame during Easter Sunday Pontifical High Mass.

Priests and some of the ten thousand worshippers chased the false friar, a man of 22 named Michel Mourre, from the cathedral. As he ran, Mourre tried to take off his white homespun Dominican cassock which was tripping him, while the organist played with all bass stops open to drown the shouting. He was caught by the police in the square outside the cathedral and taken to the local police station. There he was charged, on the complaint of Monsignor Maurice Feltin, Archbishop of Paris, with illegally wearing ecclesiastical garb and with disturbing a religious service.

In a Dominican robe hired from a fancy-dress shop, Mourre stood at the foot of the pulpit until Archbishop Feltin had finished chanting the Creed. In the silence that followed, the white-robed figure mounted the pulpit and addressed the congregation in a loud voice. "I accuse the Catholic Church of turning our thoughts towards an empty sky. The Church is the canker of the West," he said.

The rest of his address was drowned by the organ, famous for the power of its bass which can make the Cathedral vibrate. Three young men tried to stop acolytes and worshippers who were struggling to reach the man in the pulpit so that he might have a chance to escape.

Mourre, who had shaved his head and was still wearing his Dominican robes on entering the police station, deceived even the inspector, who came forward to greet him respectfully before realising that he was under arrest.

Mourre, who is an ex-soldier in receipt of 10,000 francs (just under £10 sterling) monthly disability pension, said he had studied for the Catholic ministry in a seminary until he was 18, when, he told the police, he had a "revelation" that he should found a new religion. He wished to launch it in Notre-Dame. He described himself as a philosopher, and a "citizen of the world". He was remanded in custody.

APRIL 10, 1950

TELEVISION TASTES

FEW SWITCH OFF ITEMS THEY DISLIKE

OWNERS OF TELEVISION sets seldom switch off even programmes which they admit to disliking, so that the extent to which television is watched seems to depend only to a limited extent upon the nature of the programme transmitted, said Mr Robert Silvey, head of Audience Research, BBC, when he addressed the Manchester Statistical Society last night on methods of viewer research employed by the corporation.

Mr Silvey said the programme preferences of viewers offered no guide to their listening behaviour. There was a considerable difference, for example, between the

number of viewers who expressed a liking for, say, plays, and the number who professed a liking for ballet. Yet when the ballet was transmitted it was usually viewed by audiences which, though smaller than those for plays, must include "a vast number" who had little taste for it.

At the end of 1949 plays and newsreels were the most popular programmes, 83 per cent of viewers saying they liked the first and 84 per cent that they liked the second "very much". Ballet was the least popular programme, only 25 per cent of listeners liking it "very much".

Tastes were found to vary with income and age groups. Ballet was most popular with children from seven to eleven years old . . . The taste for studio plays, for opera, or for talks varied little with income groups: that for light entertainment and ballet did. Only 25 per cent of viewers with incomes of £1,000 or more approved music hall, against 65 per cent of viewers with incomes of less than £350.

DECEMBER 14, 1950

UPS AND DOWNS OF AN ENTERTAINER

AL JOLSON DIES ON CREST OF A WAVE

BY ALISTAIR COOKE

AL JOLSON DIED in San Francisco last night too late to hit the headlines of the morning papers, but in the evening papers today he swept everything before him, including President Truman at the fifth anniversary of the United Nations.

At sixty-four he was the luckiest man in show business. He went from minstrel show to blackface, from vaudeville to Broadway before he hit a fabulous prosperity as the most sentimental of all sentimental singers, a poor Russian cantor's son daubed with burnt cork and down on one knee sobbing for the "mammy" he had never known in a south that nobody ever knew.

For twenty dazzling years he was "as corny as Kansas in August, high as a flag on the fourth of July." He knew it, he revelled in it, and then the fashion slumped. Jazz overtook ragtime, vaudeville languished, the "era of wonderful nonsense" exploded as flat as a bottle of Texas Guinan's forty-dollar-a-bottle imitation champagne. Jolson was out on the sidewalk and soon out in the hinterland picking up one-night fees in crummy night clubs a thousand miles from the Broadway he had ruled.

FIRST "ALL-TALKING" PICTURE

His last brief vogue was after he had starred in 1927 in *The Jazz Singer*, the first full-length "all-talking", all-squawking picture. He had little to offer to the fast-maturing sound film, but he bawled and whinnied for a while over the equally adolescent radio networks. Then radio too broke through the creaking stereotypes of vaudeville back-chat and old Kentucky homes into the vertiginous comedy of the Marx Brothers, the whimsicality of Jack Benny, the relaxed and urbane mockery of the Bing Crosby show. By the late thirties Jolson was the most thorough has-been in the American theatre.

During the war he tried to pick himself up again but there were few takers. Only a Hollywood producer, mulling over the ups and downs of Jolson's life, took what was thought to be a suicidal risk in filming a movie of it. It was one of the box-office champions of 1946–7. It

inspired a sequel, made famous an obscure movie actor who impersonated Jolson, and catapulted Jolson himself back to Broadway, to the radio and to the big money.

Asked how he had planned his comeback, he replied: "That was no comeback, I just couldn't get a job." Once again he was called "the world's greatest entertainer." He was a guest star on every star radio programme. For a reason no one has ever satisfactorily explained, his records, old and new, started to sweep the hit parade and sell in the tens and hundreds of thousands.

An enforced bachelor after three unsuccessful marriages, he married again, a lovely 21-year-old brunette. He gave a banquet for her, "only because it'll give me a chance to show her how I work with an audience. She's too young to have seen me." A guest congratulated him on his pretty daughter. "Mister," Jolson said, "she's too young to be my daughter. She's my wife."

HIS DEATH

He had one last hour of glory. He offered to fly to Korea and entertain the troops hemmed in on the United Nations precarious August bridgehead. The troops yelled for his appearance. He went down on his knee again and sang "mammy", and the troops wept and cheered. When he was asked what Korea was like he warmly answered, "I am going to get back my income tax returns and see if I paid enough."

He had been back only a month and last night was in a San Francisco hotel, on his way to Hollywood to be the guest on Bing Crosby's radio show. It was ten o'clock. He was playing gin rummy with three friends. He felt a little off colour and asked a friend to go out and get him some bicarbonate of soda. He lay down. Before they called the doctor, he said, "It looks like the end." The friends ridiculed his scare but Jolson remarked that he "had no pulse." He invited the doctor to "pull up a chair and hear a story or two." Then he said, "Hell, Truman had only one hour with MacArthur. I had two." A few minutes later he died.

OCTOBER 25, 1950

NO TRACE OF MISSING STONE OF DESTINY

BY OUR LONDON STAFF

SCOTLAND YARD HAD no further news tonight of the Coronation Stone, the Stone of Scone, or the Stone of Destiny as it is variously called. There is "absolutely no trace" of it, but the police are still busy all over the country — especially on northward routes — looking for it.

The stone was stolen in the early hours of Christmas Day from Westminster Abbey. One theory is that the thieves (or, from the point of view of certain Scotsmen, "liberator") hid in a chapel overnight in readiness for their coup. They had first to prise the stone out of its housing under the Coronation Chair, which is behind the High Altar. Then the stone — which weighs four hundredweight and measures roughly 26in. by 16in. by 11in. — had to be carried round to the Poet's Corner door where, presumably, it was loaded into a car.

SCOTTISH ACCENTS

The police are looking for a man and a woman in a Ford Anglia car, which was seen near the Abbey in the small hours of the morning. Descriptions of them have been circulated, and the police say they speak with Scottish accents. It is taken for granted that the stone has been stolen by Scottish Nationalists.

The stone, which is rectangular and is of yellowish sandstone, has two rings let into it and normally lies behind a grille under the Coronation Chair. In 1940 it was buried in the Abbey, and the secret position marked on the chart which was sent to Canada for safety.

It is believed to have left the Abbey only once, when it was taken across to Westminster Hall and used for the installation of Cromwell as Lord Protector in 1657. It has been "attacked" before and was once slightly damaged (in 1914) when a bomb was placed under the Coronation Chair during the woman suffrage agitation. Twenty-five years ago, Mr David Kirkwood was given permission to bring a bill for the removal of the stone to Holyrood Palace, but the bill went no farther.

The Coronation Chair is the oldest piece of furniture in the Abbey, and has been used for 27 coronations. It was damaged by the removal of the stone; part of it was broken and a strip of wood from the grille was found lying on the floor.

ALREADY IN SCOTLAND?

Scotland Yard sent a number of CID men, including fingerprint experts, to the Abbey today and have circulated a description of the stone. There is no official confirmation of a rumour that a wrist-watch was found near the Coronation Chair, but it has been stated that freshly carved initials, "JF S," have been found in the gilding on the front of the chair.

It seems evident that the intruders were amateurs, for they made little attempt to hide their tracks. Whether or not they will make straight for Scotland with the stone is doubtful, though one Scottish paper said this morning that the stone might already have crossed the border. It should not prove a difficult object to hide once it can be taken out of the car which is carrying it, and the police of the two countries are likely to find themselves with a difficult job — not so much in finding the culprits but in finding the stone. If anybody is brought to court either on a charge of stealing or of sacrilege, the case should produce some fine legal and historical points.

WATCHMAN "ALONE IN THE ABBEY"

Mr Andrew Hislop (47), night watchman-fireman at the Abbey, told a reporter last night how he discovered that the stone was missing:

"I was quite alone in the Abbey. The stone was there when I went round at about 11 p.m. — I always flash my torch on to it — and again at 12.15 a.m. At about 6.15 a.m. I found the Poets' Corner door, a temporary one, had been burst open and the lock was lying on the floor. It is the only possible door by which they could have broken into the Abbey . . . The stone was gone. Part of the chair was broken.

"There is a night watchman outside the Abbey as well. They used to have a burglar alarm which rang a bell if the stone was touched, but I don't think any alarm has been fitted since the stone was brought back after the war."

THE STONE'S LEGENDARY HISTORY

The history of the stone is surrounded by legend, most of it of late invention. It is of Perthshire sandstone and is thought to have been used as a coronation stone by Irish Kings before being used by the Irish speaking dynasty of Kenneth McAlpin in Scotland.

The legendary history of the stone is described in Cyril Davenport's *The English Regalia* as follows:

The stone was brought from Scotland by Edward I in 1296, after his defeat of John Baliol. All our kings since that time have been crowned upon it at Westminster, except Mary I; and when Cromwell was installed Lord Protector it

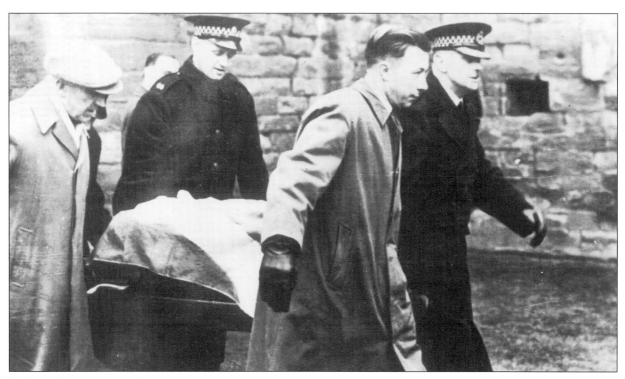

The Stone of Destiny is recovered, 1951

was taken to Westminster Hall for him. The seat holds "Jacob's stone", on which tradition says the patriarch Jacob slept in the plain of Luz.

Holinshed in his *Historie of Scotland* gives a curious history of a Greek noble, Gathelus, son of Cecrops, the builder of Athens. Gathelus, being of a turbulent and wandering disposition, went from Greece into Egypt with several companions, "*anno mundi* 2416". Here he made friends with Pharao the king, and eventually married his daughter Scota from whom it is said the name of Scotia is derived.

On the death of Pharao, Gathelus, not agreeing with his successors, left Egypt and settled at Compostella, where he was "intituled by the name of the king, and sat upon his marble stone in Brigantia." The two sons of Gathelus, however, not liking Spain, migrated to an island "lying north ouer agaynst Spayne" and landed at "Dundalke", the island being called "Hibernia", after one of them whose name was Hyberus.

The stone they are supposed to have brought with them, and it is described as being "in fashion like a seate or chayre, having a fatall destinie, as the Scottes say, following it, that wheresoever it shoulde be founde there shoulde the Scottish men raigne and haue the supreme gouernance. Hereof it came to passe that first in Spaine, after in Irelande, and then in Scotlande, the kings which ruled ouer the Scottish men receyued the crown sitting upon that stone, untill the time of Robert the First, King of Scotlande." It is said to have been taken to Ireland about 700 B.C. by Simon Brech, King of Scots. Thence it was taken to Scotland by King Fergus, about 330 B.C., and in A.D. 850 it was placed in the Abbey of Scone by King Kenneth. He found it at Dunstaffnage, a royal Scottish castle.

King Kenneth had it enclosed in a wooden chair, of which the present one is a copy made for Edward I, and particulars concerning it are to be found in his wardrobe accounts. It was originally gilded, painted, and inlaid in places with glass mosaics, traces of which can still be seen on a careful examination, especially on the back of the chair. It was dedicated by Edward I to St Edward the Confessor in 1297, and part of the Abbey in which it is kept is still known as St Edward's Chapel. Edward had an engraved plate inserted in the stone, and on it the legend:

Ni fallat fatum, Scoti hunc quoqunque locatum
Inveniunt lapidem regnare tenentur ibidem.

which may be translated:

Except old saws do fail and wizards wits be blind,
The Scots in place must reign where they this stone shall find.

This plate is now gone, but a space remains to mark the place to which it was formerly attached. A cross is cut upon the stone, and it has old handles at the ends. Another superstition concerning it was that it was said to groan whenever any of the monarchs of the Scythian race seated themselves upon it; and this must have been known to Hector Boece, who notes a fuller version of the old Scoto-Irish prophecy which being translated says:

Unless the fixed decrees of fate give way
The Scots shall govern and the sceptre sway
Where're this stone they find, and its dread sound obey.

DECEMBER 27, 1950

INVADERS THREATEN SEOUL

NORTH KOREAN ARMIES PROBE 38TH PARALLEL

SIX MONTHS AND two days after the North Korean armies first crossed the 38th parallel, invaders are again poised on the frontier of the (South) Korean Republic. Three thrusts — from north-west, north, and north-east — threaten Seoul, the South Korean capital. Five thousand civilians left Seoul on Christmas Day alone.

Of the three enemy thrusts reported, one is nearing Kaesong, 34 miles north-west of Seoul. Chinese troops have been identified officially two miles south of the 38th parallel and 28 miles due north of the capital. North Korean patrols have reached a point less than 24 miles from the city.

Facing the invaders now is a United Nations army estimated at 250,000 men and holding a front of 140 miles from coast to coast. The United States 8th Army and the United Nations 10th Corps (which completed the evacuation of its forces from North-eastern Korea during the weekend) is now a unified force under Lieutenant-General Ridgway, who arrived in Korea yesterday to succeed Lieutenant-General Walker, the 8th Army commander who was killed when his jeep crashed on Saturday.

EQUIPMENT SAVED

The evacuation of the Hungnam beachhead, completed in thirteen days, was greeted by President Truman as "the best Christmas message I have had." One hundred and five thousand United Nations troops were taken off by the evacuation fleet, together with 400,000 tons of equipment. All have now been landed at ports in the Pusan area and been assigned new roles.

This is the fact-and-figures account of the evacuation, planning for which was started by the United States Navy on November 27.

The first troops boarded evacuation vessels on December 12. As the number of troops inside the dwindling beachhead decreased, the warships off Hungnam gradually increased their bombardment of the enemy forces surrounding the beachhead.

At 9 a.m. on Christmas Eve nine thousand men remained ashore, and by midday three thousand remained. Two hours later there were only two hundred covering the withdrawal. The last to leave were the Navy's underwater demolition teams, which blew up dock installations.

In thirteen days a fleet of 193 United Nations vessels evacuated the 105,000 United Nations troops, 91,000 Korean refugees, 17,500 vehicles, and 350,000 tons of other equipment and supplies.

The withdrawing corps left Hungnam a battered, burn-ing shell containing nothing of value for the North Korean and Chinese troops who had besieged it. The great fertiliser and explosives works run by the North Koreans under Russian advice were among the buildings demolished.

MACARTHUR'S OPTIMISM

In a tribute to the 10th Corps, General MacArthur declared, "No command fought more efficiently or more gallantly, and no command could have acquitted itself to better advantage." General MacArthur said that the evacuation had completed the readjustment of the United Nations forces' positions made necessary by the entry of Communist China into the war. This redeployment, with that of the United States 8th Army, was possibly, in the general result, the most significant and fortunate of any during the Korean campaign.

General MacArthur repeated his claim that the United Nations push north of Korea's "waist" had been justified.

"We exposed before it was too late secret political and military decisions of enormous scope and threw off their balance enemy military preparations aimed at surreptitiously massing power capable of destroying our forces with one mighty extended blow."

In his general communiqué yesterday General MacArthur said that in spite of the deceptive appearance of quiet along the 8th Army front the enemy continued to make preparations for offensive operations. "Numerous reports received during the last 48 hours established the fact that Chinese Communist forces are now deployed in forward areas," the communiqué went on. "Nor does the enemy make any secret of his intentions."

"FINAL WARNING"

United Nations planes continued their attacks yesterday on enemy concentrations fifty to a hundred miles north and north-west of Seoul. Superfortresses carried out "saturation" raids on four targets before noon, including Chorwon, a principal supply, road, and railway centre fifty miles north of Seoul, and other targets fifty miles farther north. They dropped 176 tons of bombs.

A Peking radio broadcast received in Tokyo yesterday said that if the American "invaders" did not withdraw from Formosa and Korea they would be driven back by Chinese might. The broadcast said that the statement was a final warning.

DECEMBER 27, 1950

Above: US soldier fights in the Korean War Overleaf: Korean prisoners of war

'Just what is it that makes today's homes so different?' by Richard Hamilton

TURN OF THE HALF CENTURY

BY AJP TAYLOR

THE NINETEENTH CENTURY has been called the age of Hope; the twentieth century has been the age of Hope Fulfilled. In the first half of the century Western man has achieved every ambition which he set before himself since the time of the Renaissance. He has conquered space, disease, poverty. The scientific method which he has perfected guarantees that he can do anything that he wishes. Atomic energy will give him infinite power; and, if he survives long enough, he will conquer death itself. He has mastered all nature, including his own; for it is only in the last fifty years that families and therewith populations have become "planned".

In the social world, too, Western man has shaken himself free from the chains of ignorance and tradition which Rousseau denounced. In 1901 Habsburg, Hohenzollern, and Romanov still towered in Europe; now every royal dynasty, great or small, has gone, except for the few that have long had only decorative uses. Hereditary right, whether of monarch or noble, now counts for nothing anywhere in the Western world; the House of Lords is too trivial to be an exception. Every Government throughout the world claims to represent the majority of inhabitants in its country; and nearly all make at any rate a show of universal suffrage. Most of all, mankind has been prised up from its roots of custom and traditional belief. Apart from a few surviving sentiments of humanistic morality, reason and self-interest have become the sole motives of man's conduct; the exception is his readiness to sacrifice himself for the nation state — and even this seems to be dying in most of the Western world.

This is the picture in the West. Asiatic man is still a rather different kind of being. But Asia is only the West a little behindhand. What the West has gone through the Asiatic countries are beginning to go through also. Japan is already superficially Westernised: China and India are following suit.

FULFILMENT

Every dream of the eighteenth-century philosopher, every theory of the nineteenth-century radical has been fulfilled. If an Englishman could have learnt on the last day of 1850 what his descendants would accomplish in the next hundred years he would have been incredulous with admiration and delight; but it would have amazed him still more to learn that at the end of these hundred years we look forward to the next half-century with harsh anxiety, if not with despair. The first half of the twentieth century has had its share of bitter experiences for the West: two world wars, two Russian famines, the planned slaughter of millions in the Nazi gas-chambers. Yet after all these the most optimistic of us would only dare to say: "If the next half-century is no worse than the last we shan't do so badly!" A gloom hangs over the future such as the Western world has not known since the first Renaissance of the twelfth century. It is perhaps a mitigation to bear in mind that this gloom is confined to the world of Renaissance Europe which has now grown into the Atlantic community. Most of mankind outside Europe has still achieved little or nothing; and is therefore still in the age of Hope. From this point of view Asiatic communism is the last version of nineteenth-century rationalism; like its precursor, it holds out the illusion of infinite possibilities.

Europe has ceased to be the centre of the world. Though it is always unsafe to guess how the present will appear to the eyes of the future, this is a generalisation which is likely to stand the test of time; it is the greatest shift in the world balance since the upheavals of the fifteenth century. From the time of Columbus until the time

Albert Einstein, scientist and twentieth-century prophet, warns against the dangers of atomic power

of Gandhi, Stalin, and Mao Tse-tung, European man and especially the educated classes of Europe lived on the plunder of the rest of the world. The process has been running down in the last half-century; and its end is now in sight. If that were all, if our gloom was merely the gloom of a French aristocrat on the fall of the Bastille, knowing that his privileges were ending, we could find some consolation: loss of privilege for a few means greater freedom for many. No doubt the game is up for the inhabitants of this island; in the long perspective of history this would be a small price to pay if the inhabitants of Asia were to achieve in the next half-century something like the freedom from want that we have known.

But is this all? Is our gloom confined to a small area which is losing its geographical and historical privileges? Is it merely, as the Communists maintain, a symptom of the decline of capitalism? Or is it not more fundamental — a realisation that the values of Western civilisation, and not merely the privileges of Western Europe, are perishing before our eyes? The Russians and the Chinese can master our machines; will they ever have our respect for individual lives, our recognition of the human spirit in every man? The Western world called in

America to save it in two world wars; and is now looking to it for salvation in a third. Yet the Americans show none of the confidence that goes with success. On the contrary, the United States is racked far more savagely than we are in Europe by anxiety for the future. This anxiety is disguised as a hysteria against Communism; it springs more deeply from the consciousness of infinite power which man has gained and dare not use. After all, the American ideal is the refrigerator in every home; this is the Russian ideal too. The only difference is that in America the refrigerator has arrived.

NO DECADENCE

Yet there is something else which should be placed on record for the benefit of the future. Although apprehensive and perhaps despairing, we are not decadent. Claudian, writing in the fourth century A.D., was sharply aware that he was an inferior poet to Virgil. The philosophers and scientists of Western Europe are not inferior to their predecessors; even the politicians of the last half-century make a creditable showing. Nowhere in Western Europe can you point to the signs which show that a civilisation is in decline. Hitlerism was the nearest thing to it; and

this was a disease which Western Europe seems successfully to have overcome. Gibbon said of his history: "I have depicted the triumph of barbarism and religion." Western man can still hold his own against both. In fact, he is more sensible, more critical, more tolerant, more intelligent than he has ever been: he has even survived the shock of discovering that when Utopian dreams are translated into real life the perfect world is still far away.

On the whole Western man has justified the hopes of the eighteenth-century democrats: the people, it has turned out, can be trusted. It may well be that, just as Greece ceased to be the centre of the ancient world, Western Europe — or even the white nations generally — have ceased to dominate the world of modern times. In that case, the greatest historic success of the Greeks is still before us: to take our conquerors prisoner. The world outside Europe has learnt to handle our machines; it has still to be won for our ideas. At the very least, this task will provide some interest and occupation for the next fifty years. Better that than emulate medieval man, waiting for the end of the world in A.D. 1000 and sit in helpless contemplation of the universal catastrophe that may well have come before A.D. 2001.

DECEMBER 30, 1950

A Century of Images

1912 Emily Pankhurst addressing a crowd on Boston Common, August 7
1916 Battle of the Somme, The Great War
1939 'Gone with the Wind', with Clark Gable and Vivien Leigh
1945 Victory in Europe, Churchill greets the jubilant crowd
1966 England celebrates as Bobby Moore holds aloft the Jules Rimet Cup, July 30
1969 Neil Armstrong records Buzz Aldrin's first step on the Moon, July 20
1972 War in Vietnam: US casualties and (above) children flee from a napalm attack
1985 Crowds at the Live Aid Concert, Wembley
1997 Tributes to Diana, outside the British Consulate in New York, August 31

'She's free of the restrictions. Certainly you can see that.'

1950 | 1960

ONE SIDE OR THE OTHER

WINSTON CHURCHILL

"WHAT A REMARKABLE position of superiority is that occupied by the editor of the Manchester Guardian. (Handclaps) On the one hand are ten million or twelve million or more of reactionary Tories . . . On the other are ten million or twelve million of ignorant Socialists . . . Meanwhile, around his knees the little Liberal spaniel leaps and plays to whom he gives an affectionate pat, or from time to time a cuff for some unfortunate indiscretion. (Prolonged laughter) . . . So long as an unending flow of brilliant articles are produced putting everyone in their place and often stating all the arguments on both sides of every question the editorial duty in the world is done. But I think this is a time when all true Englishmen must choose their side . . ."

[Report of a speech in Manchester on the eve of the 1950 election. The Guardian leader writer (editor AP Wadsworth) refused to support any party whole-heartedly. Attlee's Labour won, but soon went downhill.]

FEBRUARY 21, 1950

The Guardian front page, Manchester, Monday August 24, 1959.

This one won't bite … the growing demand for mink

MINK AND MONEY

THE FUR SHOW

THE FIRST POST-WAR show of home-bred live mink was held at Beaver House yesterday. If the majority of the unexpectedly large crowds of spectators had seen mink before, only as expensive fur coats and wraps, they quickly marked the notice to take care not to be bitten.

The beautiful and slender animals, each in a narrow wire cage, looked deceptively soft and harmless until they bared long sharp teeth to hiss and scream at the visitors. A number of "standard black" mink were in the show but the majority were "mutation", the breeders' name for any variation on this standard, in white, pastel and the much-sought-after silver blue. The highest quality furs are densely piled and even in colour.

A nucleus of about five Mink farms survived in England after the war; there are about a hundred today. The minority are run as a full-time concern, the others are a spare-time hobby. Few of the pelts reach the home market as there is 105 per cent purchase tax, and in the twelve months to February, 1951, £42,000 worth of British-bred mink and silver fox were exported.

Many of the visitors were making inquiries about keeping mink in their back gardens. A start with a trio of two females and one male costs about £75. They mate only once a year with an average litter of three or four and those not kept for breeding are killed at five months. As the dried pelts fetch only about £6 the outlay will not be recovered the first year; but profits can be made with a larger number of animals, and it is possible for a small breeder to keep, say, a hundred if he has the space. The skins are sent to a fur company or centre, like the Hudson Bay Company in London, and these are matched into bundles.

Feeding costs are not high as these ferret-like animals eat fish-heads, liver, and some cereals. No grooming is necessary or, indeed, possible as they can only be handled when one is wearing thick leather gloves.

APRIL 7, 1951

MILK AND MORALS

A NUISANCE BUT NOT DEPRAVED

BY NORMAN SHRAPNEL

SEARCHING FOR DEPRAVITY among the milk bars is a quest that could happen in no time and in no place but ours. We are in Graham Greeneland, among the morose haunts of former innocence. It is here, in the fun fairs and the soft-drink establishments and the once-gay places with entrance halls of distorting mirrors at which nobody laughs any more, that corruption waits to strike.

Can Greenery curdle even a milk bar? Dr JL Burn, medical officer of health for Salford, seems to think so. He sees some of them as rather sinister places where "young people flock at night when they ought to be in bed." Illegitimacy is on the increase. Partly to blame, he suspects, is the growing number of "snack bars and milk bars of an unsatisfactory type." Not all milk bars, he hastens to add: some of them are as candid as on the day they were born. But there is what he darkly calls "the other kind".

Setting out to find "the other kind" is a suitable pastime for a January night, nagged by an indeterminate wind and spattered with icy rain. You start, on the final stroke of nine, in the region of dog-meat shops, corner pubs, Chinese laundries, and people who stand brooding and sniffing at the ends of streets for no reason that they seem able to remember. Very soon you understand the lure of the milk bars. Anywhere showing a light has an irresistible attraction. You flutter towards it damply and blindly; you grope for the door and stumble into a place that is warm and bright, at any rate in comparison with the street outside.

This is a snack bar. It says "Open until after midnight, including Sundays" and you wonder why. It is empty but for a couple in a corner, eating snacks in a forbidding pool of private silence that does not seem to merge into the public silence of the rest of the establishment, and a woman behind the counter who regards you without welcome. She has indigestion, and you do not wonder. She

stares with what is probably a good deal less like open hostility than it looks, and she hiccups. Perhaps she does not have to speak, for directly above her head is a notice which says "Wishing you all a Happy New Year."

A thin line of paper streamer circumnavigates the brown walls and at the end of the long counter is the mighty geyser-like apparatus that gives such places their definition and rank. It fumes and mumbles to itself, like a symbol of the strictly private life that goes on here.

"Mind the step," says the woman as you carry off your tea. These are her first

Dens of iniquity?

and last words. You wonder how many people, bemused by endless soft drinks or blinded by half a lifetime of snack-bar steam, have fallen on their faces at this point. You leave swiftly, stumbling up the step, and find not far away a milk bar that might be one of the sort the health officer had in mind. It is full of children in their teens, some obviously at the lower end.

They look nice children. The boys are bright-eyed and gay and the girls wear bright headscarves and excitedly discuss

the rival merits of this place and others of its kind. It is obvious that most of them are *habitués*. You cannot feel that corruption has yet struck deeply here, though one or two of the older boys hold their drinks a shade ponderously, like Humphrey Bogart. On the serving shelf the drinks stand ready poured out, like whiskies at a brisk dance, suggesting rapid sales — soft drinks in all their enchanted colours, yellow, and black, and pale and hectic red. Ices are popular, too. You shudder more deeply into your damp coat collar as you watch the sleet patterning the blackness of the uncurtained windows and wonder anew at the extraordinary habits of the English.

The table-tops are scrawled with what may count as sociological data, but it looks too innocent for anybody's report. At any rate it would be considered so if scrawled on the tolerant bark of trees. You read conjoined names like Jim and Betty, Walter and Flo, with here and there a message, a bucolic message scrawled on a milk-bar table, a midwinter's night's dream, perhaps.

What looks at first like the oldest inhabitant — twenty if a day, with thick soles and draped mackintosh — hangs over the chromium-edged bar with an air of dissociation. Such kid's stuff is not for him. Soon he is joined by a girl of his own age, incredibly tense and self-conscious and stupid-looking. The really sad thing here seems to be that the cheery little boys and girls will one day be like these.

Policemen are likely, in confidential moments, to call the places "a bit of a darned nuisance with all those youngsters hanging about." But the police do not appear to regard them as hatching-grounds for crime or any serious misbehaviour. Asked if any special eye is kept on them, an officer said, "We don't go out of our way." He added that as "long as they don't obstruct the pavement outside they don't particularly worry us."

APRIL 28, 1951

BENTLEY'S APPEAL DISMISSED

"LET HIM HAVE IT"

THE APPEAL OF Derek William Bentley (19) against his conviction of murdering Police Constable Sidney Miles during a gun fight on the roof of a Croydon warehouse was dismissed yesterday by the Court of Criminal Appeal. Bentley had been tried at the Old Bailey with Christopher Craig (16), who was similarly convicted and ordered to be detained during Her Majesty's pleasure. Bentley was sentenced to death.

Mr FH Cassels said the first ground of appeal was that the Lord Chief Justice

Derek Bentley . . . lost appeal

had failed adequately to put Bentley's defence to the jury. The only reference to Bentley's defence in the summing-up was that he did not know Craig had a gun, a denial that he had said: "Let him have it, Chris," and the statement that he did not know Craig was going to shoot.

Bentley's defence was that the whole of his behaviour in the gun battle on the rooftop, which went on for between twenty and twenty-five minutes, was not consistent with that of someone in concert with Craig but was that of a person who was taking a passive part.

JANUARY 14, 1953

CHILLED BEEF FROM ARGENTINA

IT WAS ANNOUNCED at the Treasury last night that a new Anglo-Argentine meat agreement had been signed in Buenos Aires. Under this agreement Britain will receive 230,000 tons of meat a year at an average price of approximately £130 a ton. The average price paid under the old agreement was £97 10s.

JANUARY 14, 1953

A RARE OLD DAY FOR ENGLAND

ASHES AFTER YEARS OF WAITING

BY NEVILLE CARDUS

IN SUNSHINE WHICH might have come to us from an August at Kennington Oval more than a quarter of a century ago, a victory for England over Australia was vociferously celebrated today.

The result on paper suggests that after all the prize came to us fairly comfortably, but as a fact every run to the end needed hard work and determination to get. The Australians fought vehemently until a boundary hit or two would settle the issue. Then Hassett bowled like a gallant captain and opponent who chivalrously chose to be the first to present the laurel wreath.

Had the gentlest wind of chance blown Australia's way the finish would have unsettled the nerves and, possibly, unseated judgement. WA Johnston, Australia's only spin bowler, missed taking important wickets by inches, for several mishits from him eluded a field which on the whole, appeared as omnipresent as avid and brilliantly safe.

TOO MUCH FOR JOHNSTON

But though no patriotic spectator dared take events for granted, the die was all the time cast against Australia. Ably and manfully though Johnston worked away, over after over, the wicket called for spin at the other end of the pitch as well. England needed too few runs with no need for hurry. No single bowler not a genius in his class could have won the match by dint of his own arm in the circumstances which alleged and brought

the best out of Johnston, as splendid and sterling-hearted a cricketer as Australia ever sent to us.

Hassett, in a humorous speech to the crowd, paid his generous tribute to England. He has the philosophy to ask himself, now the battle is done, if he did not make a mistake in going into action at the Oval in so crucial an engagement with inadequate reserves of spin.

AUGUST 20, 1953

SEXUAL BEHAVIOUR IN THE HUMAN FEMALE

DR KINSEY'S BOOK

ALTHOUGH NO DOUBT the advertisement was repaying, the early sensational newspaper accounts of the Indiana University inquiry associated with Dr Kinsey's name hardly did him justice. The full book is serious and factual, with a vocabulary well above the heads of most of the diligent searchers after scientific information to whom the "popular" papers addressed themselves in August.

It is of fascinating interest as a survey of current American morals and it opens up many suggestive lines of inquiry for the psychologist and teacher, to say nothing of the Churches. It could even be studied with profit by those whose business it is to catch the public fancy through the film and the press. The diagnosis of the differences between what appeals to the male and what appeals to the female will suggest to the cynical that many of our eminent practitioners in the

art of mass-appeal have been wasting their time. If they want to enter the fantasy life of the female they must adopt a quite different technique from that directed to the male: "cheesecake" has its limitations.

The English reader may feel that the statistical analysis of the evidence from the 5,940 "case histories" is over-elaborate, often to the point at which it ceases to have significance. But the main defect is the lack of correlation with social, ethical, and class distinctions. This could have been pushed much farther. Even in a small country like Great Britain we should expect to find regional differences, and American mores are probably no more standardised. None the less the Kinsey report is a brave attempt to let in light on dark places and to open the way to honest and fresh thinking.

DECEMBER 4, 1953

Screen kiss … Gregory Peck and Audrey Hepburn

NEW FILMS IN LONDON

ROMAN HOLIDAY

EVEN NOW, WHEN the world of the cinema has lost some of its illusions and its raptures, the advent of new stars is proclaimed with incautious frequency. Nevertheless it is impossible to resist the notion, shared with others who have seen William Wyler's *Roman Holiday* (at the Carlton) that Audrey Hepburn, the young British actress who, having had scant attention in British films, has taken the leading role in this American one, has star quality. William Wyler is, of course, one of the very best American directors; not every other director would have helped her to give so enchanting an account of herself. Yet much credit must go to Miss Hepburn herself.

The story of *Roman Holiday* is an inversion of *Cinderella*; it is not a poor waif who escapes to a royal ball but a princess who, during a State visit to Rome, escapes from her surroundings of pomp and circumstance to find brief liberty among the Romans. She is, in fact, found by Gregory Peck, a none too prosperous American journalist, who, with his attendant photographer (Eddie Albert) realises that he has fallen on a wonderful scoop. But when, after a dizzy day, the time comes for this royal Cinderella to return to the prison of her embassy, the gentlemanly Mr Peck is in love with her and, being Mr Peck and a gentleman, he knows that his scoop will not go to press.

It is, of course, a story dear to any sentimental heart, but it has been given quite exceptional distinction, partly by Mr Peck's competent and experienced acting, largely by Mr Albert's rich touch of humour, largely, too, by Mr Wyler's use of the beautiful Roman scene (the film was made in Rome), but most of all by Miss Hepburn. She shows dignity and innocence, pathos, and a sense of fun. This may be no more than an unimportant little fantasy in substance, but thanks to its Cinderella it has that blend of tears and laughter which is the true stuff of comedy.

AUGUST 22, 1953

NOT JUST "SHORT BACK AND SIDES" NOW

MULTIPLICITY OF HAIR STYLES FOR MEN

BY OUR CORRESPONDENT

THE EXTRAORDINARY GROWTH of men's hair styles since the war received full recognition yesterday with the opening of the National Hair and Beauty Week. Side by side in shop windows in town and country the latest fashions for men and women demonstrated the full range of "the art and craft of hairdressing", from the Evening District Attorney and countless variations on the Tony Curtis theme for men to some of the less elaborate "creations" that women go in for.

CURLS AND STREAKS

Manchester, with one of the most ambitious projects during the week, intends to take this equality of opportunity a step farther. A pageant in the city showing 94 styles through the ages will take the male, trimmed, curled, and waved, from Mark Antony to the City Cut.

The male interest in hair styles is now quite as feverish as any woman's, according to Mr LM Lawrence, secretary of the committee which is organising the week's events in the Manchester area. "Some men are even keener than women," he added, opening two great volumes that gave details with pictures of the more popular of the forty male styles in demand in Withington.
Youths in their teens and early twenties are keenest on the styles of Tony Curtis, a square-browed, dark-haired film actor, whose photographs show "one curl at the front and occasionally a bunch of curls". For an average of 2s. 6d. this is officially rendered as "sides fairly straight; curls forming into a peak drop softly on to the forehead . . . "

Subtle variations on that or the District Attorney (which was originally known as the Duck's Anatomy but had to be renamed because some critics called it

by "slang expressions") are fashioned to suit the client's type of face and personality. The crew cut which came from the lumberjacks of Canada and America can be rendered "round", "square", or "British or American". Some of the older

men in the suburbs no longer seek a simple "back and sides" but sit back for such improvements as permanent waving, "silver and gold streaks", "tipped gilt ends", and give the most complicated directions to enhance their masculine features.

Many middle-aged men, prematurely grey, "particularly the commercial-traveller type", are erasing the signs of age at the roots and going home a different colour — blond, red, brown, or whatever they fancy. The younger men, the experts think, are going in for more elaborate "hair-dos" partly as a revolt against the standardisation they had to submit to in the forces but "the mass of men" are just simply becoming "more hair-conscious".

"Give me a Dale Robertson" was the latest request in a Manchester hairdresser's yesterday, and, after a photograph of Mr Robertson has been produced and carefully studied, the customer's very straight hair was "permed" into the right shape for 15s. He wanted a "Dale Robertson" because he was getting married next week, and his fiancée was so pleased with the result that she came in later in the afternoon to congratulate the hairdresser on his work.

For those who are not so easily pleased some other titles suggest the scope available to them for matching their coiffure to their position in life. They include the Director ("Slight wave on the crown of the head . . . sideboards fairly full"), the Academician (". . . high side part to counterbalance the broad forehead . . . "), the Author, the Olympic, and the Continental. Even the Editor with "a large head and fairly full round face and fairly straight hair" has a style named after him with "a high side part, both sides swept back with the part immediately above the ears going back fully."

JANUARY 2, 1954

MR ERNEST HEMINGWAY IN MISSING PLANE

WRECKAGE SIGHTED

BY OUR CORRESPONDENT

A CHARTERED PLANE carrying the novelist Mr Ernest Hemingway and his wife crashed near Murchison Falls on the Victoria Nile, in North-West Uganda yesterday. Wreckage of a plane, believed to be the Hemingways' was sighted today three miles below the falls, and the pilot of a BOAC. Argonaut air liner flying from Entebbe to Khartum, which was diverted to search for the missing Cessna aircraft, said he saw no signs of survivors.

The BOAC pilot added that "it looked like the chap did a neat job of landing. The plane plopped right into scrub trees growing about 20 feet high along the river valley." He doubted if those aboard were killed in the crash. "One wheel of the undercarriage was broken, but otherwise the plane appeared little damaged," he said. The river was only 300 yards away, he said.

A police rescue party immediately set out to move up the Nile by launch from Butiaba, on Lake Albert, into the wild country where the plane came down. It is the least accessible part of Uganda,

thick with big game.

Police and aircraft started the search for the Hemingways' plane when it failed to arrive at Masindi to refuel on a flight from Entebbe to Murchison Falls.

Mr Hemingway, whose home is in Cuba, arrived in East Africa last August with his wife. He then said that he had no plans then to write about the Mau Mau terrorists but might write a feature article on them for an American magazine. After his arrival in Kenya he spent several months touring the Kikuyu country, the scene of most of the Mau Mau operations. Then he began a big-game and fishing trip.

Ernest Hemingway, 55-year-old writer and war correspondent, won last year's Pulitzer Prize for fiction with his novel *The Old Man and the Sea*. His story of Kenya, *The Snows of Kilimanjaro*, was filmed recently.

He has been married four times. His present wife was formerly Miss Mary Welsh, a Chicago-born war correspondent.

JANUARY 25, 1954

THE MILE IN 3 MINUTES, 59.4 SECONDS

BANNISTER'S TRIUMPH

ROGER BANNISTER, AGED 25, today became the first man to run a mile in less than four minutes. His time at the Iffley Road track, Oxford, in the annual match between the Amateur Athletic Association and Oxford University, was 3 minutes, 59.4 seconds.

Bannister, a former president of the Oxford club and now a medical student nearing qualification, ran as first string for the visiting side against his old university. Bannister received considerable assistance by the intelligent pace-making of CW Brasher, a former Cambridge runner, who led the field through the first quarter-mile in 57.3 seconds and reached the half-mile in 1 minute, 58 seconds. with Bannister three yards in the rear. From there CJ Chataway took up the lead and reached the three-quarter mile mark in 3 minutes, 0.4 seconds with Bannister at 3 minutes, 0.7 seconds. Bannister took the lead with some 350 yards to go, passed one unofficial timekeeper at the 1,500 metre mark in 3 minutes, 43 seconds equalling the world's record for that distance, and thereafter, throwing in all his reserves, he broke the tape in 3 minutes 59.4 seconds.

7 MAY, 1954

PICTURE THEATRES

THE UNUSUAL THING about *On the Waterfront,* which is certain to be one of the year's outstanding films, is that Marlon Brando's performance is only one of many striking bits of acting; and for this the chief credit seems to go to its brilliant director, Elia Kazan, who has fanned this murky dockside jungle into life (or as it used to be, we are told) down to the last docker and bartender. Brando himself shambles, rambles and mumbles together (few can have so nicely underplayed the *sotto voce*) a masterly portrait of the diffident but tough ex-pugilist who finally scotches the tyranny of the trade union bosses. But behind him always, essential background, is a wonderful collection of craggy, life-worn faces whose acting is just as subtly relevant to the strong, measured tread of this picture.

NOVEMBER 9, 1954

Roger Bannister breaking the world record

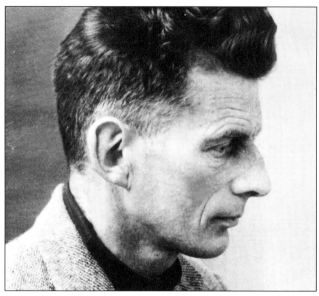

Samuel Beckett . . . writes in French for preference

WAITING FOR GODOT

CONUNDRUM OR NONSENSE?

BY PHILIP HOPE-WALLACE

WAITING FOR GODOT at the Arts Theatre Club is a play to send the rationalist out of his mind and induce tooth-gnashing among people who would take Lewis Carroll's Red Queen and Lear's nonsense exchanges with the fool as the easiest stuff in the world. The play, if about anything, is ostensibly about two tramps who spend the two acts, two evenings long, under a tree on a bit of waste ground—"waiting for Godot".

Godot, it would seem, is quite possibly God, just as Charlot is Charles. Both tramps are dressed like the Chaplinesque zanies of the circus and much of their futile cross-talk seems to bear some sort of resemblance to those music-hall exchanges we know so well: "You know my sister?" "Your sister?" "Yes, my sister," and so on, ad lib. One of the tramps is called Estragon, which is the French for tarragon herb: the other is called Vladimir. On the first evening their vigil is broken by the arrival of a choleric employer called Pozzo (Italian for a well) and a downtrodden servant Lucky, who looks like the Mad Hatter's uncle.

On the second evening this pair reappears, the former now blind and led by the latter, now a deaf mute. As night falls on both sessions a boy arrives to announce that Godot cannot keep the interview for which the tramps so longingly wait. And at the end of it, for all its inexplicit and deliberate-ly fatuous flatness, a curious sense of the passage of time and the wretchedness of man's uncertainty about his destiny has been communicated out of the very unpromising material.

The allegorist is Sam Beckett, who was once James Joyce's secretary and who writes in French for preference. His English version bears traces of that language still. The language, however, is flat and feeble in the extreme in any case. Fine words might supply the missing wings, but at least we are spared a Claudelian rhetoric to coat the metaphysical moonshine.

The play bored some people acutely. Others found it a witty and poetic conundrum. There was general agreement that Peter Hall's production did fairly by a work which has won much applause in many parts of the world already and that Paul Daneman in particular, as the more thoughtful of the two tramps gave a fine and rather touching performance. Peter Woodthorpe, Timothy Bateson, Peter Bull, and a boy, Michael Walker, the mysterious Godot's messenger, all played up loyally. There was only one audible retirement from the audience, though the ranks had thinned after the interval. It is good to find that plays at once dubbed "incomprehensible and pretentious" can still get a staging. Where better than the Arts Theatre?

APRIL 3, 1955

PRIESTLEY'S PURGATORY

THE ADVENT OF ADMASS

BY ALASTAIR HETHERINGTON

"THE SOCIETY THAT does not know what it wants and is lunatic." The epitaph is Mr JB Priestley's, and the society is ours today. It is a form of society most fully developed in the United States but spreading rapidly in England and Western Europe. Mr Priestley has coined a word for it, "Admass". High-pressure advertising, mass communications increasing productivity, and rising material standards all help to create "the mass mind, the mass man". He finds it typified in the highway from Fort Worth to Dallas, Texas, with miles and miles of trailer courts, motels, gas stations, supermarkets, bars, drive-in movies, drive-in restaurants and thickets of television aerials. He says that the people of "Admass" are dissatisfied, restless, and secretly bitter — especially the women, who discover life to be a glittering treachery.

Mr Priestley and his wife, Jacquetta Hawkes, have sustained their attack on "Admass" throughout their book, which is an account of their travels last year in Texas, New Mexico, and Colorado. Mr Priestley spent most of his time in the cities while Miss Hawkes was studying Indian pueblos and pre-history. Their book is eminently readable, gaining much from the juxtaposition of their two styles of writing. (Miss Hawkes is the sharper observer of the two and the closer-knit in thinking.) But the underlying attack on our society does not stand examination. The pattern of life being produced in America and spread from there is not so empty and frustrating, nor is individuality so lacking.

Let Mr Priestley compare the cities of the United States with their counterparts in the industrial north of England. "Admass", of course, has its horrors both on the Fort Worth–Dallas road and in the kind of ugly suburban shopping centres with which England abounds. But what English industrial city has anything to compare with the lakeside parklands of Chicago — free of advertising, open, green, and spacious — or its Cook County Forest Preserve? Or with Central Pittsburgh, where whole blocks of buildings have been cleared away to make a park, flanked on one side by the rivers and on the other by a gleaming line of

JB Priestley . . . too much travel?

aluminium skyscrapers? Or with the boulevards of Baltimore or with the vistas of Seattle? These American cities are of the "Admass" age; the English are of an earlier period and much uglier. Even today if Manchester's authorities had a fraction of Chicago's foresight they would not be turning the banks of the Mersey into a rubbish dump, and if its pre-"Admass" citizens were not sunk in stupor they would have organised something like the Allegheny Conference on Community Development in Pittsburgh. It is worth noting, too, that the great industrial corporations — those whose advertising and productivity are at the heart of "Admass" — were among the foremost promoters of the Pittsburgh reconstruction. The "Admass" society has a creative side which the Priestleys seem to have missed.

Mr Priestley's political analysis also is faulty. He writes with understandable sorrow about the intolerance and unreason and sheer ignorance of the political views held by some Texans whom he met, but he concludes that a "radio spellbinder" could enlist mass support and by enticing millions of dollars from the oil tycoons could let loose totalitarian forces. Senator McCarthy was such a spellbinder, and he was well financed in Texas. Where is he now? Deflated and discredited. The mass of Americans have too much sense and too much decency to be fooled for long by such men.

People are the decisive factor. Mr Priestley in the cities found a lot of them unhappy and restless, and among the women he detected bewilderment, even despair, behind their flashing and dashing manner. "They were still girls in a mining camp," he says. One wonders. That may be true of some groups in urban society, especially in the extremes of Texas; but there are certainly a great many people, even in Dallas and Houston, who are living happy and fruitful lives.

One's impression, of course, depends largely on the individuals whom one meets. Mr Priestley seems to have been unlucky. Or was it that too many parties and too much travel gave him a tummy ache?

OCTOBER 1, 1956

Budapest waits in dread as Soviet tanks roll in

SOVIET TANKS CRUSH RESISTANCE

FIGHTING ENDS IN BUDAPEST AFTER ULTIMATUM

AT EIGHT P.M. yesterday the Soviet High Command in Hungary ordered Mr Nagy's Government to surrender by noon "or Budapest will be bombed." Soviet armoured forces then went into action. Just after 1 p.m. Moscow radio announced, "The Hungarian counter-revolution has been crushed."

A mid-afternoon Moscow radio bulletin said that "negligible groups of insurgents" were offering resistance in Budapest but were being crushed. The radio also announced that a new "Revolutionary Workers' and Peasants' Government" had been formed under Janos Kadar, the former "Titoist" who became first secretary of the Communist party at one point in the rebellion.

Budapest radio had gone off the air at 8.10 p.m. with a woman's appeal to "help Hungary . . . Help, help, help . . ." In mid-afternoon a Vienna monitor picked up what was apparently the last rebel-held radio station in Hungary. It broadcast repeated calls for help.

"Civilised people of the world. On the watch tower of a thousand-year-old Hungary the last flames begin to go out. Soviet tanks and guns are roaring over Hungarian soil. Our women — mothers and daughters — are sitting in dread.

They still have terrible memories of the army's entry in 1945.

"This word may be the last from the last Hungarian freedom station. Listen to our call. Help us — not with advice, not with words, but with action, with soldiers and arms."

The last news from Budapest itself reached the British Foreign Office in mid-afternoon. This said that Soviet troops were in control of key points and bridges in the city although gunfire was still in progress. Other reports said that Mr Nagy, who attempted to restore democracy in the country after the insurrection, was under arrest together with members of his Government.

Mr Nagy had given news of the Soviet attack to the world in a dramatic broadcast over Budapest radio. He spoke in English and then repeated his message in Hungarian. "This is Imre Nagy speaking," he said. "In the early hours of this morning, Soviet troops started to attack the Hungarian capital with the apparent purpose of overthrowing the democratic Government of the Hungarian People's Republic." After broadcasting frequent appeals to Russian troops not to fire on peaceful citizens, the radio then went off air.

NOVEMBER 5, 1956

"ELVIS THE PELVIS" AND THE BIG BEAT

THE RATIONALE OF ROCK 'N' ROLL

BY DW BROGAN

THE AMERICAN PEOPLE have, like us, a great many serious things to think of now, but one of the less serious but not totally unimportant things they debate is the Elvis Presley phenomenon. Is he a credit to his state, as the Governor of Mississippi has asserted, or is he only too representative of that most backward and savage of American commonwealths? Should he be paid nearly as much as Miss Mary Martin on television? Is he going to get married? Is he about to be drafted?

Such are some of the questions that the American public, in a muddled and often angry frame of mind, puts to itself. And it has, on the whole, rejoiced when it has learned that teenagers in Manchester have wrecked a cinema under the inspiriting influence of Rock Around the Clock and that our adolescents are ready to give to "Elvis the Pelvis" the same adoring reception that the two-way stretch girdle age-group gave to Liberace. We are all in the same boat, so it is gladly believed. Not only American kids are crazy, and English parents will know, do know the reproach of being "squares".

In one way there is no novelty in the Presley boom. In its most preposterous form it recalls Frank Sinatra of ten years ago, as Liberace recalls the Valentino of nearly a generation ago. The Charleston and The Black Bottom were as much a source of scandal as Blue Suede Shoes, and the American child is quite ready to tell Mom or even Grandma where she gets off. These infatuations are no novelty, and having to listen in to only too many discussions of Elvis, I recalled that day in New York when the Sinatra fans stormed Times Square, tearing each others' clothes off when deprived of the chance of stripping and

Previous page: Elvis in uniform; above: the rock look

perhaps dismembering their hero.

After all, the Bacchae had been there before. And my taxi-driver, philosophical in spite of the hold-up, had found the right answer for a sulky colleague — "What has he got that we haven't got?" "I don't know, but I sure wish I had it."

The screaming adolescents who wreck cinemas and terrify ministers and parents are disciples of the goddess "to whose bright image nightly by the moon Sidonian virgins paid their vows and songs."

"What," asked a lawyer friend of mine of his Irish-Catholic office girl, "What does your mother think of your rushing off to see Elvis Presley?" "Oh, she doesn't mind; she doesn't know anything." "But what about the wiggle?"

"Oh, that's just his way of expressing himself." Today, as we know, to cripple self-expression is a sin.

In spite of the prayer meetings and the refusal to hire halls that are reported, self-expression rages. Yet Elvis is a good boy; he doesn't smoke or drink; so what? In the William Faulkner country which he comes from, that is all the law and the prophets. It is, indeed, probably only an accident that had made him a master of Rock 'n' Roll and not a gospel-singer or a minor warbler of "country music" (not "hillbilly" songs).

Already someone unknown is on Elvis's trail. For leadership in this world is "a garland briefer than a girl's." Only death can confer real immortality, as the cult of James Dean shows. "Somewhere some young musician is working on something which will make Rock 'n' Roll sound like the genteel tinkling of a spinet," says a Rock 'n' Roll organ. This is the Big Beat that is on the way. We have been warned.

NOVEMBER 8, 1956

NASSER: WE SHALL FIGHT

EGYPTIANS DETERMINED

PRESIDENT NASSER, CONTENDING that "free people everywhere" were now behind him, said today that Egypt would accept no condition infringing her sovereignty or honour.

The Egyptians would fight to the last man to preserve their rights.

Addressing the congregation of the Islamic University of Azhar after prayers, he said: "We have been betrayed once and shall not allow ourselves to be taken by surprise again. Egypt wants peace but will not surrender."

He gave a day by day account of the battle in the Sinai peninsula and the Anglo-French air and land action aimed "at the destruction of our main forces."

"Arab nationalism," he said, "was a power today as proved by offers of help from King Saud, King Hussein of Jordan, and President Shukri el Kuwatly of Syria. Arab nationalism had co-operated with the Egyptians everywhere against imperialism. The Arabs had emerged from the events of the past ten days "united, strong and determined."

NEHRU, TITO, SUKARNO

He emphasised that navigation in the Suez Canal had been working "effectively" before the Anglo-French-Israeli attack. For this aggression Britain, France, and Israel stood today "condemned" by the conscience of world public opinion. Mr Nehru, President Tito, President Sukarno of Indonesia, and all free people had condemned it.

President Eisenhower had warned Israel and Israel had agreed to withdraw from Sinai. A similar warning had been given earlier by Marshal Bulganin, but,

President Nasser said, "the battle goes on." It was a political as well as a military battle against "perfidy and tyranny." Egypt would preserve her sovereignty and the entire world was with her.

"Egypt will accept no condition infringing her sovereignty or infringing her honour," he said. "Egypt is determined to preserve her sovereignty, independence, territories, and dignity.

"PEACE" AND "HOLY WAR"

That was what he meant by the political battle.

"As for the military battle, we are all of us to the last man in the country, prepared for it. We have proclaimed . . . that we shall not allow the repair of the canal and we shall not begin to clear the canal, as long as there is a single foreign soldier on our soil. This, my countrymen, is our attitude today.

"Our feelings today, my countrymen, are: determination, resolution, and faith. We want peace, and for peace we shall fight. Our feelings today are: unity, force, work, determination, struggle, and holy war. The entire world, free people everywhere, are behind us.

"You are told that the world today is passing through the most critical stage in its history, in the history of all humanity, but Egypt is not the cause of it, for Egypt did not attack anyone. Egypt defended her sovereignty.

"Those who are hurling threats at humanity today are treaders of wars or aggressors. Today our feelings are: we shall fight, we shall fight in the defence of our homeland."

NOVEMBER 9, 1956

THE SUEZ CRISIS

FIRST UN TROOPS READY

PRESIDENT NASSER ANNOUNCED yesterday that Egypt would not allow the clearing of the Suez Canal "as long as there is a single foreign soldier left on Egyptian soil." Nor would she accept any condition infringing her sovereignty. "We shall fight in defence of the homeland," he said.

ADVANCE UNITS TO ITALY

In New York it was reported that advance units of the United Nations force for Egypt will be flown to a temporary staging area in Italy "probably within 24 hours." The force, for which more than a dozen countries have offered troops, and for which more than five thousand men have already been promised, is expected to be in Egypt "in strength" within ten days.

"APPROPRIATELY ARMED"

Mr Hammarskjold said the first units would be rather small, but "appropriately armed", and would come from Denmark and Norway. Other advance units from Canada, Colombia, Finland, India, and Sweden would follow them a day later. American planes were being used to take the units to Italy, but Swissair would be asked for DC-6 aircraft to carry them on the last leg of their journey into Egypt.

NOVEMBER 10, 1956

SARTRE REPUDIATES COMMUNISM

JEAN-PAUL SARTRE, the writer, who has been a frequent and honoured visitor to Moscow, announced today that he was breaking off relations with Soviet writers because they had failed to protest against their Government's action in Hungary. He was also leaving the Franco–Soviet Friendship Society and would have nothing further to do with the French Communist party. M. Sartre commented: "One can no longer have any friendship of the ruling members of the Soviet bureaucracy. Horror dominates."

NOVEMBER 10, 1956

GIRLS DO NOT LIKE SCIENCE

DANGER BUT NO GLAMOUR

MISS M MILES, headmistress of Mayfield Comprehensive School, Putney, London, told a conference of the Association of Scientific Workers in London on Saturday of some of the reasons why girls did not care for science: it was too dangerous, too factual, not glamorous, and had no scope for self-expression. One girl said that men avoided scientists because they preferred not-so-clever women.

Employers and parents were reluctant to let girls do what they assumed was normal for boys, said Miss Miles. Parents were only too ready to encourage their daughters to "get a nice clean job in an office at the exorbitant wages which are at present paid to office juniors." Miss Miles added:

"We must educate parents, employers and headmistresses, who, on the whole, tend to be dyed-in-the-wool arts graduates like myself, so that girls of good general ability are steered towards science. We hear heart-rending appeals for girl technicians, but experience shows that by no means all firms are prepared to give girls the same chance as boys."

DECEMBER 10, 1956

"GARLIC AND OLIVE OIL HOLIDAYS"

BRITISH HOTELS DEFENDED

THE PRESIDENT OF Scarborough Hotels Association, Mr Harry Lund, is annoyed with people who praise foreign holidays at the expense of holidays at home, and he is also annoyed with the Government. At the association's annual meeting last night he said:

"We appear to have two implacable enemies — the garlic and olive oil gang of the press and radio and the Government. By the garlic and olive oil gang I mean those writers, usually women, who happily accept on the Continent the sort of carpetless room with iron bedstead, flock mattress and early Victorian plumbing which they would raise all hell about over here. Imagine what they would say if instead of bacon and eggs and the incomparable meats and vegetables of England we were to give them starch-loaded Continental breakfasts and main meals consisting of dollops of spaghetti with a little tomato sauce. If they are willing to put up with that sort of thing over there it's their own look-out. What we do object to is that they should then be given good space in journals and valuable time on the air in which to drool about how much better and cheaper foreign hotels are than our own."

SUBSIDISED TOURISM

Mr Lund said that staffs in this country had to be paid more than "sweated foreign labour" abroad, where the tourist trade was usually subsidised by the Governments. In Britain the reverse was the case, with high rating and purchase tax on the tools of their trade. In addition the Government here subsidised inland hotels in that their guests' bills came off income tax so that they did not mind what they had to pay. As a result hardly a first-class hotel in the country charged less than 37s. 6d. for bed and breakfast, while first-class seaside hotels had to struggle to get 35s. for a whole day's keep. Inland hotels had few people there at weekends, which lessened the problem of staff days off, whereas seaside staffs had often to be kept on all year round while establishments were empty for 60 per cent of the time.

Mr Lund spent a holiday in Spain after the hotel season this year.

DECEMBER 11, 1956

THE OUTSIDER PHILOSOPHY

A MODERN TYPE

BY IRIS MURDOCH

IN HIS FIRST BOOK, *The Outsider*, Mr Colin Wilson studied various types of man to whom the triviality of life had become unbearable because of the vision of something larger. It was suggested there that every Outsider was a religious man in embryo. In his second book, *Religion and the Rebel* (Gollancz, pp. 333, 21s.)Mr Wilson studies the "developed" Outsider who has advanced into the religious situation . . .

I enjoyed the book, but found it on the whole disappointing and unconvincing: not personal enough to be a challenging credo and not exact enough to be a persuasive analysis. What Mr Wilson does succeed in presenting (and it is worth study) is a picture of an important type of modern mind . . . The liberal attaches value to the world of ordinary virtues, while the Outsider philosophy rejects this region with contempt . . .

OCTOBER 25, 1957

USE OF SYNTHETIC HORMONES

ANXIETIES OVER MEAT SAFETY

A DECISION IS expected soon on the Ministry of Agriculture's attitude to the use of synthetic hormones to increase the yield of meat in beef cattle and sheep. There has been some anxiety recently among wholesale and retail meat dealers, and among certain sections of the public, about the possible effects of these hormones on humans.

It is generally agreed — by the Medical Research Council as well as other bodies — that with normal doses these is no danger to humans who eat meat from hormone-treated cattle or sheep. A veterinary officer of the Boots Pure Drug Company, Nottingham, which is producing these hormones in "quite large quantities", has calculated that one would have to eat 6.5 cwt of meat to obtain one daily dose. There are already comparatively large quantities of these hormones — known collectively as "oestrogens" — present in the human body, particularly in females.

DECEMBER 10, 1957

ROCKETS POINTED
AT BRITAIN

SOVIET WARNING

MR KHRUSHCHEV HAS issued a warning that the Soviet Government will establish nuclear rocket bases aimed at the British Isles if the British Government permits the establishment of similar American bases on its territory.

In a letter published in the magazine *International Life* he said the British decision was "tantamount to plans for a war of aggression," and added: "If the Soviet Union should suffer tremendous losses as a result of this aggression, crushing retaliatory blows would bring about still greater losses for the British Isles."

The Labour party and the TUC have called on the Government to give an immediate lead to other nations by suspending for a time nuclear tests. A joint declaration issued yesterday also says that as a first step the Government should try to hold summit talks soon.

The United States yesterday rejected Russian proposals for a limited Foreign Ministers' meeting as a prelude to a summit conference. It also reaffirmed its determination to have the question of German unity aired at any new summit meeting.

At the same time, the United States made public the text of a Soviet memorandum of February 28 which proposed drawing in representatives of East and West Germany but rejected German unification as a summit subject.

MARCH 7, 1958

TELEX TROUBLE

LONDON CALLS MOSCOW

BY MICHAEL FRAYN

MANCHESTER LIFTED THE Iron Curtain an experimental inch or two yesterday, and was disconcerted to find something remarkably like the first dress rehearsal of an Ionesco comedy going on on the other side.

The city's Commercial Library chose yesterday to test the recently established direct Telex link between Britain and the USSR by an experimental greetings call to Maschinoimport, Moscow. Telex is a teleprinter service connected through exchanges; there are 75,000 subscribers in the world, and there seemed to be no reason why one should not try getting through to one of the twenty or so of them listed in Moscow.

The experiment started with quiet commercial efficiency at 11 a.m. sharp, when the Telex operator at the library asked the exchange for a line to Moscow. For twenty minutes nothing happened. Then the exchange said that the Moscow operator was repeatedly replying "MOM" (the "wait" signal), and added that the Moscow end "now advise London that the Moscow subscriber has gone to lunch".

The Manchester exchange asked courteously if there was any other subscriber who would serve the purpose. Not to be thwarted, the library selected from the incredibly misspelt list of Moscow subscribers Moscow 1010 — the Telex Information Office. Moscow 1010, it seemed, had no appetite for lunch that day, and tapped out slowly: "Hat do du wish??"

Encouraged, the library fired off its prepared greetings message, explaining that it was one of the most important centres for commercial information in Northern England, and would be very pleased to help with any information which might be required on the import and export of industrial goods.

This was too much for Moscow 1010, who sent "MOM please", and paused for reflection. Then, relieved perhaps to find it was all so unsubversive, they replied gaily:

"Oh we k we very glad to meet you on our Telex we shall cu connect you with the subs who which will interest you. Please tell me what number are interested you??"

The library asked for Moscow 1086, which the list gave as the number of Maschinoimport. Maschinoimport, now back from lunch, were given the prepared message. The line went dead halfway through, but was brought to life again. It was 11.30 a.m.

There was a pause at the end of the transmission, and then Moscow 1086, perhaps suffering from indigestion through bolting lunch, replied testily: "I am not information service of Moscow."

"Are you Maschinoimport?" asked Manchester quickly.

"No," said Moscow 1086 coldly, "I am Maschinoexport."

He switched the call to his import twin, who turned out to be a much more cheerful person. "Hi," said Maschinoimport, "this sub is open today."

The prepared greetings were transmitted once again. This time there was no reply at all. It was 11.37 a.m. — about time, it seemed, to throw in the sponge. One could only conclude that the Russians did not want to be said hello to, even by Telex.

DECEMBER 5, 1957

POETRY BEYOND A JOKE

BETJEMAN'S COLLECTED POEMS

BY PHILIP LARKIN

CHARMINGLY BOUND IN blind-tooled ivory cloth, with gold Baskerville on the spine and a rose top-edge, this collection finally puts to flight the notion that Betjeman is no more than a dealer in a few preciosities such as Anglicanism or ghastly good taste. No doubt the photographs and rubrications of his early books helped to foster this view of his work as "amusing" yet infantile pastiche: since 1940, however, a succession of more chastely designed volumes has ousted the element of undergraduate hoax, of Osbert Lancaster and Arthur Marshall, and after A Few Late Chrysanthemums we have had to accept that what poets are supposed to do Betjeman does — not perhaps, in ways we think proper or ways sanctified by recent example, but which henceforward must be marked — or remarked — on the map.

Yet it would be wrong to claim that the later poems represent any radical alteration of poetic method. The first poem in the book, published in 1930, might have been written yesterday:

> She died in the upstairs bedroom
> By the light of the ev'ning star
> That shone through the plate glass window
> From over Leamington Spa.

Only mediocrities develop, Wilde said, and if Betjeman could hit the target so unerringly at 25 he had clearly no need to change. What he did was enlarge his range of subjects. Little in the earlier books presages the discoveries of the forties:

> The gas was on in the Institute,
> The flare was up in the gym,
> A man was running a mineral line,
> A lass was singing a hymn.

> On the floor of her bedroom lie blazer and shorts
> And the cream-coloured walls are betrophied with sports,
> And westering, questioning, settles the sun
> On your low-leaded window, Miss Joan Hunter Dunn.

> Rumbling under blackened girders, Midland bound for Cricklewood,
> Puffed its sulphur to where that Land of Laundries stood.
> Rumble under, thunder over, train and tram alternate go,
> Shake the floor and smudge the ledger, Charrington, Sells Dale & Co.,
> Nuts and nuggets in the window . . .

To love and topography the fifties added a deeper sense of time and mortality and a chantableness towards ordinary people that in no way blunted his feelings about the Age of the Common Man. And now, so far from being the laureate of a few private fads, Betjeman goes further than anyone else towards summarising "Dear old, bloody old England. Of tele-graph poles and tin" simply because no one else has his breadth of poetic reception. Betjeman picks it all up: the decay of surviving nineteenth-century institutions, the decline of the Church, the altered countryside and ways of living, sub-topia and socialism, and all the tiny vivid little manifestations of sadness and snobbery and silliness, and with his simple loving enthusiasm transmutes it to poetry. He is a subtle poet, but not a sophisticated one. Poetry for him is not a moral or sociological gymnastic, but a spontaneous overflow of natural feeling which directs his choice of words and informs them when found:

> Cancer has killed him Heart is killing her.
> The trees are down. An Odeon flashes fire
> Where stood their villa by the murmuring fir . . .

Those who 25 years ago tried to dismiss Betjeman as "bourgeois taste at its most corrupt" now call him a remarkable minor poet it would be a disservice to overestimate. This seems to me to ignore his particular worth at this time. Almost alone among living poets, Betjeman has knocked down the "No Road Through To Action" sign; he is in the best sense a committed writer, whose poems spring from what he really feels about real life, and as a result he brings back to poetry a sense of dramatic urgency and a jumble of properties it had all but lost. In the 36 lines of Felixstowe, or The Last Of Her Order, to for instance, or Eunice, there is a whole life it took delicacy to perceive and subtlety to express, and its impact has the fullness of a novel. Similarly, the quality in his poetry loosely called nostalgia "is really that never-sleeping alertness to note the patina of time on things past which is the hallmark of the mature writer:

> And from Greenford scent of mayfields
> Most enticingly was blown
> Over market gardens tidy,
> Taverns for the bona fide,
> Cockney anglers, cockney shooters,
> Murray Poshes, Lupin Pooters
> Long in Kensal Green and Highgate silent under soot and stone.

For this reason it is my considered opinion that it would do no harm to overestimate Betjeman's poetry for a bit. Some people have been puzzled by Edmund Wilson's remark last May that Auden, Thomas, and Betjeman were the best post-Eliot English poets: to me it seems eminently sensible, and my only regret is that he did not add that, of the three, Betjeman is the only one who is still a positive poetic force.

JULY 2, 1959

LEARNING THE HARD WAY

POLICE OFFICER'S COMMENT ON SHARPEVILLE RIOTS

BY OUR SPECIAL CORRESPONDENT

"I DON'T KNOW how many we shot," said Colonel J Piernaar, the local area police commander at Sharpeville. "It all started when hordes of natives surrounded the police station. My car was struck with a stone. If they do these things they must learn their lesson the hard way."

An official at Vereeniging hospital put the casualties at 7 p.m. tonight at 56 dead and 162 injured. Forty-four people seriously injured are in this hospital and the other 118 injured have been transferred to Baragwanath hospital, near Johannesburg.

Meanwhile there were reports from newspapermen in Langa, an African township near Capetown, that an unknown number of Africans were shot dead and many wounded when a riot broke out there tonight.

Seven buildings, including two schools, were said to have been destroyed by fire in the riot.

The newspapermen were at Langa police station, where they had been besieged by a crowd of Africans for more than two hours. They reported that Army units arrived just before 7 p.m. to help the police.

Mr Owen Hodges, a commercial traveller who drove through the Vereeniging area today, said African men egged on by women pelted cars with stones and fruit. Sharpeville police station was "literally besieged" by thousands of African men and women and police could only make contact with it by forcing their way through with Saracen armoured cars. Aircraft which dived over the area in an attempt to disperse the crowd only seemed to anger the Africans.

LIKE NINEPINS

The first African was shot dead and four Africans and several policemen were injured after the police had been stoned. The Africans retaliated, causing casualties among the police. The police then opened fire with sub-machine guns, sten guns and rifles, and eye-witnesses said that the front ranks of the crowd fell like ninepins. The crowd then retreated, leaving their dead and wounded in the street.

Mangled bodies of men, women and children lay sprawled on the roadway of the square. One policeman described the scene as "like a world war battlefield". A Johannesburg news photographer, whose own car was riddled with bullets, said "I took pictures of more bloodshed than I have ever before seen in South Africa."

The South African Press Association said one police officer instructed an African to collect pieces of a mangled body in a hat with a shovel and then spread sand over pools of blood in Sharpeville Road. A couple of African Salvation Army workers in uniform tried to help some of the victims.

The police seemed to be rather shocked themselves at the scene. Traffic policemen and motor cyclist police patrols led ambulances and fire appliances and police trucks to and from the African hospital at Vereeniging and the police station at Sharpeville. Roads outside the police station were literally covered in blood.

African bodies strewn across a road in Sharpeville

Police officers went to the scene, including Brigadier Els, the Witwatersrand assistant commissioner of police. There were at least six Saracen armoured vehicles ranged around Sharpeville police station and it was understood more were being called in for tonight.

WAILING OF WOMEN

An African minister of religion took a piece of iron and scraped sand over the pools of blood. The scene of shooting after it was all over, was relatively quiet, But in the background the wailing and screaming of the women could be heard.

Hospital wards were crammed with casualties — at least twelve corpses were in the mortuary and there was a shuttle service of ambulances. Some of the wounded were lying covered with blankets on verandahs of buildings near the casualty wards. Authorities of the Vereeniging hospital's non-European section issued an urgent SOS tonight for blood for the wounded.

MARCH 22, 1960

BAN ON COLOURED PERSONS ENTERING MAISONETTES

LANDLORD CAN DO LITTLE IN LAW

BY OUR LEGAL CORRESPONDENT

ENGLISH LAW, IN its incomparably, empirical manner, provides a just answer to the problem of the tenants of the maisonettes in The Ridgeway, St Albans, who are under covenant not to allow any coloured persons on their premises.

The law does not, however, as it should, provide a straightforward prohibition against such forms of racial discrimination. The reason for this absence of any prohibition against racial discrimination is largely, but not wholly, because the relationship between landlord and tenant is a private arrangement. There are aspects of public law which, similarly, do not provide protection to religious or racial minorities.

Shut out ... Blacks discriminated against

The most usual form of discrimination against people on the grounds of their race or religion is found in leases where the landlord does not wish to have as his tenant's successor any "undesirable" person. It is therefore not uncommon to find an absolute prohibition against subletting or assigning of the property to coloured persons.

MAY 17, 1960

Nikita Sergeyevich Khrushchev ... accuses the US of spying

US ADMITS PILOT WAS SPYING

MR KHRUSHCHEV'S EVIDENCE

THE UNITED STATES, making the best of a bad job, admitted on Saturday that one of its U-2 weather planes had been on a spying mission over the Soviet Union, as Mr Khrushchev had alleged earlier in the day.

Faced with a pilot "alive and kicking" in Moscow, the State Department after eleven hours' thought acknowledged that he had been trying to obtain information "concealed behind the Iron Curtain."

It justified this activity — and similar missions had been carried out "along the frontiers of the free world" for the past four years — on the grounds of Western security; it was compelled to take precautions against the possibility of surprise attack.

The statement emphasised, however, that this flight had not been authorised by President Eisenhower or other officials in Washington and this, together with Mr Khrushchev's evident desire not to blame Mr Eisenhower personally, is taken as meaning that Summit prospects may not suffer too much as a result of the incident.

Mr Khrushchev had told the Supreme Soviet that the plane was shot down 1,200 miles inside Soviet territory on a flight from Pakistan to Norway. The pilot, instead of using his ejector seat (which would have killed him) had parachuted down. He had taken photographs of Soviet military installations and airfields.

MAY 9, 1960

1960 | 1970

ALL THAT IS SOLID
MELTS INTO AIR

ANTHONY BURGESS

"FIVE BRANDIES," SAID the bartender, "and three beers." This was me, generous on Third Avenue. "And one Scotch-on-the-rocks." What he did then was to tot it all up on a piece of paper. Yes, I thought; that's the sort of thing that happens in a dollar country. A British barman will add up the most fantastically various major round in his head; get among the decimals, and out come paper and pencil. It's something to do with the fact that decimal money isn't real; it isn't solid enough to visualise.

The British people will undoubtedly (not that they have much choice in the matter) accept decimalisation just as they have accepted other, undreamt-of-even-after-a-cheese-supper, irrationalities, insults, and con-tricks. But their true life is lived in spite of the creep of totalitarianism, in the community and not in the State.

DECEMBER 24, 1966

THE GUARDIAN

London   Monday July 21 1969   6d

9.17 pm, July 20, 1969: Man makes his first space landing

On the moon after perfect touchdown

EDWIN ALDRIN—Apollo 11 lunar module pilot

By ANTHONY TUCKER, our Science Correspondent

Men are on the moon. At 9.17 last night, within two minutes of the planned time, the lunar module, with Armstrong and Aldrin at the controls, curved gently down over the Sea of Tranquillity. With a hop to clear a crater "the size of a football pitch" it dropped smoothly to the surface, and soon the astronauts—who ate man's first meal on the moon at about 11.30 p.m.—announced that the first walk on the lunar surface would take place earlier than expected.

The landing was a moment of extraordinary tension heightened by the unruffled casualness of the astronauts and mission control at Houston. The culmination of eight years of intense dedication and the fulfilment of a dream which men have shared since the beginning of recorded history was marked for ever in the flat tones of Armstrong: "Contact light; engine stopped . . . the Eagle has landed."

From 300 feet above the surface, with only two minutes in which to select the final landing site and aware that an error—or an enveloping jet-blown cloud of lunar dust—could lead to irretrievable disaster.

The landing was perfect. Spacecraft Centre and the world seemed momentarily stunned by emotion : only Armstrong, Aldrin—and above them, Collins—seemed unmoved at the end of the drama which began with a characteristically laconic acceptance of the "go."

Apollo 11 landing site (ringed) on the southern border of the Sea of Tranquillity close to the lunar equator. This area is one of seven chosen because of its comparative absence of obstacles. The other landing sites, some of which would bring men on to the surface close to or earlier, unmanned moon-landing spacecraft, will be used in later Apollo missions.

Coolest men off earth land beside crater

From ADAM RAPHAEL : Houston, July 20

Apollo 11's lunar module swept in low over the moon tonight to land in a depression beside a large, shallow, rocky crater. Scar nearly down range from the lunar area in the Sea of Tranquillity. Overthrust found announced craft Luna 15, refuelled less that 10 miles above on its mysterious mission.

Don't forget earth—Pope

The Pope told pilgrims outside his summer home at Castelgandolfo yesterday that war and hunger around the world should not be forgotten in the race to conquer outer space.

TV by 'fiddle'

The failure of the weekend of the launching of a special satellite to convey television pictures of the Apollo mission, meant that the "reserve" system used for the Royal Investiture had to be brought in.

Russia yields to Apollo interest

By our Science Correspondent

RUSSIA'S Luna 15 kept everyone guessing right up to the last moment yesterday. As the Apollo craft prepared to separate, Jodrell Bank reported that the unmanned Russian craft had gone into a new orbit, taking it to within 10 miles of the moon's surface at its closest approach, and bringing its track closer to the Sea of Tranquillity.

Timing of lunar walk

From the moment of landing Armstrong and Aldrin have worked to a carefully planned schedule which lets us walk the two hourly orbit of their mothercraft still circling the moon above them.

Loud and clear

The first look already began to blur too much passed into pulsations of astonishing lunar surface.

Jump ahead

Every step of the preparation for landing was being studied.

THE GUARDIAN'S PROGRESS

PRINTING FROM LONDON

NEWSPAPER STATISTICS, LIKE other statistics, contain pitfalls for the unwary. One or two of our fellows have fallen into a trap in commenting on sales figures for the six months that ended on December 31. The *Guardian's* average sale in that period was 245,000, which is about 33,000 up on the last six months of 1960. (*The Times's* figure for the half-year was 253,000.) The *Guardian's* figure does not, however, show the full effect so far of printing in London. We started publication in London only in the middle of September. The half-year's average included two and a half months before that date. The figure of 245,000 therefore shows less than our full growth since mid-September.

GROWTH IN THE SOUTH

In November and December the *Guardian's* sales were above 260,000. In January the gain has been held. Most of the growth since September has been in the southern half of England — in the areas served by publication from London. This is, from our point of view, a highly satisfactory and encouraging position. We did not expect to increase the sale of the *Guardian* by more than thirty thousand in the first few months of London printing. In practice we have done better than that.

END TO MISPRINTS

Some aspects of the *Guardian's* service to its readers are not yet all that we should like them to be. The "misprints man" whom we had hoped to pension off in the autumn is still with us occasionally. The quality of our pictures sometimes leaves something to be desired. And — most serious — the total amount of space available in the paper is less than we should like. This is due to a slight drop in the average number of pages in each issue, which in turn is due to a slight decline in the volume of advertisements. We hope however that the number of pages in this and other newspapers will be greater by next winter. Meanwhile we are glad that so many readers enjoy the *Guardian* as it is, and that in spite of some defects it makes good progress.

FEBRUARY 6, 1962

"THE MAN WHO PUTS THE MISPRINTS IN"

LETTER TO THE EDITOR

SIR, — SO AT last you are to print in London and your ace humorist, the man who puts the misprints in the London edition, will be out of work. I foresee many a damp eye in Dorking, not to mention lumps in throats at Loughton and Throgmorton Street. Could you not give him a job writing humorous leaders? When I read recently in your paper, "arter he left the building, Mr X . . .", I nearly wrote to applaud your pioneering spirit in printing the London edition in the vernacular. Yet all too soon, alas, it is to be no more.

However, the above is mere digression. This letter is one of protest; most violent protest. Last week, sir, you overdid it. Ventilating the Channel Tunnel may well be "bereco etao" but even if it is "cwmfyvbgkq", you had no right to say so, at least not in print. But to go on and call the whole thing "mfwy mfwm" — really, sir, these filthy four-letter Cambrian words should be left unprinted.

If I were a man of principle I would cancel my subscription to your obscene paper and take the "Daily Distress" instead. However, the salutary shock of knowing that one of your faithful readers has even contemplated such drastic action will, I feel sure, make you pull your socks up and never again print such pornographic tirades. "Mfwy mfwm" indeed! 0 tempora! 0 mores! — Yours, etc.

B. HINCHLIFFE

[It is indeed our intention to pension off our misprints man, but it is not quite clear at the moment whether he has yet reached pensionable age. — ED]

DECEMBER 6, 1962

PLUGHOLE PHYSICS

A MELBOURNE PHYSICS professor thinks he knows why the bath water gurgles out of the plughole in clockwise direction and not counterclockwise. It all depends where and how the plumber set the plughole, he believes.

"At least that is the factor which counts most,' said Professor Caro, aged 39. "This is one experiment where the layman is on exactly the same terms as a scientist," he added.

APRIL 30, 1962

"BASTA CON LIZ" FOR ITALY

ROME SAYS GOOD RIDDANCE

THE FORUM IS being dismantled, Cleopatra's palace is littered with empty lunchboxes, and Caesar's war galley is lying off Ischia amid the flotsam of the Battle of Actium. Another couple of hours' shooting tomorrow in the studios at Cinecitta and *Cleopatra* will be finished.

As far as the Romans are concerned this is definitely good news. Some thousands of film extras are going to be looking for work; the "paparazzi" (freelance press photographers), who have lived on the gossipy backwash of the production

for nearly a year, will have to find new targets; and the philanthropist who let his villa to Elizabeth Taylor for £1,000 a month may have to lower his sights a little. But Rome as a whole has long since decided that it can get along without *Cleopatra*, and it is two or three months now since a Roman daily carried the tired headline *Basta con Liz* ("Enough of Liz").

Miss Taylor, who is now on overtime — $3,000 per working day on top of the flat $1 million which her original contract provided for — is understood to have no immediate plans, whether professional or matrimonial. Joe Mankiewicz, the director, and Walter Wanger, the producer, who must be the world's two most relieved men, still have several months' work ahead of them before *Cleopatra* is in final shape to storm the world's box offices.

JULY 9, 1962

MARILYN IS DEAD

A WOMAN OF INTEGRITY

BY ALISTAIR COOKE

MARILYN MONROE WAS found dead in bed this morning in her home in Hollywood, only a physical mile or two, but a social universe, away from the place where she was born 36 years ago as Norma Jean Baker. She died with a row of medicines and an empty bottle of barbiturates at her elbow.

These stony sentences, which read like the epitaph of a Raymond Chandler victim, will confirm for too many millions of movie fans the usual melodrama of a humble girl, cursed by physical beauty, to be dazed and doomed by the fame that was too much for her. For Americans, the last chapter was written on the weekend that a respectable national picture magazine printed for the delectation of her troubled fans a confessional piece called "Marilyn Monroe pours out her soul".

The plot of her early life is as seedy as anything in the pulp magazines, and to go into the details now would be as tasteless as prying into the clinical file of any other pretty woman whose beauty has crumbled overnight. It is enough, for summoning the necessary compassion to recall her miserable parents, her being shuttled like a nuisance from foster home to orphanage, the subsequent knockabout years in a war factory, her short independence as a sailor's wife, the unsuspected first rung of the ladder provided by a posing job for a nude calendar.

THE OUTSIDER

She talked easily about all this, when people had the gall to ask her, not as someone reconciled to a wretched childhood but as a wide-eyed outsider, an innocent as foreign to the subject under discussion as Chaplin is when he stands off and analyses the appeal of "The Little Man".

Then she wiggled briefly past the lecherous gaze of Louis Calhern in John Huston's *Asphalt Jungle* and his appraising whinny echoed round the globe. Within two years she was the enthroned sexpot of the Western world.

She completed the first phase of the American dream by marrying the immortal Joe Di Maggio, the loping hero of the New York Yankees; and the second phase by marrying Arthur Miller and so redeeming his suspect Americanism at the moment it was in question before a House Committee.

To say that Marilyn Monroe was a charming, shrewd, and pathetic woman of a tragic integrity will sound as preposterous to the outsider as William Empson's Freudian analysis of *Alice in Wonderland*. It is nevertheless true. We restrict the word "integrity" to people, either simple or complex, who have a strong sense of righteousness or, if they are public men, of self-righteousness. Yet it surely means no more than what it says: wholeness, being free to be spontaneous, without reck of consistency or moral appearances. It can be true of forlorn and bewildered people as of the disciplined and the solemn.

REFLECTIONS

In this sense, Marilyn Monroe was all of a piece. She was confused, pathologically shy, a straw on the ocean of her compulsions (to pout, to crack-wise, to love a stranger, to be six hours late or lock herself in a room). She was a sweet and humorous person increasingly terrified by the huge stereotype of herself she saw plastered all around her. The exploitation of this pneumatic, mocking, liquid-lipped goddess gave the world a simple picture of the Lorelei. She was about as much of a Lorelei as Bridget, the housemaid.

This orphan of the rootless City of the Angels at last could feel no other identity than the one she saw in the mirror: a baffled, honest girl forever haunted by the nightmare of herself, 60 feet tall and naked before a howling mob. She could never learn to acquire the lacquered shell of the prima donna or the armour of sophistication. So in the end she sought the ultimate oblivion, of which her chronic latecomings and desperate retreats to her room were token suicides.

AUGUST 6, 1962

THALIDOMIDE BABIES APPEAL

MOVE PROVOKED BY GUARDIAN

A RECENT ANNOUNCEMENT by the *Guardian* that the National Fund for Research into Poliomyelitis and Other Crippling Diseases was prepared to take up the cause of the "thalidomide babies" has resulted in a national appeal being started on their behalf.

Lady Hoare, the Lady Mayoress of London, is opening today a special appeal for children born crippled after their mothers had taken thalidomide during pregnancy.

Money raised through the appeal will be used to finance research into the causation and prevention of these congenital abnormalities and to develop new types of apparatus and techniques to help those born cripples. A suggestion from a teacher, after reading the *Guardian* on July 7, is that a comfortable residence for the babies might be provided near the Ministry of health limb-fitting centres (such as Roehampton) where the children could stay while undergoing training. Contributions to the new fund can be sent to the Lady Hoare Appeal, Mansion House, London EC1.

AUGUST 1, 1962

BRITAIN'S ROLE IN WORLD

"PLAYED OUT"

MR DEAN ACHESON, former United States Secretary of State, asserted today that Britain's role as an independent Power was "about played out."

He told a conference on American affairs at West Point Military Academy that Britain had lost an empire and had not found a role. He added:

"Britain's attempt to play a separate power role — that is, a role apart from Europe, a role based on a 'special relationship' with the United States, a role based on being the head of a Commonwealth which has no political structure or unity or strength and enjoys a fragile and precarious economic relationship — this role is about played out."

Mr Acheson is President Kennedy's special adviser on NATO affairs.

DECEMBER 6, 1962

SOVIET SHIPS ON WAY TO CUBA

THE MISSILE CRISIS

THE US SECRETARY of defence, Mr Robert McNamara, said in Washington last night that armed boarding parties would be ready to search about 25 Russian cargo ships moving towards Cuba when the US partial blockade of Cuba comes into effect at 3 p.m. (BST) today. The proclamation giving effect to the blockade was signed by President Kennedy last night.

At a press conference in the Defence Department, Mr McNamara said he had ordered that all Navy and Marine personnel should be held on active duty for as much as a year beyond the expiration of their normal tours.

Washington sources said that the first Russian ship to be intercepted might be the *Polotavia*, apparently designed to carry missiles. Reconnaissance planes had taken photographs of the vessel, which was unescorted, and the Navy was keeping a special watch for her.

Other developments in the Cuban crisis yesterday were:

Russia cancelled all military leave yesterday after the Soviet Government had issued a harshly worded reply to President Kennedy. The Russians said that America was playing with fire and added that a most powerful retaliatory blow would follow if "the aggressors" touched off war. Other members of the Communist block have ordered military preparedness. Dr Fidel Castro issued a mobilisation order to Cuba's armed forces shortly before Mr Kennedy's speech on Monday night. A communiqué said hundreds of thousands of men were mobilised in a matter of hours.

The Security Council met last night to discuss the crisis. Mr Zorin, Russian president of the council, said the US reasons for calling the meeting were completely false, and presented a Soviet draft resolution asking the Council to "insist" that the US revoke its blockade decision. The resolution called for talks between Russia, Cuba and the US, with the purpose of "normalising the situation and removing the threat of war."

Britain, in a Foreign Office statement, accused Russia of "deception and deliberately opening up a new area of instability by placing offensive arms in Cuba." Mr Macmillan is expected to make a statement on the crisis tomorrow.

A curfew has been imposed on the British garrison in Berlin, which is taking "precautionary measures."

Prices in the London Stock Exchange yesterday suffered a further sharp setback. Much lower and wider prices were quoted to discourage heavy selling, and there was a keen demand for gold in the London bullion market.

OCTOBER 24, 1962

FIVE-YEAR TERM FOR MANDELA

"I WAS DRIVEN TO THIS SITUATION"

NELSON MANDELA, AGED 44, the "Black Pimpernel" of African nationalism, was sent to prison for five years by a special court here today for incitement and for leaving the country illegally.

Before leaving court he raised his clenched right fist in the salute of the outlawed African National Congress (ANC) and said: "When I come out I will again take up the struggle." The Court sentenced him to three years' imprisonment on a charge of inciting African workers to strike last year and a maximum of two years for illegally leaving the country earlier this year.

Mandela's impassioned address to the Court — which took the form of a political testament — cannot mostly be published in or disseminated from South Africa under the provisions of the General Law Amendment (Sabotage) Act. Mandela is a "banned person" and statements made anywhere at any time by such persons come under the provisions of the Act. The Minister of Justice, Mr Balthazar Vorster, has made an exception for statements made in court provided they are not "political propaganda".

Giving judgement today, the magistrate, Mr W. A. Helsingen, said: "There is no doubt that the accused was the leader, instigator, and main mouthpiece of the campaign to incite native workers . . . throughout the country to strike or stay at home on May 29, 30, and 31, 1961." The object of the strike, he said, was to protest against the Act proclaiming South Africa a republic. "To overthrow the Government . . . defiance of the law in this manner is the surest way to tyranny and destruction. The accused has shown no remorse for what he has done and freely declared he would continue his activities," he said.

Mandela, a former underground leader of the ANC, pleaded not guilty but called no witnesses. A tall, imposing figure in a jackal-skin cloak, Mandela said in his final address today: "I was driven to this situation."

On the charge of leaving the country illegally, Mandela said: "For the first time in my life I was a free man." In London he was received by Mr Hugh Gaitskell, Leader of the Labour Party, and Mr Jo Grimond, Leader of the Liberal Party. Mandela, himself a lawyer, said his conscience made it imperative that he oppose laws which in his opinion were "immoral, unjust, and intolerant."

NOVEMBER 8, 1962

THE PROFUMO AFFAIR

BY PHILIP RAWSTORNE

THE FIRST INSTALLMENT of what the prosecution described as the "somewhat sordid story" of Stephen Ward was told yesterday in Marylebone magistrates' court — a building designed originally for the district's public wash-houses.

It was heard by nearly fifty reporters crammed in an L-shaped gallery against the ceiling of the small blue-and-white court room, and by some twenty members of the public who had queued in early morning rain, passing the waiting hours by swapping tales of experiences at other hearings. The preface was written by the prosecuting counsel, Mr Mervyn Griffith-Jones, and on this first day the main chapters came from Miss Christine Keeler and Miss Marilyn ("Mandy") Rice-Davies. Among the names mentioned during more than four and a half hours of examination and cross-examination were those of Lord Astor, Mr Douglas Fairbanks, Mr Profumo, Ivanov, a business man named James Eylan, and another man named Charles who lives somewhere off Park Lane. Several more were masked by letters picked at random from the alphabet.

Ward, a fifty-year-old osteopath, bespectacled and wearing a dark grey suit and brown tie, appeared before the magistrate, Mr Leo Gradwell, to face eight charges:

Two of knowingly living wholly or in part on the earnings of the prostitution of Miss Keeler and Miss Davies; one of inciting Miss Keeler to procure a Miss "R"; another of attempting to procure a Miss "X"; and a fifth of conspiring to procure others. Further charges alleged that he had been a party to unlawful abortions of a Miss "W" and a Miss "M", and that he had kept a brothel at 17 Wimpole Mews, W1.

Ward stroked his chin, scribbled notes and, later in the day, appeared to do a little of the sketching for which he is known, as Mr Griffith-Jones outlined the case and Miss Keeler and Miss Rice-Davies gave evidence.

Miss Keeler, in an off-white suit and cool self-confidence, told how she met Ward at Murrays Club where, after a little indecision, she said she had been employed as "an artist." She then added: "I was a showgirl."

Her words were repeated by the clerk into a dictaphone as she went on to describe her relationship with Ward:

"We were like brother and sister . . . My life really used to revolve around Stephen. He had full control of my mind. I used to do more or less everything that he said. I thought I could never stand on my feet unless he was there and supporting me mentally."

Miss Keeler said that money for the rent of one flat she occupied was paid for by Ward with a cheque from Lord Astor — "though there was no ulterior motive in that." She had made love with Ivanov and with Mr Profumo, who gave her money for her mother. She had received money also from Eylan — "some hundreds" — and given some of it to Ward. These meetings occurred when Ward said he was short of money; and she had met, at his suggestion, a man called Charles in a mews house off Park Lane. He had given her £50.

"I never considered myself a prostitute or a call-girl. Stephen said that you have to have the mentality of a prostitute, which I didn't have, and it was not quite so wrong just once or twice sleeping with a man and having some money from him: a man I knew and liked."

Miss Keeler described how she had taken work as a model and introduced some of the girls she met to Ward:

"I introduced them because he liked girls. He used to tell me which girl he liked in a shop and say 'Go and get her'."

After relating preparations at Ward's flat for an abortion and after a short cross-examination by Mr James Burge, representing Ward, in which she said that police had taken twelve statements from her and interviewed her twice a week during the last few months, Miss Keeler left the witness-box.

She was replaced by Miss Rice-Davies in a black coat, flowery hat and white gloves, who said she had been introduced to Ward by Miss Keeler. There had been frequent intercourse between Ward and herself, she said. He had suggested they ought to get married some time.

"He always said that he did not have any money but had lots of friends. He mentioned Lord Astor's name and said 'we have always got Bill who can help us'."

The only other friend of Ward's whom she knew was Douglas Fairbanks, Jr. Ward's inference had been "fairly obvious — Lord Astor had already paid Christine's and my rent."

Miss Rice-Davies said that for some time she had lived with a Mr Peter Rachman, but after his death in October, 1962, had gone to live with Ward at Wimpole Mews.

DECEMBER 6, 1963

PRESIDENT KENNEDY ASSASSINATED

POLICE ARREST SUSPECT

BY ALISTAIR COOKE

PRESIDENT JOHN FITZGERALD Kennedy, the 35th President of the United States, was shot during a motorcade drive through downtown Dallas this afternoon. He died in the emergency room of the Parkland Memorial Hospital 32 minutes after the attack. He was 46 years old. He is the third President to be assassinated in office since Abraham Lincoln and the first since President McKinley in 1901.

In the late afternoon the Dallas police took into custody a former Marine, one Lee H Oswald, aged 24, who is alleged to have shot a policeman outside a theatre. He is said to have remarked only, "It is all over now." He is the chairman of a group called the "Fair Play for Cuba Committee", and is married to a Russian girl. He is described at the moment as "a prime suspect."

The new President is the Vice-President, Lyndon Baines Johnson, a 55-year-old native Texan, who took the oath of office in Dallas at five minutes to four at the hands of a woman judge and later arrived in Washington with the body of the dead President.

This is being written in the numbed interval between the first shock and the harried attempt to reconstruct a sequence of fact from an hour of tumult. However, this is the first assassination of a world figure that took place in the age of television, and every network and station in the country took up the plotting of the appalling story. It begins to form a grisly pattern, contradicted by a grisly preface: the projection on television screens of a happy crowd and a grinning President only a few seconds before the gunshots.

The President was almost at the end of his two-day tour of Texas. He was to make a lunch speech in the Dallas Trade Mart building and his motor procession had about another mile to go. He had had the warmest welcome of his trip from a great crowd at the airport.

The cries and pleas for a personal touch were so engaging that Mrs Kennedy took the lead and walked from the ramp of the presidential plane to a fence that held the crowd in. She was followed quickly by the President, and they both seized hands and forearms and smiled gladly at the people.

The Secret Service and the police were relieved to get them into their car, where Mrs Kennedy sat between the President and John B. Connally, the Governor of Texas. The Dallas police had instituted the most stringent security precautions in the city's history: they wanted no repetition of the small but disgraceful brawl that humiliated Adlai Stevenson in their city when he attended a United Nations rally on October 24.

The motorcade was going along slowly but smoothly when three muffled shots, which the crowd first mistook for fireworks, cracked through the cheers. One hit the shoulder

blade and the wrist of Governor Connally who was taken with the President to the hospital, where his condition is serious.

The other brought blood trickling from the back of the sitting President's head. His right arm flopped from a high wave of greeting and he collapsed into the arms of Mrs Kennedy, who fell unharmed. She was heard to cry "Oh, No" and sat there all the way cradling his head in her lap.

As some people bayed and screamed and others fell to the ground, and hid their faces, the secret service escort broke into two groups, one speeding the President's car to the hospital: and another joined a part of the heavy police escort in wheeling off in pursuit of a man fleeing across some railroad tracks. Nothing came of this lead.

The President was taken to the emergency room of the Parkland Hospital and Governor Connally was taken into the surgery. Mrs Kennedy went in with the living President and less than an hour later came out with the dead man in a bronze coffin, which arrived shortly after two priests had administered the last rites of the Roman Catholic Church.

The body was escorted by Generals Clifton and McHugh, the President's chief military and air force aides, to the Dallas Airport and flown thence to Washington.

Within an hour of the President's death, the Secret Service had found a sniper's nest inside the building from which the first witnesses swore the bullets had been fired. It is a warehouse for a school textbook firm, known as the Texas School Depository, on the corner of Elm and Houston Streets.

In an upper room, whose open window commanded the route of the Presidential motorcade, the Servicemen found the remains of a fried chicken and a foreign-made rifle with a telescopic sight. Alongside it lay three empty cartridges.

NOVEMBER 23, 1963

WHAT IS A BEATLE?

QC ASKS THE QUESTION

BY JEAN STEAD

THE WAY IN which Mr W. Raeburn, QC, turned down a free ticket to see the Beatles when he presided over the Performing Right Tribunal in London yesterday would have roused bitter envy in the soul of a teenager, if any had happened to be present. Perhaps fortunately, none was. If any had been, they would have had to endure the counsel for the Cinematograph Exhibitors' Association and other interested parties, Mr Duncan Ranking, describing their idols in terms which might have well caused them to scream.

To the attentive ears of Mr Raeburn and his colleagues, Mr Ranking sketched this picture of pop concerts: "The performers are just a few young men, occasionally with a female also. Sir, they are equipped by amplifying instruments, these instruments being a guitar or a number of electric guitars, with perhaps an electric double bass. There is also a microphone, sir, which further amplifies the sound. The music which is played has little or no melody to it and it consists of a rhythmic and monotonous beat, and while it is being played the performers sing or croon into the mike. They also play the fool on the stage, sir, by making gestures, dancing, grimacing and that sort of thing. They are often dressed in an unusual or outlandish way. A certain number of these beat performers enjoy a quite fantastic popularity."

Mr Raeburn, however, looked quite eager when Mr Ranking suggested he should make a personal visit to a cinema concert with other members of the Tribunal to form a first-hand judgement on which is the real cause of Beatlemania — the Beatles themselves, or their yeah, yeah, yeah. Mr Ranking had described how during beat concerts, the audience "instead of sitting listening quietly and attending as one would when listening to a concert of Beethoven, indulge in very loud and almost hysterical screaming."

"Where is the cinema you are thinking of?" asked Mr Raeburn quickly, and later added, "Would we be expected to scream?" Mr Ranking wasn't sure about the cinema, but assured the Tribunal that failing personal attendance, they had in court a tape recording of the Beatles which could be played to them.

After a day spent in studying programmes of concerts by Cliff Richard and The Shadows, Duane Eddy and the Everly Brothers, and listening to descriptions of Cliff Richard's pillowcases and Eddy's taste for Ivy League suits, Mr Raeburn said they were prepared to go to a Beatle concert though they couldn't spare the extravagance of a whole afternoon for it.

It was pointed out that the Beatles perform only in the evening. "I have only one free evening this week, and I don't know about the others," said Mr Raeburn. His colleagues, it seemed, had no free evenings which coincided. So the Tribunal decided to be satisfied with tape.

This is being played back at the Tribunal today as part of the case of the Association, who are contesting a claim being made by the Performing Right Society which represents composers, and publishers of music for 4 per cent of box office takings. This is an increase of more than 3 per cent.

DECEMBER 10, 1963

TWO CULTURES

DARK WARNING FROM LORD SNOW

BY NORMAN SHRAPNEL

IT WAS A technological revolution that made the Roman Empire, the Lords was reminded yesterday, and after that we had the Dark Ages. It began to look, before this debate was very far advanced, that Britain may be settling for its own Dark Age without any technological revolution.

For although both sides in Parliament are competing with each other in their professed desire to speed that revolution, the country is not going along with them. The warning came in impressively similar terms from two highly influential quarters — from Lord Todd, the Master of Christ's College, Cambridge, and a Nobel Prize winner for chemistry, and from the Government Despatch Box in the occupation of Lord Snow.

Lord Todd ... importance of technology

The Master and the New Man saw eye to eye about the perilously low status still accorded in our confused and self-deceiving society to the men who would power the technological age if we decided to have one, the applied scientist and the engineer.

The arts are flourishing in all the universities of the land. The pure scientist is considered socially acceptable in some perfectly civilised colleges. But the poor engineer, we almost gathered, with oily spanners bulging his pockets and his knuckles brushing the ground as he walks, is courted by none. The image is all wrong, and nobody — excepting always the Master, the New Man and, of course, that top technologist Lord Bowden — seems to want to put it right.

DECEMBER 3, 1964

EDWARDIAN OR JET AGE?

MR WILSON OFFERS A CHOICE

BY PETER JENKINS

AN OUTDATED CONSERVATIVE Britain ruled from the grouse moors or a modern Socialist Britain, ruled with technical skill based on equality of opportunity. This was the choice and the challenge Mr Harold Wilson threw out last night in what was designed to be the first major speech of the 1964 general election campaign.

SOCIALIST BRITAIN

Addressing a capacity all-ticket audience (1,987 at 2s. a head) at the Birmingham Town Hall, the Labour Party leader contrasted a drab picture of a class-ridden and lethargic society with a glowing vision of a Socialist Britain tailored for the scientific age. It was the theme, hammered home, of his conference speech at Scarborough: it will be the central theme of the series of campaign speeches he has now embarked upon.

INDICTMENT

He returned time and time again to his indictment:

"We are living in the jet age but we are governed by an Edwardian Establishment mentality."

TECHNICAL ABILITY

"If you fly the Atlantic in a jet you want to be sure the pilot knows his job, that he's been trained for it. If you are in a hospital you feel more confident if you know that the surgeon has given his lifetime to fitting himself for his work. Pilot or surgeon, it doesn't matter to you who his father was, or what school he went to or who his friends are. And yet in Government and in business we're still content to accept social qualifications rather than technical ability as a criterion.

GROUSE MOOR LEADERS

Mr Wilson scorned "the grouse moor conception of national leadership", ability measured by upper-class accents, and "smoothness" when it was "ruggedness" that we really needed. In place of this Labour would create "an open society in which all have an opportunity to work and serve — in which craftsmanship will be more important than caste."

JANUARY 20, 1964

"PILL" A MATTER FOR INDIVIDUAL DECISION

PLEASURE VERSUS SIDE-EFFECTS

WHETHER THE USE of contraceptive pills is justifiable is a matter of individual decision, say three writers in the current issue of the *Lancet*.

The three men — Lord Brain, president of the Family Planning Association, Professor A. S. Parkes, of Cambridge, and Dr P. M. F. Bishop, endocrinologist, Guy's Hospital and Chelsea Hospital for Women — discuss the side-effects of oral contraceptives and say there is still much to be learnt about the complex inter-relationships which underlie their effectiveness. They comment: "In general their supposed hazards must be balanced against the known consequences of using ineffective contraceptive methods or none at all — namely oppressive pregnancies, unwanted children, back-street abortions and over-population.

They say that some women experience one or more side-effects, among them nausea, headache, changes in weight and loss of libido, but point out that there are also desirable or "positive" side-effects including a sense of wellbeing and increased pleasure in sexual intercourse "which some people remark upon with gratitude."

DECEMBER 19, 1964

WHAT TO DO ABOUT SWEETS

BY MARGARET DRABBLE

NOW THAT I have children of my own, I often think of the rules, pleasures and traditions of my own childhood, and of the war, which so largely determined them ... Part of me is convinced that it is bad for children to eat sweets every day (morally bad, I mean, and not merely bad for their teeth) and another part of me feels that it is wrong to make such a triviality a bone of moral contention. The result is that six days out of seven I let them get on with it, and then on the seventh day I turn on them and deny them and tell them bitter tales of the hardships I endured, confectionery-wise, when I was a little girl. (I despise myself for doing this, but all mothers do it, I think.) ...

JULY 24, 1965

IN COLD BLOOD

THE FACT-FICTION NOVEL

BY GEORGE STEINER

WHATEVER ITS MERITS, *In Cold Blood* is already more than a book: it is a happening. It represents a fantastic publishing operation, an example of the technology of assured success at its most sophisticated. First printed in four instalments in the *New Yorker,* Mr Truman Capote's reportage has since been sold to the films and for publication in fifteen languages. Prepublication earnings have been estimated at somewhere in the region of two million dollars. The American publishers reckon that Mr Capote is being paid some fifteen dollars a word. Book clubs, world serialisations, literary awards are swinging into line. This is the "big one", the year's masterpiece; it cannot fail, for it has behind it the brilliant, tough-minded manipulation of those who pre-package so much of our sensibility.

As almost every man, woman and child literate enough to wade through a Sunday supplement knows by now, *In Cold Blood* is the exhaustive account of the murder of the Clutter family on their farm in Holcomb, Kansas (population 270) on November 15, 1959, a sickeningly slow, aimless butchery for four ordinary human beings which netted the two murderers forty dollars and a small portable radio set. Mr Capote's eye chanced across a brief newspaper report of the crime; he felt intrigued by the seeming motivelessness of so black a

Documenting life and death ...Truman Capote

deed in the heart of rural, Eisenhower America, and he went to have a look. For five years he immersed himself in the life of a small community on the far edge of the Middle West; he came to know more about the affair than anyone else, dead or alive, bending over the evidence as if to test how far the mind of an observer can empty experience of its minutiae, of its secrets and brusque oblivion.

Stendhal found the *données* of *The Red and the Black* in a crime story reported in the press; two of Dostoevsky's major novels sprang from an obscure grain of literal violence. But with a signal difference. Mr. Capote has not written a novel. He has described *In Cold Blood* as a "nonfiction

novel", as a "fact fiction" whose narrative imposes fictional techniques on rigorously documentary material. "All the material in this book not derived from my own observation is either taken from official records or is the result of interviews with the persons directly concerned." In other words, *In Cold Blood* is probably the most deliberate, the most powerfully thought-out product of a movement towards high-reportage, towards fiction-documentaries which a number of us first identified as emerging in the United States about twenty years ago (though it had its precedent in, say, Rebecca West). Sensing the increasing staleness of the prose novel, equipped with the tools and unblinking eye of the sociologist, often overwhelmed by the sheer complexity and shapeless barbarism of modern experience, a whole group of novelists or near-novelists have turned to montage. They dramatise and give psychological order to a piece of implacably authentic, documented life. It is no accident that Truman Capote thanks the editor of the *New Yorker* for backing the project; for it is with Hersey's Hiroshima, with the 'romantic documentaries' of Rachel Carson's writings about the sea, with the dramatised high journalism of Mary MacCarthy, Richard Rovere, and Edmund Wilson — all first published in the *New Yorker* — that fact-fiction or the post-novel is more closely linked.

The utter banality of the Clutter murder, the fact that it was resolved not through some acute feat of detection but by a facile indiscretion — one of the assassins had discussed the family with a cell-mate before leaving prison — make Truman Capote's radical point. Looked at minutely enough, filtered through the lens of a highly professional recorder, caught by the tape recording ear in its every inflection and background noise, the most sordid, shapeless of incidents, take on a compelling truth. Exhaustively rendered, the fact is richer than any fiction.

NOVEMBER 17, 1965

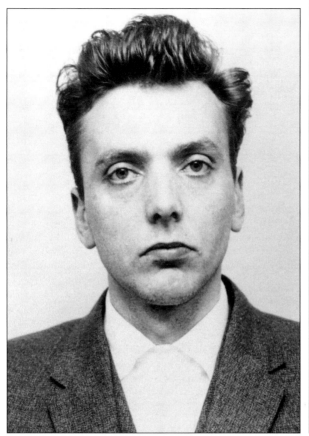

Murder charges ... Ian Brady and Myra Hindley

THE MOORS MURDERS

COURT CLEARED FOR CHARGES HEARING

WHEN IAN BRADY, 27, a stock clerk, of no fixed address, and Myra Hindley, 23, typist, of Wardle Brook Avenue, Hyde, Cheshire, appeared in court at Hyde yesterday on murder charges, the magistrates granted a defence application that the prosecution's opening statement should be in camera.

The application, which was not opposed by the prosecution, was made by Mr David Lloyd-Jones, who is defending Brady. He said that powerful emotional reactions would probably be aroused by the matters to be investigated.

Mr W Mars-Jones, prosecuting, said that after the opening statement the magistrates would be able to decide whether the evidence should be heard in camera.

After the application the court was cleared, and at the end of the day the clerk to the magistrates said that the opening statement would probably continue until 11 a.m. today, when the magistrates would decide whether the rest of the evidence should be given in camera.

Brady and Hindley are both charged with the murders of Leslie Ann Downey, 10, of Charnley Walk, Ancoats, Manchester, and Edward Evans, 17, apprentice engineer, of Ardwick, Manchester.

Brady is further charged with the murder of John Kilbride, 12, of Smallshaw Lane, Ashton-under-Lyne.

Hindley is additionally charged with receiving, comforting, harbouring, assisting, and maintaining Brady, knowing that he had murdered John Kilbride.

The bodies of Lesley Downey and John Kilbride were found on the Pennine moors near Saddleworth, and the body of Evans in a house at Hattersley, Hyde.

Mr Lloyd-Jones said: "I don't think I am putting it too highly when I say that probably never before has there been more need for an approach by the jury to such a grave issue to be unbiased and unprejudiced."

DECEMBER 7, 1965

MONEY MAKES THE WAR GO ROUND

EVERYTHING FOR SALE IN SAIGON

BY MICHAEL WALL

IT BEGINS AT Saigon airport, this feeling that it can't be real. Monstrous military machines, fat-bellied transport planes, vicious shark-nosed fighters, grotesque helicopters take off and land in alarming succession. Yet, somehow, among them the sleek, white airliners find both air and landing space to disgorge the motley array of newcomers into the confusion of Vietnam. The diminutive Vietnamese air-hostesses, pretty as dolls, trip their way over the tarmac, brilliant spots of peacock blue against the ferocious background of armed, military might. In front of the terminal a gardener waters a patch of grass; a young arriving passenger carries two squash rackets and an American struggles under the weight of a bag of golf-clubs.

The road into Saigon is a slow moving jumble of traffic. Huge army lorries with supplies, jeeps with cigar-smoking GIs, jeeps with the small, neat Vietnamese soldiers in striped jungle dress which makes them look like friendly little tigers. There are small blue and yellow taxis of beetle shape, cyclos and *pousses* — the names given to the cycle and motorised rickshaws — bicycles, scooters, carts and horses. They all push forward nose to tail, into the chaos of Saigon.

Nearer the city we pass what were once the villas of the French officials and settlers, villas which have now lost their elegance and pride, many surrounded by fences of high wire which reveal where the Americans are billeted. Then, standing on stilts along the banks of the sluggish, filthy river tributary, are wooden shacks which serve as houses, then apartment blocks which once must have gleamed in the sunlight, but now have the look of decay. It is Saigon.

In the city the heat is damply sticky.

"Wait until March and April," the old hands say, "then you will know what hot means." Cigarettes, paper money, stick to the hands; furniture and bed linen are damp to the touch and whether it is night or day, perspiration runs. The utter confusion of the city centre adds to the feeling of unreality. Here again are the military vehicles, the men in uniform, the outward signs of war. Yet now they are pushing their way through an apparently thriving, flourishing town whose inhabitants are devoted to the business of making money.

Everywhere there are shops and stalls and pavement merchants — elegant shops which alone retain the flavour of France. Here, exquisitely groomed Vietnamese women, wearing the *ao dai* dress — a high-necked garment reaching down to the ankles and seductively split to the waist on either side to reveal the long silk pyjama-type trousers — examine jewels or silks or perfumes.

Along the pavements of the wide, tree-lined boulevards the stalls are piled with leather and skin wallets and belts, sunglasses, cheap jewellery, cigarettes and contraceptives. Among the cheap shirts are bottles of American whisky. Tins of army ration food stand beside plastic flowers. The traffic is an insane mêlée, the pavements are seething with strangely assorted humanity.

Everywhere there are American males, in uniform, in T-shirts, in sports shirts. Americans with duties in Saigon, Americans on leave from the battle areas, American civilians who drive tractors, teach in schools, construct wells in villages, build houses and airstrips, who dispense money and medicines, who are caught up in the confusion of Vietnam.

The Vietnamese women should have a book to themselves. Diminutive, delicate-looking they may be, but the strength of their character shows in their faces and it is clear that Madame Nhu was no phenomenon in Vietnam. One notices the American men, picked out by their crewcuts and their size among a small people. But one notices too the Vietnamese female, whether walking with head held high, serene, graceful and proud in rich silks — or even struggling along under the weight of a pole with two baskets of fruit, laundry or rubble from a building site, dressed almost in rags. The women in Vietnam, they say, dominate their families. With the flower of Saigon's male population away and at war, the women dominate the city.

In the streets where they sell puppies, monkeys, caged birds, luxuriant plants, smoked fish, coffee beans, second-hand clothes, old women with wrinkled parchment skin stretched tight over high cheek bones survey all with sharp, dark eyes. Outside the bars the girls stand, perhaps to escape the dark and the smoke inside, more likely to attract in the foreign men who need relaxation after weeks of compound life and unnerving operations.

The number of bar-girls in Saigon must be extraordinary. Perhaps twenty will be at work in one bar at one time — serving the drinks, chatting to each other in harsh, high-pitched voices, repeating their parrot-like English phrases in broad American accents to the clients. They carry paper and pencil to play noughts and crosses, or cards to play poker or gin rummy. "If you lose, you buy me drink . . . if me lose, me buy you drink." Their drink, a thimbleful of cold tea — cost to client 10s.; client's drink, a beer — cost to girl 1s. 3d. If client wins, girl throws down pencil or cards. "You cheat."

JANUARY 10, 1966

THE DEATH OF CHE

BODY IN THE HANDS OF US INTELLIGENCE AGENCIES

BY RICHARD GOTT IN BOLIVIA

THE BODY OF Che Guevara was flown into this small hill town in south-eastern Bolivia at five o'clock last night.

From the moment the helicopter landed bearing the small figure strapped in a stretcher to the landing rails, the succeeding operation was to a large extent left in the hands of a man in battledress, who, all the correspondents here agree, was unquestionably a representative of one of the United States intelligence agencies.

He was probably a Cuban exile and so Che Guevara, who in life had declared war almost singlehanded on the United States, found himself in death face to face with his major enemy.

The helicopter purposely landed far from where a crowd had gathered and the body of the dead guerrilla leader was hastily transferred to a van. We commandeered a jeep to follow it and the driver managed to get through the gates of the hospital grounds where the body was taken to a small colour-washed hut that served as a mortuary.

The doors of the van burst open and the American agent leapt out, emitting a war cry of "Let's get the hell out of here." One of the correspondents asked him where he came from. "Nowhere," was the surly response.

The body, dressed in olive green fatigues with a zippered jacket, was carried into the hut. It was undoubtedly that of Che Guevara. Ever since I first reported in January that Che was probably in Bolivia I have not shared the general scepticism about his whereabouts.

I am probably one of the few people here who have seen him alive. I saw him in Cuba at an Embassy reception in 1963 and there is no doubt in my mind that this body was that of Che. It had a black wispy beard, long matted hair, and the shadow of a scar on the right temple, probably the result of an accident in July when he was grazed by a rifle shot.

On his feet he wore moccasins as though he had been shot down while running fleet-footed through the jungle. He had two wounds in the lower part of the neck and possibly one in the stomach. It is believed that he was captured when seriously wounded, but died before a helicopter could arrive to take him out of the battle zone.

My only doubts about the identity arose because Che was much thinner and smaller than I had recalled, but it is hardly surprising that after months in the jungle he had lost his former heavy appearance.

As soon as the body reached the mortuary the doctors began to pump preservative into it, and the American agent made desperate efforts to keep off the crowds. He was a very nervous man and looked furious whenever cameras were pointed in his direction. He knew that I knew who he was and he also knew that I knew that he should not be there, for this is a war in which the Americans are not supposed to be taking part. Yet here was this man, who has been with the troops in Vallegrande, talking to the senior officers on familiar terms.

One can hardly say that this was the factor with which Che failed to reckon, for it was his very purpose to provoke United States intervention in Latin America as a way of bringing help and succour to the embattled Vietnamese. But he certainly did fail to estimate correctly the strength and pervasiveness of the US intelligence agencies in this continent, and this more than anything else has been the cause of his downfall and that of the Bolivian guerrillas.

And so he is dead. As they pumped preservative into his half-naked, dirty body and as the crowd shouted to be allowed to see, it was difficult to recall that this man had once been one of the great figures of Latin America.

It was not just that he was a great guerrilla leader, he had been a friend of Presidents as well as revolutionaries. His voice had been heard and appreciated in inter-American councils as well as in the jungle. He was a doctor, an amateur economist, once Minister of Industries in revolutionary Cuba, and Fidel Castro's right-hand man. He may well go down in history as the greatest continental figure since Bolivar. Legends will be created around his name.

He was a Marxist but impatient of the doctrinal struggles between the Russians and the Chinese. He was perhaps the last person who tried to find a middle way between the two and attempted to unite radical forces everywhere in a concerted campaign against the US. He is now dead, but it is difficult to feel that his ideas will die with him.

OCTOBER 9, 1967

Name of legend . . . Che Guevara

GROOVY FOR THE DROP-OUTS

HIPPIES IN LONDON

BY CHARLES MAROWITZ

ANYONE WHO HAS been following the vicissitudes of the London "underground" scene is beginning to look a little peaked. It is not the spectacular soirées and relentless pop accompaniment that gets one down but the gradual realisation that, to stay alive, the "movement" is as dependent on blood-transfusions as Count Dracula ever was.

Many bystanders believe the London hippies who flame in the cellars of UFO on Tottenham Court Road or the Round House in Chalk Farm are nothing more than the Beats having a second wind. But whereas the Beats, for all their dissociation from mainstream culture, ultimately enriched that culture with their work, the hippies' speciality is not work but "freak-outs" and "raves", i.e. elaborate clambakes where the maximum amount of distraction is supposed to create an optimum of personal awareness.

By refusing to acknowledge the prevailing commercial totems, writers like Ginsberg, Corso, Ferlinghetti and Burroughs were at least making a comment upon them. In the London hippie-scene one finds the same social evils syruped over with a fraternal mysticism in which euphoria is supposed to equal love. But what a wet kind of love it is! Devoid of taste or sinew, it has all the charm of a Labrador puppy slobbering over the fingers of a disinterested master. At the vortex of the Beats, there were mystics and poets, clowns and stylists, but at the centre of the London Scene one finds mainly self-aggrandising displaced Americans with flairs for publicity and an inexhaustible *bonhomie* as shallow as it is pervasive.

FUZZY CONCERN

Many of London hippies are not only "drop-outs" (people who have rejected any form of social or political activism) but "cop-outs" — people who equate mind-erasure with the dissolution of social problems. ("When I'm stoned, there's no Vietnam and no Bomb, man, it's groovy.") Still a fuzzy sort of political concern climbs to the scene. Often this is a result of the admixture of CNDers and hippies, the hippie flank being so

The hippy and the unhippy . . .

insubstantial in itself it tends to take on the complexion of almost every faction that joins it. Political fervour fastens on to issues like drug-prohibition and censorship, but these are not aspects of a general liberal outlook — they are personal preoccupations that erroneously imply the existence of wider political beliefs.

They react with uncharacteristic aggression, when attacked by the media-boys or the CID or the Narcotics Squad, but having no ideological base they haven't the means of combating these attacks. When they occur, it just seems to them that people are sending out "bad vibrations" and are "coming on all square and unhippy." It is a political naiveté which may be adorable in the abstract, but is infuriating to those who battle the same enemies with conviction and a thorough understanding of who and what they are up against.

At the moment with the overpowering realities of Vietnam, the Middle East and the failure of nerve in English politics, the Scene seems trivial to point of obscenity. Continually urged to action, it can only bleat second-hand Greenwich Village shibboleths ("tune in — turn on — drop out") and foist slightly-soiled American heroes; Dr Timothy Leary, the LSD guru, Andy Warhol, pop-artist extraordinaire, Ginsberg and Burroughs, honoured alumni. When social pressure is really laid on and it comes to the crunch, acid and pop-spectaculars is its ultimate deterrent.

The underground soirées at UFO, Electric Garden, etc., are highly indicative of this disaffiliation. They are unique Theatres of Total Distraction where sound, sights, music, painting and pot all combine to bombard the sensibility and displace the present. The *summum bonum* is the higher consciousness these raves are trying to induce. The irony is that the higher consciousness seems to have validity only as a means of transcending reality, not grappling with its complexities. Throughout the Scene there is a tacit assumption that simulated reality is somehow superior to the grimy here and now, and that private hallucination is the cool antidote to disturbing external circumstance.

JUNE 24, 1967

WARHOL, WARHOL, ON THE WALL

BY NORBERT LYNTON

"ANDY WARHOL," SAYS the catalogue; "born Philadelphia 1930, lives in New York." That is all. The last item is right, the second is questionable, the first in its implications problematic. According to some sources he was born in 1927, which would put him on the unglamorous side of forty. No matter, as long as it is Andy we have before us, but here the difficulty arises: no one shows less of himself in his art.

Note the paradox. We all know about him — telly, colour supplements, art magazines, word of mouth. And what do we know about him? Nothing. His is the most secret, as well as the brightest, stardom in the art business.

The Rowan gallery is showing a selection of his photo-based, silk-screened faces. Two sorts: criminals, taken from the rough half-tones of the New York police gazette, full-face and profile, also four unposed snapshots. And, Marilyn Monroe in a series of ten prints, the same photo used ten times in different colour combinations.

They are the "Most Wanted Men". The enlarged half-tone fascinates visually. Close to it, resembles some complex contructivist programme of varyingly intense spots of paint and of intervals on a grid. We draw away and are surprised at our conceptual agility. With the most immediate of compulsions we translate a dot cluster into tone and tone into features and features into personality. They

look like television actors, French intellectuals, the young man next door, a headmaster. Only one of them looks thuggish and he has a ghastly bruised eye, more thugged than thugging. To society they are criminals. There but for the grace of God.

On the other wall, the most wanted woman. Her at least we know: her name evokes a swarm of film and newspaper images, sportive and sad. Yet, looking at Warhol's reproductions of that familiar face, we lose the familiarity. Each version is different because of the colour and tone values and the way the register is allowed to drag a little. They are Marilyn but they contradict each other and we lose sight of her behind the suave and garish surfaces. In the end it is as though she has been exorcised from her own public image, and suddenly the twinges we all felt at her death seem narcissistic.

Whether Warhol himself at any point touched any of these pictures does not matter: in some way or other he made them exist, and they touch us. Or, strictly, they are there for us to enter into dialogue with or not, as we wish. He has said "Some day everybody will think just what they want to think, and then everybody will probably be thinking alike." His pictures invite us to think what we will — a mass media Bruegel, he holds up mirrors.

MARCH 9, 1968

MR POWELL ON THE RACE BILL

THOSE WHOM THE gods wish to destroy, they first make mad, said Mr Enoch Powell, Opposition spokesman on defence, on Saturday. He added: "We must be mad, literally mad, as a nation to permit the annual inflow of some fifty thousand dependants."

It was like watching a nation "busily engaged in heaping up its own funeral pyre," he said at the annual meeting of the West Midlands Area Conservative Political Centre. He called for an immediate reduction to "negligible proportions" of the present immigrant inflow, and an "urgent" encouragement of re-emigration.

In a reference to the Race Relations Bill, Mr Powell said that to enact legislation of this kind was "to risk throwing a match on gunpowder." He continued:

"In fifteen or twenty years, on present terms, there will be in this country three and a half million Commonwealth immigrants — and their descendants. That is not my figure. That is the official figure given to Parliament by the spokesman of the Registrar-General's office.

"There is no comparable official figure for the year 2000, but it must be in the region of five to seven millions, approximately one-tenth of the whole population, and approaching that of Greater London. Of course, it will not be evenly distributed. Whole areas, towns and parts of towns will be occupied by different sections of the immigrant and immigration-descended population . . ."

The Race Relations Bill [Powell said] was a means of showing that the immigrant communities could agitate and campaign against their fellow citizens, and overawe and dominate the rest with the legal weapons which the ignorant and the ill-informed had provided. "As I look ahead, I am filled with foreboding. Like the Roman, I seem to see 'the River Tiber foaming with too much blood'."

APRIL 22, 1968

PARIS GRIPPED BY INSURRECTION

BY JOSEPH CARROLL

AN INSURRECTION, THERE is no other word for it, swept a stupefied Paris last night in the hours that followed General de Gaulle's television address.

The most dramatic moment in a night of unbelievable happenings was the invasion of the Bourse (Stock Exchange) by a mixture of Trotskyites, Anarchists, and revolutionary students who hoisted the Red Flag over the building of the "Temple of Gold", as it is called, built as it is in the classical Grecian style. After singing the Internationale, the invaders set fire to the inside of the building, but it was extinguished soon afterwards.

Paris riot police battled throughout the night with the demonstrators made up of students, workers, and goodness knows who else. But their technique of breaking off the engagement and rushing to another quarter in small, highly mobile groups of about fifty, baffled the less nimble police who had to run to their vans and take off in pursuit.

POLICE BULLDOZER

Thousands of students turned the Latin Quarter into a besieged camp in the early hours of this morning, building dozens of barricades along the wide Boulevard St Michel and in the streets around the Sorbonne.

At 1 a.m., a police bulldozer began moving up the Boulevard St Michel under the cover of continuous fire of tear-gas grenades. The bulldozer was followed by large forces of police well protected by their vans moving slowly up the boulevard. Their aim was to reach the junction of Boulevard St Michel and Boulevard St Germain, where the largest number of demonstrators had assembled.

The police, advancing slowly and deliberately, elbow to elbow, protected themselves with black shields. The demonstrators on the boulevard had created a scene of utter desolation, having sawn down most of the trees, pulled up wood seats on the pavement, and ripped up the paving stones, all to reinforce their barricades. From minute to minute, the riots were becoming more and more spectacular.

MAY 25, 1968

DR LUTHER KING SHOT DEAD

BY OUR CORRESPONDENT

DR MARTIN LUTHER KING, the Negro civil rights leader, died in hospital here yesterday after being shot in the head by a sniper outside his hotel room.

Police put out a wanted bulletin for "a young white male, well dressed", who was seen running from a brick building across the street from the Lorraine Hotel, where Dr King was shot while standing on the balcony of his second-storey room.

Officers surrounded the car and the hotel. He was taken to St Joseph's Hospital. Early reports indicated that police have possession of the weapon. Police said his assailant had dropped the weapon, while running down Main Street, about a block from the shooting. The man had jumped into a blue car and driven off.

NEWS STARTS RIOTS

Police reported that sporadic acts of violence broke out in the Negro section of the town, as news of the shooting spread.

Dr King, aged 39, held the 1964 Nobel Peace prize. He was in Memphis to lead marches by striking garbage workers. His march on Wednesday ended in violence, in which one person was killed, 62 injured and two hundred arrested. Dr King had been the subject of repeated assassination threats over the past ten years, and there had been at least two serious attempts on his life.

APRIL 5, 1968

MAN WALKS ON MOON

QUIET DRAMA AT TRANQUILITY BASE

BY ANTHONY TUCKER

MEN ARE ON the moon. At 3.39 a.m. this morning — nearly four hours ahead of schedule — Armstrong, the lunar module commander, opened the hatch and clambered slowly down to the surface of the moon. Minutes later Aldrin followed him down the steps of the ladder — already renamed Tranquility Base — to join in this moving, clumsy culmination of eight years of intense dedication. It was the fulfilment of a dream which men have shared since the beginning of recorded history.

The decision to walk early was made three hours after the lunar module Eagle had made a perfect landing at 9.17 p.m., four miles downrange from the chosen site. The spacecraft was steered manually to clear a boulder-strewn crater "the size of a football pitch." It was a moment of extraordinary tension and silence. The lunar module curved gently down over the Sea of Tranquility, the drama heightened by the calm, almost casual voices of the astronauts and the mission controller at Houston.

The casualness was deceptive: from 500 ft. above the surface and all too aware that an error could lead to irretrievable disaster, Aldrin brought the spacecraft down under Armstrong's direction. At the moment of approach Armstrong's heartbeat rose from its normal 70 to 156. Yet his voice was calm and flat: "Contact light: engines stopped . . . the Eagle has landed."

The landing was perfect. Spaceflight Centre and the world seemed momentarily stunned by emotion: only Armstrong, Aldrin — and above them, Collins — seemed unmoved at the end of the drama which began with a characteristically laconic acceptance of the "go" for separation of the lunar module shortly before 7 p.m.

"You got a bunch of guys who're about to turn blue," said the Houston space controller, when the module had landed. "We're breathing again. Thanks a lot."

Within a few minutes of landing Armstrong was saying they did not know exactly where they had landed. Houston replied "We'll figure it out for you."

Armstrong reported that the site was pitted with craters, "in the five to fifty feet range" with rocks of five to 10 ft., and ridges of five to 30 ft.

Ten minutes after landing Aldrin radioed: "We'll get to the details of what's around here, but it looks like a collection of just about every kind of rock. Colour depends on what angle you're looking at . . . rocks and boulders look as though they're going to have some interesting colours."

The close look already began to belie the image gained from centuries of examining lunar reflectivity — for that is what we see by — and the more detailed examination from orbit by man and camera. And from there, in the Sea of Tranquility, the colourful earth is simply bright. "It's big, and bright and beautiful," said Armstrong.

They said they had no difficulty in adapting to the moon's gravity. The conversation from the moon's surface came through loud and clear.

Separation began on this side of the moon, but the descent itself — the journey to which President Kennedy committed his nation eight years ago — began with a firing of the lunar module's motor after a long separating half-orbit on the far side of the moon and out of touch with the control centre back at Houston.

The world waited for the static-filled radio silence to be broken by an astronaut's affirmative. After what seemed on earth to be an age, the disappointed millions who had hoped to watch the first steps of separation on television, at last heard a calm and distant Armstrong confirm that the landing trajectory was good. The first minor miracle had been performed.

From that moment, with the tension mounting second by second and with the minimum of interrogation from earth, or from the orbiting Collins, the lunar module bore Armstrong and Aldrin downward, using its motor as a brake and slowly tilting until it was upright and ready for landing.

On and down, past "high-gate" at 7,000 ft. with the braking phase complete and the spacecraft rotated so that its windows faced forward — the point at which the final approach began. Still onward and down, but more slowly now, the spacecraft moved with the astronauts checking, checking and checking again that all systems were "go".

Visual approach, but still under automatic control, began at 500 ft. with all forward motion stilled and the descent rate only two and a half feet. a second, the spacecraft seemed to pause as Armstrong searched the ashen-grey landscape for the hidden flaws, a sudden rock which would shatter the landing.

With a permitted tolerance of 12 degrees about the horizontal — a tilt of 6 degrees in any direction — if the spacecraft was ever to rise again, the search for a landing area had to be as knowledgeable and as perfect as man could make it. A few minutes later, although time seemed to have slowed down, we knew that it had been good. The tilt was four and a half degrees. A second minor miracle had been worked.

Every step of the preparation for landing yesterday went smoothly. Armstrong and Aldrin transferred from the command module — codenamed Columbia — to the lunar module "Eagle" during the tenth orbit, and on the eleventh orbit Glynn Lunney, the flight controller at Houston, told the world that all spacecraft systems were "operating just fine."

With the deceptive casualness which is now a hallmark of spacecraft control, he added that the astronauts were "a jump ahead in their work."

JULY 21, 1969

1970 | 1980

HOSPITALS WORK BY CANDLELIGHT

NATIONWIDE POWER CUTS averaged 31 per cent yesterday, with 40 per cent in some areas, and hospitals faced their most critical 24 hours of the strike so far with staff struggling to keep going by candle and battery power.

Sir John Eden, Minister for Industry, said at a lunch in London yesterday that nothing could justify the widespread disruption caused by the work-to-rule and added that he could not believe that the men intended to endanger human life.

He warned that organised industrial unrest on the scale now being witnessed had grave consequences for the economy as a whole and as such it would be firmly resisted.

The most anxious staff were those in children's hospitals. At the Great Ormond Street hospital, with 350 patients ranging from premature babies to seriously ill eleven-year-olds, stocks of emergency respirators were brought into the wards.

"We have hand-pump breathing apparatus ready for immediate use," a hospital official said.

DECEMBER 10, 1970

Above and overleaf : bloody scenes in Londonderry

BLOODY SUNDAY

13 KILLED AS PARATROOPS BREAK RIOT

BY SIMON WINCHESTER

THE TRAGIC AND inevitable doomsday situation which has been universally forecast for Northern Ireland arrived in Londonderry yesterday afternoon when soldiers firing into a large crowd of civil rights demonstrators, shot and killed 13 civilians.

Seventeen more people, including a woman, were injured by gunfire and another woman was seriously injured after being knocked down by a speeding armoured car.

The army reported two military casualties and said that their soldiers had arrested between fifty and sixty people, who had been allegedly involved in the illegal protest march.

After the shooting, which lasted for about 25 minutes in and around the Rossville Flats area of Bogside, the streets had all the appearance of the aftermath of Sharpeville. Where, only moments before, thousands of men and women had been milling around, drifting slowly towards a protest meeting to be held at Free Derry Corner, there was only a handful of bleeding bodies, some lying still, others still moving with pain, on the white concrete of the square.

The Army's official explanation for the killing was that their troops had fired in response to a number of snipers who had opened up on them from below the flats. But those of us at the meeting heard only one shot before the soldiers opened up with their high velocity rifles.

And while it is impossible to be absolutely sure, one came away with the firm impression, reinforced by dozens of eyewitnesses, that the soldiers, men of the 1st Battalion The Parachute regiment, flown in specially from Belfast, may have fired needlessly into the huge crowd.

Miss Bernadette Devlin said it was "bloody cold blooded murder." Mr John Hume said it was "another Sharpeville," and he demanded the immediate withdrawal of all these "uniformed murderers." Mr Michael Canavan of the Derry Citizens' Central Council said "It was impossible to say who fired first. Personally I am sure it was the army, but it doesn't really matter. What was so terrible and so tragic was that the soldiers fired into a huge crowd of people, and fired indiscriminately at that. The death toll must show us that their firing was indiscriminate."

The death toll at 7.30 p.m., three hours after the shooting, was said to be 12, all men, and all said to be in their mid-twenties. A thirteenth victim was reported later.

JANUARY 31, 1972

JOURNALIST TOLD LIES, SAID GENERAL

THE JOURNALIST JONATHAN Aitken had told lies and "behaved in a dishonourable manner" in copying a confidential military report on the Nigerian war, the Fleet Street secrets case was told yesterday.

The accusation came in a letter from General Henry Templar Alexander, the former Chief British Officer in Lagos, to Colonel Douglas Cairns, one of those accused in the trial at the Central Criminal Court. Aitken is accused of receiving the report from General Alexander and communicating it to the *Sunday Telegraph*.

When the case resumed yesterday before the jury, who had been out since Tuesday during legal arguments, Colonel Cairns said the general wrote to him: "I am very sorry about this matter of the paper. I have become a very good friend of Aitken and he has dined with me on several occasions.

"On December 22 he had dinner with me and at the end of the port session, I offered to lend him the document and to treat it in the strictest confidence for background information only.

"He returned it the next day, but it appears he had it copied. I fear he has told a good many lies, and has behaved in a dishonourable manner."

The case continues today.

JANUARY 22, 1971

THE FEMALE EUNUCH

BY CATHERINE STORR

IN HER OUTPOURINGS on the subject of women's liberation Germaine Greer does not hesitate not only to use those old four-letter words but also to descend to personal — and in one case certainly unjustified as well as bitchy — abuse of women currently in the public eye. She writes volubly, making her points several times over, she's not always accurate in her facts, she generalises wildly, but at the same time she has some interesting things to say.

She thinks women have been "eunuchised" by the culture which teaches them to be passive, almost asexual, beings in every sphere. She writes to stir them up to think for themselves, to demand independence, to reassess their position, to emerge from the pupa case which once protected but now restricts them.

Behind the stridency, this makes sense. But it amazes me that [she] apparently blame[s] man for having imposed the pupa image on women without recognising that while women were obliged to spend most of their lives bearing and rearing children in order to ensure the survival of the race, it was an image which was not only necessary but salutary for them.

It is only now, when the drop in infant mortality and The Pill have set them free, that we can begin to assess what women are really capable of. Every previous supposition — including that of there being absolutely no difference between the mental and emotional equipment of the sexes — should be scrapped. We have got to learn all over again, from as unprejudiced a stance as possible, what women are like; and probably, because of the relationship of the sexes, we shall emerge with some new ideas about the nature of men as well.

DECEMBER 10, 1970

WOULD YOU KILL THIS?

THE HUNT SABOTEURS

BY JILL TWEEDIE

THE SUN BEATS down on Dorset — green meadows spread under even blue skies and, in a pleat of a hill, one grey church steeple. A perfect summer's day and what more traditional a way to pass a perfect summer's day than watching, say, an otter being torn to pieces? . . .

[A youth from the saboteurs confronts a hunt follower:] "Are otters pests?" "No," says the lady. "Well, do they taste good when you cook them?" The lady's eyes, glazed until then, clear. She regards her kibitzer with warm amusement. "My dear boy, you don't eat otters. Oh ho ho ho no."

"Really?" says the youth in his thick way. "They're not pests and they can't be eaten. What do you kill them for, then please?" The lady's smile sets and she gazes with a consuming interest on the horizon. Beside her the Major — a fine specimen of an Englishman with a curling mousatache and a florid complexion — gazes with her. They are not related but they could be twins, two C Aubrey Smiths, incredibly noble, with faces made for the quelling of natives or felling lions at a glance. They don't make 'em like that any more.

JULY 3, 1971

PRISONER OF IDI AMIN

FOUR DAYS IN MAKINDYE

BY JOHN FAIRHALL

THE LIGHT WAS switched on, the steel door opened and we were led into a 50 ft. long room with high barred windows. Fifteen or so Africans were lying on blankets on the concrete floor. At a shout from the guards some of them threw us each a blanket and we were told to lie down. A moment later the steel door grated shut, the light went out, and we were left for the night.

The night was warm, but the combination of shock and the hardness of the concrete under the blanket made sleep near impossible. In the almost pitch black one of the African prisoners came to whisper questions about who we were and where we had been arrested. Stretched out side by side we whispered to each other.

Outside we could hear soldiers shouting and vehicles coming and going throughout a very long night. The whole camp was as tense as we were. There was no way of telling what was going on — all we knew was that that morning's news bulletin had announced that a thousand Tanzanian troops had invaded Uganda.

In the first light of dawn through the barred windows high above us I saw two Africans across the cell silently go through the Moslem ritual of prayer, standing and kneeling towards Mecca. Following the example of the African prisoners we folded up our blankets and sat on them, leaning against the wall.

In the early Monday afternoon some food arrived outside. The Africans filed out for a plate or mess tin of cooked beans, but the supply ran out before all were served. We had no plates, anyway. But we were given a packet of the hard army biscuits and that, with water in a borrowed mug, was lunch. There was another meal in the early evening — rice and meat — and by then we had acquired a mess tin, but could eat nothing.

Other meals were posho (maize meal cooked to a stiff porridge) and meat, rice and beans, or a mug of tea and a hunk of bread. As far as I could tell it was standard army rations, but still difficult to eat.

One mealtime we filed out into the compound to queue up at the bath of food. In the next wire compound troops were shooting. I saw a coloured man, lighter skinned than an African, running from one soldier to another. He sat on the ground as a soldier first screamed at him and then twice swung his rifle butt down on to his head or shoulder. The particular thud and rattle of a rifle butt and mechanism accompanied by hysterical shouting became one of the standard noises that we lay and listened to in the long days and longer nights in our cell. The Africans could understand what was being shouted and would whisper that another lot of prisoners was being brought in.

One night the lights went on and two Asians were brought in. One had a cut chin and blood all over his shirt. He said three of them had been driving into Kampala. They cleared four road blocks after documents were checked. At the fifth were military men in plain clothes. The three were made to lie on the ground and were then kicked on the head. One said their companion had been badly cut about the head — the blood on his shirt mostly came from carrying him and the guards had said they would take him to a Kampala hospital.

When the cell door was opened at mealtimes and through the Judas window (the spy hole) in the door we could see that the next cell held Ugandan Army men. At first they were only men on disciplinary offences in fatigue kit, but then I saw men in uniform being brought in. African prisoners said these were men who had been involved in the fighting with the army.

One day orders were shouted to the troops in the next cell. These were translated to us as being orders to turn out and unload bodies from a truck. One of the African prisoners looked through the Judas window and turned away shuddering to whisper that he could see a truck with bodies in civilian clothes.

We had listened earlier to noises like wooden clubs being wielded but had no way of telling what they were.

No shots were ever heard in the prison. African prisoners told me that the normal method of execution was by "tapping" a man's skull with a 20 lb. hammer. One said he knew of twenty prisoners who died in this way. He said he had seen one group made to lie down. Then the first man was forced at gun point to get up and smash the skull of another prisoner. Each was made to kill the man beyond him and a soldier dispatched the last. The prisoner who described this was a highly intelligent and articulate man who had seen it happen not long previously. He himself seemed to have been arrested quite casually because he was not carrying documents.

Several prisoners went, to be replaced by others . . . It was obvious, too, that people were brought into the prison and were killed or held almost carelessly. Communication was one problem. French-speaking Africans were bawled at in Swahili and expected to understand orders to stand or sit. One NCO asked me who I worked for. I said the *Guardian*. "Are you a soldier?" he asked. I said I was a journalist. "*Guardian*, is that the name of your regiment?" he wanted to know. I told him it was an English newspaper that was sold in Kampala.

The cell door opened, we were ordered out . . . Our shoes and suitcases were restored, after careful investigation and signing, and we waited at the gatehouse for long checking of names against deportation orders. As we waited we heard someone screaming. Inside a ring of laughing soldiers we could see a woman wielding a whip. She lashed at someone hidden inside the ring of soldiers, first with one hand, then with both. Then an African in a ragged shirt ran through the troops, making animal noises of terror. The soldiers roared with laughter.

SEPTEMBER 22, 1972

THE WATERGATE BURGLARY

PRESIDENT'S AIDES ACCUSED

BY PETER JENKINS

SENSATIONAL NEW REVELATIONS now link Republican espionage and subversion during the election campaign directly with the White House.

Both *Time* magazine and the *Washington Post* connect one of President Nixon's close personal aides with the activities of Mr Donald Segretti, a Los Angeles lawyer, who had earlier been identified as one of the undercover agents working for the committee to re-elect the President. *Time* magazine further alleges that payments of more than $35,000 to Segretti were made through President Nixon's personal attorney, Mr Herbert Kamlebach.

There is still no direct evidence linking the President with the Watergate burglary and the other criminal or covert activities of the Republicans, but the finger is beginning to point in his direction.

(Seven men are awaiting trial for their part in the Watergate affair, which involved the bugging and breaking into the Democratic National Committee offices.)

Time magazine cites Justice Department files and says the White House aide who recruited Segretti in September, 1971, was Mr Dwight Chapin. The *Washington Post* quotes the sworn testimony of a lawyer friend of Segretti to

whom Segretti said: "Dwight Chapin was a person I reported to in Washington."

Mr Chapin is the President's appointments secretary. He has easy access to Mr Nixon and sees him most days . . .

The *Post* quotes its official sources as saying that criminal offences in connection with the Republicans' undercover activities would be difficult to prove in court. But the officials described them as despicable and vicious.

According to these FBI and Justice Department sources the espionage and sabotage "represented a basic strategy of the Nixon re-election effort."

The activities included forgery, distribution of false information, disruption of Democratic campaign schedules and meetings, investigating Democratic party workers, and placing agents provocateurs in Democratic organisations. The activities were conducted across the country and throughout the primary election campaign.

At a press conference in June Mr Nixon said that the methods used at Watergate had "no place whatever in our electoral process." The White House "had no involvement whatsoever," he said.

OCTOBER 16, 1972

DANCING TO VICTORY

ALI OUTWITS FRAZIER

BY DAVID GRAY

AT MIDNIGHT AT Madison Square Garden Muhammad Ali saluted his victory over Joe Frazier by reading a long poem called "Truth" that was symbolic. Almost everyone had told the truth about the fight, said Ali — "that we would win" — and all the best judges had agreed. But no one had believed that Fight Two, a contest between two great but ageing former champions, would quite match the quality of their first classic meeting three years ago.

Ali won — the judges were unanimous — but it was another of Time's familiar triumphs. Frazier was an easy target. He always has to take punishment to get himself into the position to hit, but last night his feet seemed heavier than usual and it took him longer to set up punches. Ali could strike and go, could play the role of a 212 lb will-o'-the-wisp without often straying into trouble.

He was delighted by his own performance. "A little dancing, a little slugging, a little more dancing, and a little more slugging. I was faster and I hit him harder. It was a better fight than last time. There wasn't any clowning on the ropes." But if there was more stinging than floating this time it was because it was easier to sting and there was less need to float. Angelo Dundee, Ali's manager, may have cried, "You've got to stop him to win," as they went into the twelfth round, but that can only have been an attempt to spur him into making sure that absolutely nothing went wrong.

Ali hurt Frazier with some good rights. "You know why he left himself open to those punches? Because he read too many newspapers," said Ali. "You wrote that I had an injured right hand, but I tricked you all. I punched him with that right. There wasn't nothing wrong with it."

Certainly it was not all change and decay. Often Ali made the science seem sweet. The style is still there, even if the reflexes are not what they were. For a big man he still moves marvellously, but understandably he tired towards the end. "Snake. Rally with him. Dance, Ali, dance," shouted his brother urgently from the front row. And so Ali did. . . .

JANUARY 30, 1974

WE'RE IN BUT WITHOUT THE FIREWORKS

BY DAVID MCKIE AND DENNIS BARKER

BRITAIN PASSED PEACEFULLY into Europe at midnight last night without any special celebration. It was difficult to tell that anything of importance had occurred, and a date which will be entered in the history books as long as histories of Britain are written, was taken by most people as a matter of course.

The principal party political figures maintained their familiar postures of hope and optimism or head-shaking despair. Mr Heath was starting back from Ottawa, where he had gone for the funeral of Mr Lester Pearson, at about the time that Britain, along with Denmark and Ireland, officially became members of the European Community.

In a spate of pre-recorded interviews, he expressed his own hope and satisfaction at the successful outcome of the long march towards Europe with which he had himself been so closely associated for so long.

Yesterday the latest opinion poll on the Market, by Opinion Research Centre for the BBC, suggested that 38 per cent were happy about embarking on what Mr Heath depicted as an exciting adventure, while 39 per cent would prefer to get off. Twenty three per cent had no opinion at all.

PRAGMATISM

Mr Heath believed that enthusiasm for the market existed predominantly among the young. Elsewhere he detected no more than good old British pragmatism. He had been impressed by people he had met who did not expect immediate benefit for themselves but looked forwad to a better life for their children and grandchildren.

"If you allow yourself to be bedevilled by your fears, you are paralysed by them. The only future lies in energetically seizing opportunities."

Mr Wilson, however, saw nothing to celebrate when we were going in without that fullhearted consent of the British people, which Mr Heath had made a condition of entry and when the price of admission was "utterly crippling". He defended the Labour decision not to attend the European Assembly.

JANUARY 1, 1973

THE OIL WAR

ARABS WILL CUT AND CUT AGAIN

BY PETER HILLMORE

THE ARAB STATES have used their most potent weapon in the Middle East conflict. Supplies of oil to the United States are to be cut 5 per cent, escalating each month "until Israeli forces have left the occupied lands and restored the rights of Palestinians."

FRIENDS OF ISRAEL

Late last night the Foreign Office and the oil companies were trying to find out whether Britain was included in the "other industrial countries" friendly to Israel which will also have their supplies cut.

Sheik Yamani . . . will cut supplies

But amidst all the uncertainty, one thing is certain: petrol prices will go up by at least 1.5p–2p a gallon, and this could well rise to a staggering 9p a gallon following an earlier decision by the oil states to raise the price of oil.

BALANCE OF PAYMENTS BLOW

Quite apart from any oil cut-off fears, the price rise is a crippling blow both to the balance of payments and the Government's anti-inflation policy, which is firmly based on a belief that the price of raw materials will drop. Britain uses 817 million barrels of oil a year, and the increase demanded by the Arabs is 50p a barrel — representing an extra £408 million drain on the balance of payments.

OCTOBER 18, 1973

THOUSANDS OF UNSOLD CARS

WHAT THEY MEAN FOR BRITAIN

BY FRANCIS BOYD

IN THE SEARCH, which we must all now be making, for a simple explanation, or a vivid visual image, of the facts that control our take-home pay, our standard of living, and our prospects for the future, an aerial press photograph published on Friday told me more, at one glance, than I found comfortable.

It showed some of a batch of ten thousand cars, parked near Coventry because they could not be sold. The company is said to have produced thirty thousand vehicles which are so far unsold. All these cars — and more also from other makers — are awaiting buyers who would have to drive them on our crowded roads using petrol which must be imported, is too expensive for economic use, and could be made still dearer or quite unobtainable at one strike from OPEC. At the same time, some workers in the car industry are striking to protect their standard of living, as Hugh Scanlon explained yesterday.

No one photograph could show more concisely the flimsy assumptions on which so much of our society is based:

1. That more and more people will earn enough to be able to afford cars;

2. That the public will support the spending of enough social capital to finance the road and parking system needed for so many cars;

3. That we shall always be able to import enough petrol at a reasonable price to run all these cars;

4. That an increase in car ownership is a condition of the fuller life that all the politicians, Communists included, promise us;

5. That since we had cheap petrol once, Britain must be made strong enough to get it again.

No political party, and no trade union, has made a point of warning its members that it is at least risky for a country which has had, so far, to import all its petrol, simply to bank on producing more and more cars. Naturally, Coventry, Oxford and Luton want this to happen. The unions and investors in the car industry want it to happen, and the politicians want it to happen so that vast redundancies in the car industry can be avoided.

To look from the air at that field of unwanted cars made me wonder, for a moment, how Britain ever became rich in the first place. The British car industry, like that of the Japanese, depends on a one-way flow towards the importers, and this is flat contrary to the pattern of trade on which Britain grew rich. Our ships once left British ports with valuable merchandise and came back loaded with the goods of foreign parts for use here, or for processing and re-export. With oil the story is quite different. The tankers come, unload (at mounting cost to consumers here) and sail away — empty.

The mind clouds at the thought of what the shipmasters of London, Glasgow and Bristol would have said, one or two hundred years ago, about the arrival in a British port of the equivalent of one modern tanker, say, the Globtik Tokyo (476,292 tons), which unloaded and then departed without even half a pound of Orkney cheese on it to sell abroad.

Britain grew rich over the years because of her wool, fish, tin, coal, her seamen, her fighters, her small population, her craftsmen and inventors. The imports she needed could be bought cheap for a variety of reasons, including colonialism. The terms of trade and politics have now changed. The British are not the only people who want sugar, for example.

No one can blame the coalminers at home for cherishing what remains of their economic power. One of Kipling's jingles, like a TV advertisement, points to our change of life:

> "Oh, where are you going to all you Big Steamers,
> With England's own coal, up and down the salt seas?"
> "We are going to fetch you your bread and butter,
> Your beef, pork and mutton, eggs, apples and cheese."

In Kipling's time, "England's own coal" could buy quite a lot of groceries overseas. Between 1909 and 1913 the annual average export of coal was 65.5 million tons, with a peak of nearly 73.5 million tons in 1913; total exports in 1973–4 were 2–1 million tons, having fallen from a postwar peak of 19.2 million tons in 1949.

I am not one of those who believe that the British are now the idlest people in the world, and have lost in luxury the inventive power and enterprise they once had. Most of us do not live in luxury even yet, and an inventor will invent: certainly the criminal finds ways to outwit the security technologists. But nobody should waste a single moment in the belief either that the world will guarantee us an easy living because we are so nice, tolerant, democratic, and poetic; or that we can ever again force the world to behave in that way.

JANUARY 14, 1975

MRS THATCHER TAKES THE HELM

DREAMY, SAYS THE NEW LEADER

BY GARETH PARRY

"FOR ME IT'S like a dream," said Mrs Margaret Thatcher last night, swivelling skilfully and with waxwork-like composure before a wall of cameras so that each one had a full frontal portrait.

Looking decidedly cooler than a vase full of daffodils which almost visibly wilted in the sauna heat of television lights the new lioness of Conservatism faced her first public press conference at Central Office.

Mrs Thatcher arrived in Smith Square in an atmosphere of near carnival, considerably coloured, if not poisoned, by the blue smoke from television generators.

Stepping with the utmost skill from a friend's yellow MGB GT sports car, she was immediately into a barrage of questions. The queen-like figure in black taffeta — a pinkish tulip providing the only decoration — gave as good as she got. How did she feel about facing Mr Wilson? "About

the same as he feels facing me.

"There is so much to be done and I hope you will allow me time to do it thoughtfully and well. Yes, there are going to be some changes — a blend of continuity and change."

Was Mrs Thatcher aware of scepticism surrounding the appointment of a woman to the chief Tory job? "Give me a chance.

"I'm not making any decisions about the Shadow Cabinet yet but I'm pledged to offer Mr Heath a place as well as the other candidates in the ballot."

Was this a victory for women's lib or for Margaret Thatcher? "Neither — it's a victory for someone in politics."

A Canadian correspondent asked whether Mrs Thatcher had received a message from the Queen. "Oh, no, one doesn't on these occasions." Mrs Thatcher stamped on an anonymous quote earlier in the day that her election would ensure the

Conservatives remaining in Opposition for ten years. "I think they are wrong."

If the Labour majority was eroded would she seek coalition? "Let's wait and see." She would be campaigning to keep the country in Europe.

"I've got a lot of work to do and the champagne will have to wait tonight. In any case we haven't got any at home." Then Mrs Thatcher left in the MG for the House, the committee stage of the Finance Bill, and a late night supper with her husband.

Yesterday was altogether a fraught one for the Thatchers. Twin daughter, Carol, aged 21, was in no mood for celebration. She is in the middle of her law finals. Her brother, Mark, said at home in Flood Street, Chelsea: "It's fantastic and words can't really express how delighted I am. I'm thrilled."

FEBRUARY 12, 1975

LAST NIGHT'S TELEVISION

CHURCHILL'S PEOPLE

BY NANCY BANKS-SMITH

BOW-LEGGED UNDER the burden of its song, Little Winston's History of England (or, officially, Churchill's People, BBC1), has little to offer us but blood, horsehair and history. Though a hell of a lot of each. When a man cannot wake up without musing "How pitiful that I, Tiberius Claudius, governor of York, ex-commander of an undefeated legion . . .", or visit the barber without learning that "the Saxons have entrenched themselves in the coastal towns and the Picts have reached the Wall", the story flow is bound to be sluggish.

The decline of the Roman Empire in Britain was amply explained by their fondness for studio discussions. No good can come of a tendency to sit around in circles quarrelling with hand-picked members of representative organizations ("argue with that, Viventius!"). The decision of the Saxon captive to seize a sword and run amok among the debaters is one that will strike a chord in every viewer's heart.

Robert Muller's tendency to insert little jokes in the script to cheer himself up — "Do you like it? It's a genuine antique" or "our little local difficulties" — suggests that he too found it more a burden than a song. There are twenty-four more episodes to come. As Macbeth remarked on a similar occasion: "What, does the line stretch out to the crack of doom? I'll see no more!"

JANUARY 7, 1975

TIMOR INVADED

INDONESIANS CAPTURE CAPITAL

BY CHRISTOPHER SWEENEY

AN INDONESIAN-SUPPORTED force launched a full-scale attack by air and sea on the former Portuguese colony of Timor at dawn today.

More than one thousand army commandos parachuted into the capital of Dili in the first wave of the attack and by tonight controlled it and all the approach roads.

AIRPORT SECURE

A radio broadcast monitored in Darwin reported that Indonesian troops had secured the airport, the military headquarters, and the former Portuguese administrative buildings within four hours of the first landings.

Up to four Indonesian warships steamed into Dili harbour at first light. They shelled the town and discharged regular Indonesian marines in landing craft.

There was only sporadic resistance, according to monitored radio reports. The Indonesians were supported by an unknown number of Timorese from two right-wing movements, the Timorese Democratic Union (UDT) and the pro-Indonesian Apodeti party.

BATTLE FOR CONTROL

The invasion came almost five months to the day after the left-wing nationalist movement Fretilin defeated two right-wing conservative local movements in a bloody internecine battle for control of the mini-colony after independence from Portugal. Indonesia, with one of the most phobic anti-Communist Governments in Asia, immediately began assisting the anti-Fretilin forces with arms and training.

BETRAYAL OF TIMORESE PEOPLE

Today's invasion had been expected for some weeks. The Fretilin spokesman in Sydney, Mr Christivao Santos, accused Australia of betraying the Timorese people and said Dr Kissinger knew of the invasion and gave it his encouragement. President Ford and Dr Kissinger left Jakarta yesterday.

DECEMBER 8, 1975

JUBILEE LIGHTS UP

QUEEN LIGHTS THE TORCH

BY MARTIN WAINWRIGHT AND MARTIN WALKER

A SPARK JUMPED from the Queen's torch to a train of gunpowder last night and set the Royal Silver Jubilee officially alight. Flames leapt 50 ft. into the air from the pinewood beacon on Windsor Hill where the Queen arrived escorted by a vast and colourful carnival procession.

Unofficially, the jubilee had sparked to life a minute earlier many miles to the north on Axe Edge, rising to 1,800 feet out of the rain and mist alongside the A53 Buxton to Leek Road. A chain of Beacons across Britain should have been lit in sequence but Axe Edge jumped the gun, unaware that the Queen's lighting of the Windsor beacon had been delayed from 10 p.m. to 10.14 p.m.

At Windsor, two minutes after the Queen had lit the beacon, tiny points of flames winked from the north-east and south-west as the beacons on Dunstable Down and the Hogs Back, which should have been the first of a countrywide chain of 102 were fired.

The fifty thousand people on the hill, some of them perched in trees to make sure that they saw the Queen, erupted into cheers and shouts as the sky ripped open in a breathtaking explosion or Royal fireworks.

Like the people of Britain elsewhere, grumpy with inflation and austerity but now joining in the jollity, however crack-brained, of the jubilee, the crowds on the hill had been growing desperate for fun.

JUNE 7, 1977

SLATER FACES COURT APPEAL

FINANCIER ON FIFTEEN CHARGES

THE DEPARTMENT OF Trade is to appeal against the acquittal of financier Mr Jim Slater on 15 charges alleging contravention of the Companies Act. Mr Slater, former chief of the Slater Walker group, was cleared in February of charges of misusing more than £4,000,000 of his company's funds in share deals when the magistrate decided that there was no case to answer.

MARCH 24, 1977

PUNK RECORD IS A LOAD OF LEGAL TROUBLE

BY NICHOLAS DE JONGH

THE MANAGER OF a record shop in Nottingham who displayed in his window the new best-selling LP record by the Sex Pistols, which displays on its sleeve the title "Never mind the Bollocks, here's the Sex Pistols" has been charged with offences under the 1889 Indecent Advertisement Act.

Managers of record shops in Notting Hill and Marble Arch, London, have been charged with contravening the Indecent Advertisement section of the 1824 Vagrancy Act, for displaying the sleeve.

Another record shop, Small Wonder records in Walthamstow, East London, has had a visit from the police and has covered up the offending word.

Both the managers charged in London are at shops owned by Virgin Records, the company which produces the Sex Pistols' recordings. The two men, Mr David Martin and Mr Johnnie Fewings, refused to take down the record displays after being warned by police, according to a record company spokesman.

Mr Al Clarke, press officer for Virgin Records said: "The LP was released eleven days ago. It brought in £250,000 before it was even released, and went straight to number one in the charts."

Melody Maker, the musical paper, had covered up the word "bollocks" in an advertisement, and two national newspapers had printed the word as a series of asterisks. Mr John Mortimer, QC, was to represent the company in all three cases. Mr Clarke said "We have agreed under protest to take down the display in Nottingham, but elsewhere we will keep up the displays."

The Independent Television Companies' Association (ITCA) and the Association of Independent Radio Contractors (AIRC), the trade associations which examine advertising for commercial television and radio have banned advertisements for the record. A spokesman said: "We considered the record itself was unsuitable for advertising on family media like television and radio."

The BBC said last night that it had banned none of the tracks on the record, but a spokesman for Capital Radio said that it had been advised by the Independent Broadcasting Authority not to play four of the tracks — Bodies, New York, Seventeen, and Submission. The IBA said later that the ultimate decision was for individual companies.

Capital also said that it had banned one track, Holidays in the Sun, because it felt that a comparison likening holiday camps to Belsen would cause offence. ITCA and AIRC said that they would have banned any reference to "bollocks" in a broadcast advertisement.

The word "bollocks" appears in the supplement to the complete Oxford English Dictionary, where its meaning is defined as testicles. The dictionary says that the first recorded use of the word was in 1744 in *The School of Venus* by D. Thomas, who wrote: "You can now without blushing call prick, stones, bollocks, c—t, arse (*sic*), and the like names."

However, a detailed Shakespearean knowledge may be needed to appreciate the full implications of the record's title. For in Henry V, Act Two, Scene Two, loud-mouthed, thuggish Pistol says:

"I do retort the solus in thy bowels. For I can take, and Pistol's cock is up, and flashing fire will follow."

Johnny Rotten on stage with the Sex Pistols

NOVEMBER 10, 1977

THE FILM THAT PUTS THE PAP INTO POP

GREASE IS THE WORD

BY DEREK MALCOLM

"IF YOU CAN'T be an athlete, be an athletic support," says someone in *Grease* (Empire, A). It's one of the new funny lines in this all-conquering movie but then, such is its lack of real panache, one is not quite sure whether it understands the double meaning. The Robert Stigwood film, already pre-sold to countless millions, is a grave disappointment to anyone in search of style or substance. But one thing this botched fifties pastiche does achieve is an increased affection for George Lucas's *American Graffiti*.

Based on the pop musical which took Broadway by storm in 1972, which *Time* correctly described as "like an old yearbook in the carton of high school memorabilia we all keep stored somewhere in the back of our lives", the film shrewdly but impertinently inserts a huge dose of seventies disco music into the score and populates its high school with some of the oldest pupils one is ever likely to see this side of the Open University. Moreover, it

is directed by thirty-year-old Randal Kleiser who not only can't possibly know what the fifties were about but is a graduate from television with only the remotest idea of how to handle a wide screen.

The consequences of this are profound, and even reflect on the performances of the two starry principals. John Travolta, whom God and Hollywood preserve in case the world takes suddenly against him, can display only half the animal energy he exhibited so sexily in *Saturday Night Fever* as dangerous Danny, the boy sweet little Sandy (Olivia Newton-John) wishes so much was just a regular guy. He poses like some forlorn young stud in a bedroom full of chastity belts.

As for Olivia, the Sandra Dee substitute for the seventies, she acts and sings prettily but her final metamorphosis as a leather-clad siren makes You're the One That I Want sound like an invitation to a snogging session behind the Vicarage. And don't ask me about the dancing or I'll

explode. The Busby Berkeley stylisations are grim enough, but the high school lawn-mowing has to be seen to be disbelieved.

Still, there are compensations — as indeed there must be to keep so many customers happy for so long. One of them is undoubtedly Eve Arden as Principal McGee (a real performance this) and the fleeting, not very meaty cameos accorded to other fifties stalwarts like Frankie Avalon, Sid Caesar and Edd Byrnes. Stockard Channing is fine too but about fifteen years too late for her part.

The rest is pure pap, admittedly enlivened by hit songs in the wrong style. Great fun no doubt if you don't give a damn for the cinema but disappointingly full of holes if you do. The central theme, which is really Pat Boone and Sandra Dee versus Elvis Presley and the groupie syndrome, is certainly sketched out. But whoever held the pencil seems incapable of drawing a straight line through the dross.

SEPTEMBER 14, 1978

THE BOAT PEOPLE

A DISMAL EXODUS

BY MARTIN WOOLLACOTT

REFUGEE OFFICIALS AND diplomats call them "the boat people". Some are indeed fishermen, but most are city folk who, before they slipped away from their homes in Saigon and other towns with hearts knocking and gold and dollars sewn into their clothes, they knew nothing of the ocean or its dangers.

Nobody knows how many have drowned or been murdered by pirates. But more than two years after the fall of Saigon, they are still coming, and in increasing numbers. They run the gauntlet of the pirates to the Thai coast where the Thais, their camps already full of Cambodians and Laotians, are beginning to turn them away. They arrive hopefully off Singapore which, until recently, they have wrongly seen as a haven, to be ordered out — at gun-point if necessary.

A few blunder down into Indonesian waters, and some head for the Philippines or Hong Kong. But for those who go south, there is now one preferred final destination — Australia,

where the arrival earlier this week of a modern trawler with 180 people aboard, including seven Vietnamese soldiers who were overpowered and locked up, has caused political consternation and a diplomatic incident.

The lush little island of Tengah, eight miles off the Malaysian coast, could have been the setting for *South Pacific* and, indeed, a neighbouring island was the location for that film. Now its palm trees and white sand beaches are the scene of a genuine drama, for the Malaysian government has set it aside as a concentration point for Vietnamese refugees.

"When will it end?" a Malaysian diplomat asked plaintively, back in Singapore. The answer is almost certainly that it will get worse. There are reckoned to be some 100,000 boats up and down South Vietnam's long coastline, so this is one problem that is not going to go away.

DECEMBER 3, 1977

LUCAS IN THE SKY WITH DIAMONDS

BY DEREK MALCOLM

"I HAVE WROUGHT my simple plan / If I give some hour of joy / To the boy who's half a man / Or the man who's half a boy."

Thus saith Arthur Conan Doyle in his preface to *The Lost World*, and thus quoteth Bob Dingilian, Executive Director of National Publicity, Twentieth Century Fox Film Corporation as a preface to his production notes for *Star Wars* (Dominion and Odeon Leicester Square, U). And I must say, it about sums up the picture, except that it gives some two hours of joy, and will probably also be appreciated by girls who are half women and women who are half girls too. Bob, you're a genius.

Quite whether George Lucas, of *American Graffiti* fame, is also a genius is another matter. Viewed dispassionately — and of course that's desperately difficult at this point in time — *Star Wars* is not an improvement on Mr Lucas's previous work, except in box-office terms. It isn't the best film of the year, it isn't the best science fiction ever to be translated to the screen, it isn't a number of other things either that sweating critics have tried to turn it into when faced with finding some plausible explanation for its huge and slightly sinister success considering a contracting market.

But it is on the other hand, enormous and exhilarating fun for those who are prepared to settle down in their seats and let it all wash over them. Which I firmly believe, with the extra benefit of hindsight, is more or less exactly what the vast majority of the cinema-going public want just now. Last year it was *Jaws*, which gave us more dangerous *frissons*, and not long before that it was *The Exorcist*, with enough green slime to give us all nightmares. Inevitably 1977 was going to be the year of safer pleasures. *Star Wars*, let me tell you, wasn't given its U certificate for nothing. The only exclamation the producers want from you is "Wow!"

So how do they get it? Well they start by saying "A long time ago, in a galaxy far away," which really means "Don't worry, it's only a fairy story." And then they tell us a tale about a pretty princess (Carrie Fisher) who gets kidnapped by wicked chaps who want to control the galaxies with whom a pretty ordinary bloke, or ordinary pretty bloke (Mark Hamill) falls head over ski-boots in love. Then there's this nice old retired knight (lucky old Alec Guinness with 2 per cent of the financial action) who teaches our hero to "stretch out with your feelings" and observe the Force of Good pulsing in his otherwise bloodless veins.

Added to that, there are two funny (no, quite funny)

robots, see Threepio (Anthony Daniels) and Artoo-Detoo (Kenny Baker), an ace pilot (Harrison Ford) who represents our disbelief by proving a sceptic, an apeman or "walking carpet" (Peter Mayhew) who looks as if he's come straight out of a Neolithic pantomime, and an assortment of villains so unterrifying that it looks as if you'd only have to pinch them to produce a fit of giggles (but who would dare do any such thing to Peter Cushing?).

Finally, ladies and gentlemen (or should I say boys and girls ?) are the special effects. And now I want you all to rise from your seats and salute since they were all Made in Britain. I can't say there's anything very new around in this direction, compared, say, to Kubrick's *2001*. But *Star Trek* it is not. Besides, Lucas has been clever enough not to make the mistake of explaining everything. All the hardware is taken for granted by the characters, which means we'll wonder at it the more. Let us not forget either the very traditional music score from John Williams, which eschews electronic bops and bleeps in favour of magical airs and graces, just to keep us in touch with some kind of reality.

But I haven't mentioned the film's chief sleight of hand, which is that (unlike most super popular movies) it makes itself into something fashionable enough to prevent buffs feeling like shlocks when they join the queues. This is done, quite deliberately, by looking back into the past rather than forward into the future. Every conceivable convention of the genre is shamelessly brandished rather than concealed. *Star Wars*, as Lucas himself has remarked, seeks to generate a "high level of fantasy". And you can't do that nowadays by blowing the mind without suitable references. These are legion — there is a space-age Western saloon, there's swashbuckling with laser beams, there's slapstick which reminds one of Laurel and Hardy and sentiment that reeks of *The Wizard of Oz*. There are lines which are almost, if not quite taken from old movies and direct allusions whipped from everything from *The Searchers* to *Triumph of the Will*. It's an incredibly knowing movie. But the filching is so affectionate that you can't resent it. Whatever else you think about *Star Wars*, you can't call it the height of originality. The entirely mindless could go and see it with pleasure. But it plays enough games to satisfy the most sophisticated. It opens on Boxing Day, by the way, so don't all rush at once. And Force, friends, Force.

DECEMBER 13, 1977

THATCHER TAKES OVER NUMBER TEN

RESULTS SMACK OF "TWO NATIONS"

BY DAVID MCKIE

MRS MARGARET THATCHER looks certain this morning to be the next tenant of 10 Downing Street and the first woman prime minister in the Western world.

Yet the measure of her victory seemed likely to fall below her party's hopes. The strong surge of Tory support for which she had been hoping materialised right across southern England, but in the North swings were low and in Scotland it was Labour who gained ground, displacing as they did so Mrs Thatcher's likely Scottish Secretary, Mr Teddy Taylor.

These were the most diverse results of any British election since 1945, and they had a distinct smack of "two nations" about them.

In North Devon the former leader of the Liberal Party crashed to defeat at the hands of his Conservative opponent. Mr Jeremy Thorpe, who faces trial at the Old Bailey on Tuesday charged with conspiracy to commit murder, lost his West Country stronghold by eight thousand votes. The campaign was distinguished by the huge number of "other" candidates, ranging from Mr Auberon Waugh of the Dog Lovers Party to Dr Frank Hansford Miller of the English National Party.

The extraordinary divergence of the results region by region upset the computers and led to displays of extreme caution by some of the party leaders. Mrs Thatcher, acknowledging the applause as her own result was announced at Finchley towards 2 a.m., said: "The night is yet young and we don't know what it will hold." Mr Callaghan in Cardiff made no comment.

At one point the ITN computer was indicating a Tory majority of around fifty while the BBC computer was putting it in single figures. An ITN poll by Opinion Research Centre at the polling station doors had at the start of the evening indicated a Conservative majority of over sixty on a 6.1 per cent swing. But it looked as though the established precepts of British psephology had taken something of a battering in this campaign and Dr Robert Mackenzie's swingometer was in much less evidence than in past elections.

One sad feature of a night on which a woman reached the highest-ever office in Britain was a crop of casualties among retiring women MPs. Apart from Miss Jackson in Lincoln and Mrs Wise, Mrs Helene Hayman was dismissed from the Labour benches and the SNP women representation was cut from two to nil. Ms Maureen Colquhoun, Northampton North's controversial MP in the last parliament, was also defeated.

MAY 4, 1979

US EMBASSY STORMED BY TEHRAN MOB

KHOMEINI'S UNRULY REVOLUTION

BY NICHOLAS CUMMING-BRUCE

GUNMEN LAUNCHED AN attack on the US embassy in central Tehran yesterday morning, providing an example of the gun law that many fear is here to stay for some time. Trapped inside the Embassy during the attack were Ambassador William Sullivan, about 100–150 of his staff and two journalists. Although the Embassy sustained damage, only one person, an Iranian waiter, was killed. Four Americans were slightly wounded.

Another example of the gun law came last night when the Tehran radio and television complex came under attack. The radio broadcast an urgent message asking all "true revolutionaries" to go to the station and help to repel the attack. Thousands of supporters of Ayatollah Khomeini immediately poured into the streets armed with rifles, machine-guns, and bazookas, commandeered trucks and drove to the radio station. The attack was repulsed after 45 minutes of heavy shooting.

Gunmen launched a series of hit-and-run attacks on mosques, radio stations and power plants across Tehran in a direct challenge of strength to the country's three-day-old Islamic government. The lightning raids were apparently launched by extreme left-wing elements.

Violence also erupted in the provinces, where more than two hundred people were killed in the last two days, when mobs identified as pro-Shah stormed the radio station in the northwest city of Tabriz and occupied it.

Khomeini, battling desperately to preserve his hand-picked Government and his revolution, called for a total end to strikes throughout the country by Saturday, including the country's vital oilfields. Political sources said the struggle between Khomeini's Government and left-wing elements would be crystallised

The new Iran ... Ayatollah Khomeini

in the response Khomeini received to his back-to-work order.

In Afghanistan, meanwhile, the US Ambassador was killed after he had been kidnapped yesterday morning by guerillas.

No statement on the Tehran Embassy incident has come from Ayatollah Khomeini or the Prime Minister of the provisional Government, Mehdi Bazargan. But both must be deeply concerned at their ability to exercise any authority over the thousands of gunmen now roaming the streets of the capital. A further test of Khomeini's authority will come on Saturday when he has ordered an end to the strikes that did so much to destroy the power of the Pahlavi dynasty.

The attack on the Embassy started at about 10.15 a.m. when gunmen came over the walls and gates of the compound in several places under supporting fire from rooftop snipers. As they dropped inside the compound they opened up with everything from G3 rifles to machine-guns, spraying the main Embassy building and other offices with bullets.

The Embassy's US Marine guard returned fire with bird-shot to give officials time to destroy secret documents and coding equipment, but were then ordered by the Ambassador to unload and discard their weapons.

The Embassy staff, about 100 to 150, were taken to the communications room on the first floor while marines filled the ground floor with tear gas. But this had only a temporary delaying effect.

Gunmen eventually broke into the Embassy, forcing many of the staff at gunpoint to lie on the floor. Others ransacked the East wing, broke up communications equipment and smashed the main switchboard. They left the Embassy virtually without communications and without electricity or water.

After the shooting died down, the Ambassador made contact with members of Khomeini's committee and requested assistance. But it was more than an hour after the attack had started before more gunmen sent by the committee arrived.

Mr Sullivan said later after his release that there were still "some" Americans unaccounted for who had been driven away earlier by the Khomeini forces of the original attacks.

Revolutionaries said they attacked the Embassy because an agent of the now-disbanded secret police, SAVAK, had stored secret documents in the compound and were also hiding there themselves.

FEBRUARY 15, 1979

1 9 8 0 | 1 9 9 0

NEEDS AND GREEDS

SALMAN RUSHDIE

BACK IN THE 1960s, when we were stardust and golden, John Lennon solved the riddle of history. "It's easy," he sang, "all you need is love." But the B–side of that anthem of togetherness hinted that human needs might occasionally be more self-centred. It was "Baby, you're a rich man."

In *The Needs of Strangers*, Michael Ignatieff's sprightly analysis of humanity in terms of its long felt wants, the opposition between love and selfishness — or to put it his way, between our need for solidarity and our needs as individuals — becomes the central issue.

He redefines it, variously, as a conflict between our "social" and "natural" selves; as an Augustinian dilemma — the freedom to choose, or the freedom that comes of knowing one has chosen "rightly"; or, politically, as the struggle between "actually existing socialism", under which liberty is sacrificed to solidarity, and capitalism, under which the individual retains freedom of choice. And he asks repeatedly: "Is there a form of society which could reconcile freedom and solidarity?"

OCTOBER 28, 1984

KEEP THE HOOLIGAN
JUICE COMING

GOODBYE TO RHODESIA

BY SIMON HOGGART

THE PROBLEM NKOMO or Mugabe will have to face if either becomes Prime Minister is possibly not the panic of the Whites or the sudden collapse of financial confidence but the brutal disenchantment of their own people.

Meanwhile the Whites continue to live in a style unimaginable here, but all too familiar to the shop assistants, garage hands and dissatisfied bourgeoisie who have made Rhodesia their home. Around the average Salisbury bungalow is three or four acres of rich land, thick with shrubbery, flower beds, rolling lawns, arboretums: so much greenery you feel you need a platoon of Gurkhas to hack your way through to the front door.

A team of servants irons the grass each morning as the sun rises over the sparkling pool. Later vast dragonflies zoom over the blue water like helicopter gunships as the host and his guests enjoy perhaps a "wine race" — swimming a length backwards while drinking a glass of wine (Rhodesian wine probably, which is awful. It is the only alcoholic drink to give you bilharzia) — or just pushing each other into the water. Then maybe a few glasses of "hooligan juice", a large slug of brandy mixed to a slush with a scoop of vanilla ice cream.

This is what they call civilization, and it is easy for us to mock: after all, they work hard and they have fought hard. It is impossible not to admire the way they have coped with sanctions, the way they have manufactured almost everything from tomato ketchup to armoured cars. Though the cause was perhaps not worth fighting — indeed did not need to be fought — we need not grudge them their mindless pleasures, pleasures we would hugely enjoy if we could.

I recall one faintly pathetic note being struck 150 miles or so north of Salisbury. A young man, just out of the army, asked if there was any chance that the British would stay behind to help the White Rhodesians fight if the settlement went horribly wrong.

I said (fairly) that there was no chance at all, and added — unfairly — that they could expect to see Lord Soames mount the aircraft steps on March 1, write the name of the new prime minister on a scratch pad, throw it on to the tarmac, slam the door and take off for England with a screech of engines.

"Ah, what style" said the young man. "When the British wash their hands, they use only the finest soap."

FEBRUARY 9, 1980

THATCHER'S MODERN ENGLAND

BY PETER JENKINS

[Extracts from a diary of a journey through Britain]

COVENTRY

I wake up to the news of the monthly unemployment figures. The familiar reassuring voice of Jim Prior tells us that it's going to get worse before it gets better. For the United Kingdom the average is now 10 per cent. In the West Midlands it is 11.3 per cent, in Birmingham 12 per cent and in Coventry 13 per cent. Coventry, the proverbial Klondike of the post-war affluent society — the idea of 13 per cent unemployment takes some getting used to. I've heard several people say already, "we're not used to recessions like this round here" or, "unemployment is a new experience for us." It's not quite true. In the last recession, 1975–76, unemployment in the West Midlands for the first time exceeded the national average. The decline of the motor industry, on which one in every six workers depends, has been going on for a decade or more. Rolls Royce had to be nationalised in the 1971–72 downturn, in 1975 British Leyland was taken over and Chrysler

baled out, but this time it's far worse. The most apocalyptic of the "de-industrialisation" schools of thought, the Department of Applied Economics at Cambridge, has predicted that because of its dependence on manufacture, especially metals and vehicles, the West Midlands by 1983 will have become the worst unemployment blackspot in England.

I switch stations. The local commercial station — "BRMB 261, right in the heart of the Midlands" — is running a feature called Lucky Breaks. The lucky break is a job vacancy for a teenager. Today's lucky lad can be an apprentice joiner. Hurry, hurry, hurry.

BIRMINGHAM

As I go I'm dipping into Priestley's *English Journey*. He came here to Birmingham in 1934 and wrote "It looked like a dirty muddle." Now it looks like a clean muddle. Some people don't like the city centre but I do. It reminds me of Chicago although that is to flatter it architecturally. It seems to me fitting that the capital of the motor industry should have re-designed itself around the motor

car. I like the violent irregularity of the skyline, the brash mixtures of old and new, and the confident equation of wealth and concrete. Birmingham is one of the few English cities to have completed its inner redevelopment before the party ended.

Priestley was neither the first nor the last traveller to write the premature obituary of the English class system. In the thirties he was as impressed by Woolworths as people were with Marks and Spencer in the sixties, seeing it as the symbol of a new democracy of consumers. He noted cinemas (of which Birmingham has some marvellously kitsch examples) and dance halls in the way that we note discos and steak houses. He remarked the advent of the buffet pub; now it is the wine bar which is taking over with all the young people drinking a drink called drywhitewine.

Our highest hopes for equality and for classless society were vested in education and for two decades the schools have been in a turmoil of reform. For teachers and children the process of reorganisation has been almost as disruptive as the collectivisation of the farms and a whole generation of pupils may have suffered in

the cause. Nor is the aggravation at an end; in Birmingham, like many other cities, the school rolls are failing and the secondary schools are increasingly unable to sustain viable sixth forms: economic logic dictates a third educational tier, the sixth-form college . . .

Birmingham is a city of metals and nostalgia. Wandering around Victoria Square and Chamberlain Square it is impossible not to feel its sense of civic self-importance. The buildings here are worthy and solid, no Gothic follies; the statues recall the golden age of enterprise. It is that vanished entrepreneurial world which Margaret Thatcher would like to restore and so would Neville Bosworth, the leader of the Conservative Group on the City Council. He has the voice of a Churchill although with a Brummagem accent and a similar squat bulldog-like appearance. His father was a district engineer with the municipal water department; he is a solicitor.

Who was Chamberlain? he asks me. Who were Guest, Keen, Nettlefold? Who was Austin? Local businessmen. Nowadays there were too many big combines and too few individual personalities. We needed to get back to the days when the governor knew all his people by name. The smaller the unit the better it could be managed. Under Mrs Thatcher there was a revival of small business taking place. Was there? "Yes," he assures me, "lots and lots of small businesses and I mean lots — are springing up, in spite of the recession, gaining momentum. Many of them are using the new technologies."

Where? I ask. What sorts of businesses? "All sorts, many kinds. Some employing ten or twenty, some only four or five."

Birkenhead. Fog has made us late. Now the sun is shining brightly.

Opposite the gates of Cammell Laird's is the Royal Castle Hotel. The original pub was built in 1640 but it was rebuilt in the Victorian manner in 1898. In a back room a dozen or so shop stewards are waiting for Frank Field, the local MP.

Because I'm going to be there — the press! — the Cammell Laird management has refused permission for the meeting to be in the yard. In the chair is a man called Gerry Reeves. He is vice-chairman of the stewards' committee. He is a strong and handsome Lawrentian figure of a man with a square-cut beard. On the table before him is a pint and the latest issue of the *Militant*.

LIVERPOOL

There is too much of past glory about Liverpool. The smell of the sea makes it worse. Economic decline is turning the place into a Carthage. There is little of Birmingham's throb here; the streets are dirty, the people look shabby and depressed. Past and present sit uneasily here. The city centre has an air of work suspended about it. The "T" has already fallen off the side of the St George's Hotel, a tatty piece of architecture to put so close to the St George's Hall and its adjacent cluster of magnificent neoclassical buildings.

Shades of the Labour Party too. It was here in 1964 that Harold Wilson held his great eve-of-poll rally and afterwards marched by torchlight back to the Adelphi. The cheering crowds that night wouldn't let him leave the balcony of his suite. The Adelphi Hotel is a deserted morgue of marble today. It was here in the early hours of October 16, 1964 that some of us opened a bottle of champagne for the new Prime Minister, the man who was going to build the New Britain.

FEBRUARY 17, 1981

FALKLANDS? MALVINAS? IT'S A WAR OF WORDS

THE LANGUAGE BARRIER

BY ALAN RUSBRIDGER

THE TROUBLE WITH this sort of thing is that you can so easily sound like Professor Colin McCabe. But it is interesting, is it not, to observe the kind of language being used — no names, no pack drill, but mainly in the *Sun* — to chronicle the unhappy goings on in the South Atlantic.

OUR BRAVE BOYS

Nothing terribly new about this. Paul Fussell, in his book *The Great War and Modern Memory*, drew up his own list of poetic and euphemistic language used in that conflict. A few examples: A horse was a "steed" or "charger"; to conquer was to "vanquish"; the front was the "field"; warfare was "strife"; to die was to "perish"; the army was the "legion"; the dead were the "fallen".

And so on. "This system of 'high diction'," commented Fussell, "was not the least of the ultimate casualties of the war."

He was being premature. The last few days have turned up a list just as impressive as Fussell's Great War catalogue, and the shooting has only just started. A few

examples: The Union Jack is "The Flag of Freedom"; the South Atlantic is "the cruel waters"; British soldiers are "our brave boys"; British commandos are "our tough guys".

BLASTED TO SMITHEREENS

The language is unashamedly discriminatory. British casualties tend to be the "price of victory", which doesn't seem to be true of Argentine casualties. Sea Harriers tend to be "lost" or "shot down"; while Mirages and Sea Hawks are, as a general rule, "blown out of the sky".

Argentine gun boats, by the same formula, are "blasted to smithereens" while British ships are generally "sunk". Britain's "brave planes" carry out bombing raids or strafe enemy ships; Argentine pilots, by contrast, embark on "desperate suicide missions" or carry out "merciless air onslaughts".

MAY 27, 1982

"THE ENEMY WITHIN"

BY PETER JENKINS

MY FRIEND LIVES in what is hopefully called Sunny Avenue, South Elmsall. The mining villages in this part of Yorkshire are strung together in small conurbations, never quite town or country. South Elmsall, South Kirkby, Upton, Hemsworth all merge into one another, eventually becoming part of Doncaster which is the capital of what sees itself as the most militant district of the Yorkshire coalfield.

As the villages sprawl together on the surface, their pits, Frickley (which belongs to South Elmsall) and South Kirby, meet underground. Yet they are separate worlds. The pit in Upton closed a few years ago. "Upton is a ghost town now," a miner's wife informed me. Her husband had transferred to Frickley from Upton. "You either have to move or travel," she said. Upton is all of two miles away.

Bill travels to work at Hickleton in Thurnscoe, which is four miles away. He is a colliery joiner. His wife Janet has a secretary's job in Doncaster. They both come from local mining families. Bill's brother is a police inspector in Sheffield who has been in charge of policing Cortonwood. Hickleton, which has a reputation as a left-wing pit, was the first to vote to support the Cortonwood men when the strike was triggered there in March.

At Hickleton it takes some 1,400 men to produce a bit under a million tonnes a year. It is the deepest pit in the locality and very hot down below; the men take salt tablets and work in four-foot seams. At the new super-pit at Selby 2,200 men can get 10 million tonnes a year. "If those are the economics of mining, where are all the men to go?" Bill asks.

The Coal Board calculates the cost of production at Hickleton at £123 a tonne which, if so, makes it a champion uneconomic pit. Bill disputes this. Like nearly all miners he is a great expert on his own pit. "This dispute hasn't happened overnight," he says. His economic history of Hickleton goes back over eight years, a story of investment starvation and manpower reduction. Management has made the pit uneconomic in order to close it.

There is not much point in trying to check the facts and figures. All the miners say much the same thing. They say it not because Arthur Scargill says it but because of what they

Enraged miners strike out

think is happening at their own pits. They would agree with Rousseau who said, "The nature of things does not madden us, only ill will does." They believe the policy of the Board and the government is to run down their pits and then sell off the good ones, such as Selby, to private enterprise.

What the government calls economics offends against what these miners call morality. The moral assumptions of Thatcherism are utterly repugnant to them. Working underground makes it seem self-evident to them that life is about mutual dependence. They set no store by economic individualism. Their saying is "good seams make good colliers."

The productivity bonus scheme is offensive to them because — they quote Scargill — "it sets men against men." Bill thinks it is right that low cost pits should help the others. He says, "This isn't just an argument between Arthur Scargill and Maggie Thatcher. It goes deeper than that. It is about the government being ready to help people because people are dependent."

At the Miners' Welfare Club old couples are dancing the Anniversary Waltz. Bill introduces me to some friends including local NUM branch officials. They are back from court in Pontefract giving evidence on behalf of pickets. If they were witnesses they had attended a mass picket, said the Stipendiary, and bound the lot of them over for "besetting".

They were full of complaints about the police and the media. Frank's children had seen the recent World in Action programme. "They wanted to know 'were you there, Dad?' They're going to think I'm some kind of law-breaker."

"His father's either a thug or television's wrong," said Roy.

Reg said, "I'm thirty-six and I've never been in trouble with police all my life. Now I'm the enemy within. Some kind of criminal. My kids know that's not me. So does my wife. They resent it."

Nothing is more resented, I discovered, than the Prime Minister's remark. A typical comment from a much older miner was "they didn't call us enemy within when we were digging for fucking victory." Margaret Thatcher's insult to the miners of Great Britain will not be soon forgotten.

DECEMBER 19, 1984

BOB GELDOF PROVES THE GOVERNMENT WRONG

THE LESSONS OF LIVE AID

BY HUGO YOUNG

GOVERNMENTS, NONE MORE than this one, believe their voters to be bottomlessly mean. They tend to take a dim view of people all round, but in the matter of giving aid to poor countries their estimation of what the public will stand for is at its lowest. This deep-seated cynicism is convenient. Construing itself to be free of any pressure, moral or political, to treat Third World poverty, starvation and death with anything approaching due seriousness, government has much more money to play with at home. As long as the rhetoric of aid was left to politicians, this was perhaps a true interpretation, it was, after all self-fulfilling. Against this background, however, the Live Aid concert was hardly a triumph, as the ministerial patter has felt obliged to say. Rather, it was terrifying, and Mr Bob Geldof is a prince of darkness. For it suggested that government assumptions over all these years are capable of being proved wrong.

Far from being mean, many thousands of people showed themselves extraordinarily generous. Together, they gave a vast sum for African famine. Individually, as their letters to aid agencies show, many altered their lifestyle in order to do so.

No doubt famine is a special crisis. Images of passive, helpless human beings evoke a straightforward response. And no doubt also the concert itself, a fantastic event, gave people something worth paying for. But Mr Geldof has exposed a telling paradox. The crisis which governments take least seriously is the one which, in certain circumstances, the people take most seriously.

For no other imaginable cause could a pop concert have raised £5 million in this country, or £50 million around the world. For not one single piece of self-improvement at home would it be remotely possible. Not for schools or hospitals, on which this Government tries hard not to spend too much.

A kind of magic ... Freddie Mercury

Certainly not for tanks or the police benevolent fund which, on behalf of the taxpayer and voter, it places at the top of its priorities. It is for the item at the bottom that this great outpouring suddenly occurred.

This is why Live Aid frightens ministers. It shows that public opinion can be galvanized — the very thing the politicians do not want to happen, as the present Government revealed in its earlier days. Its first act of butchery on the overseas aid budget was to cut the money spent on "development education" — i.e. on telling people how bad the problem is.

Presiding over this budget is Mr Timothy Raison. Beside Mr Geldof he cuts an especially pathetic figure. He is a good man, as Tories go. He would like the aid budget to be bigger. He speaks the language and understands the problems of development, and he has been to Ethiopia as often as any pop star. But he has no messianic presence, and no support in Government. He knows better than anyone how utterly at odds his budget is with the spirit of Wembley. Yet, under the curse of the politician, he must shuffle from airport to television studio defending it.

One place he would hardly have dared to do so was Wembley on Saturday afternoon. A truthful account of what has happened was the only thing that might have caused a riot at that signally joyous and peaceful occasion. Since 1979, the British aid budget has been cut, in real terms, by 18 per cent. I'll say that again. Eighteen per cent. In 1984 it was allotted 0.33 per cent of the gross national product, the lowest ever. In the current year the budget, which was being fixed just as the famine was first reaching the television screen, is 3 per cent less than it was last year.

With one exception, every emergency pound the government has given Ethiopia and the Sudan has been taken not

Bob Geldof succeeds where politicians fail and raises millions to help the starving in Ethiopia

from the defence budget or the motorway budget or the budget which buys pictures or refurbishes country houses or puts the finishing touches to the other essential artefacts of the British way of life. Nor did it cost the taxpayer an extra penny piece. Except for the cost of RAF planes distributing supplies, we paid Ethiopia by starving Tanzania or depriving Bangladesh.

Nor is that the end of the generosity which the politicians deem prudent. Most aid is tied, putting more stress on British jobs than on foreign improvements. Increasingly, from the United States but also from Britain, the aid is also tied by ideology. The colonialism of ideas, and especially of free-market economics, has replaced the colonialism of possession.

Further, there is the debt crisis. A small thunder-crack echoed through Whitehall this week, when Mr Peter Walker ventured to suggest that it might be better for all sides if the governments of the industrialised world found ways of writing off Third World debt — The sense of this proposal is equalled only by the certainty of it being rejected as eccentric. The Sudan will need at least $100 million of emergency aid this year. The Sudan has $237 million of debt repayments to make this year. Behind all the murmurings of horror from Western ministers, that irreconcilable absurdity, which is within their power to cancel out, stands.

One should not, of course, underestimate the complexity of the aid equation, or the pitfalls in wait for those who try to crack it. It is rather easier to put on a global concert and make £50 million than to ensure that it bypasses corrupt governments, overcomes horrendous transport problems and reaches those who need it — although the evidence is that Band Aid, working with established agencies, has followed through to good effect.

Nor can the invincible hostility of certain politicians be overlooked. Mrs Thatcher may feel it expedient, with quite

brazen hypocrisy, to trumpet Britain's record in being "first" into Ethiopia and the Sudan. But in her guts she sees aid supplicants as scroungers. At the Commonwealth Conference in 1983, Britain resisted all efforts to produce a serious collective commitment to any transfer of resources from north to south. Tanzania was advised to prove its worth by first adopting monetarist principles of economic management.

The anti-aid lobby, indeed, is gaining ground in establishment intellectual fashion. The Government is even attacked for giving too much. Lengthy disquisitions find easy newspaper space, contending that all aid is corrupt and futile. Far Left meets Far Right in a familiar, venomous compact of misbegotten ideas.

Most politicians, however, are not as bold as that. They pretend, at least, to care. They are expert producers of the clichés of compassion. But they make the people their excuse. They resemble the employer who says he would be overjoyed to take on more Blacks, if only the Whites would let him. More aid might well be desirable, says the better class of minister, but the democratic will of the people does not favour it.

This is the alibi on which Geldof casts doubt, the bluff which he has called. Live Aid was a political event. It has political repercussions, changing the agenda long set and most sedulously protected by professional politicians. It showed that their excuses were empty. Mountains could be moved, satellites could be deployed, performers could be mobilised, millions could at electrifying speed be raised — provided that the will to achieve all these things could be assembled.

Governments will die in the last ditch pretending this cannot be done. Geldof exposed the hideous truth: that they do not want to do it.

JULY 18, 1985

THE BIG BANG

CHAMPAGNE AND BMWS TO LURE CITY STAFF

BY MARGARETA PAGANO

HIRING A HELICOPTER to swoop down on the Alps to track down a wanted financial high-flier or delivering champagne with the doorstep milk to woo a star analyst are some of the more Bond-like devices used to lure top performers from rival City firms.

There's the bank which switched its entire fleet of six-month-old BMWs to Lamborghinis because that was the fancy of the incoming team of analysts just bought out at astronomical football transfer-fee prices.

Dual contracts offering payment both in the US and the UK, provided by foreign firms with London branches, have been commonplace in the City to avoid British tax. But now head-hunters are talking about triple or even quadruple contracts as a more sophisticated tax avoidance. Many banks and brokers offer the prospective recruit a tax consultant who is invited to sit down with the potential "remuneration package" — strip it — and put it back together again with all the latest loopholes man can devise.

Stories of incentives to persuade and devices to delight abound in the Square Mile which has never seen such a merry-go-round of poaching activity. In a matter of years the average salaries of City folk have at least doubled to catch up their peer levels in Tokyo and New York. London is still way behind Wall Street's millionaire numbers but there must now be a couple of dozen top international bankers who are pulling in the £1 million package for the pleasure of leading firms into the post Big Bang era.

Much of this has of course been fuelled by . . . the *"panier des crabes"* syndrome: bankers, brokers and dealers scrambling over each other in the mad dash to double salaries overnight by offering themselves — or teams — to rival firms. In the process they helped each other talk up salaries and perks over lunch tables (perhaps its breakfast now).

First, came a dizzy rush by UK and US firms to buy out the couple of dozen top Stock Exchange broking firms to tuck under their wings and build into new securities conglomerates. It was this phase which brought us the memorable "golden handcuff" which was just a method of ensuring that newly acquired partners stayed with the new firm for at least a year or so after he had stashed his pot of gold into farms in Gloucester or little hideaways in the sun.

Then came the turn of the "marzipan" layer — the men and women — just below partner level who probably made up the real skills of the firms. They had to be enticed to stay on — many with superb salary increases overnight and hefty bonuses.

Analysts, perhaps the real soothsayers of the latter end of the twentieth century, continue to be some of the most sought after individuals.

OCTOBER 22, 1986

SONG FOR THE SACRED LAND

THE SONGLINES REVIEWED

BY ANGELA CARTER

IT IS NOW common knowledge that the people who lived in Australia before the island continent was given that name never got around to inventing the wheel because they were too absorbed in metaphysics.

This could be seen as a positive argument against metaphysics, for the contemplation of the transcendental did not equip the first Australians sufficiently against the sudden arrival of technologically adept and ethically unscrupulous invaders. But Bruce Chatwin's expository novel *The Songlines* (Cape, £10.95), is both a defence of Aboriginal metaphysics as a way of life and a piece of metaphysical speculation in its own right.

Human beings, Bruce Chatwin posits, are born to wander; indeed, the source of all evil is to settle down. Appropriately, the form of his novel is that of a journey. Its hero, an Englishman named Bruce, travels into the magical area Australians call the Centre, in order, for compelling reasons of his own, to find out what a "songline" is. His guide is a wise young man of Cossack extraction called Arkady.

Arkady is employed to map out the sacred sites of the Aboriginals so that a proposed new railway line will not destroy a single one of them. This, as he points out, is difficult, because, "if you look at it their way . . . the whole of bloody Australia is a sacred site."

A sacred site, which the totemic ancestors — the grand, original wallaby, and budgerigar, and lizard and so on — once, literally, sang into existence, stone by stone, thorn by thorn; they sang into being that vast, dry, almost supernaturally beautiful country. A country which is continually being sung into existence again and again during the ritual journeyings, the walkabouts, of the tribespeople. (I hope I've got this right. It is all very complicated.) . . .

The searcher after songlines meets and talks with strange, learned, displaced men and women, among them a policeman whose passions are weight-lifting and Spinoza; a furious old bush-crazed Communist who gives an account of the atom bomb tests at Maralinga in the mode of Black farce; a naked philosopher of the bush who gives his occupation: "Footwalking all the time all over the world."

Footwalking is Bruce Chatwin's passion, too, and, in the course of nearly 300 pages, he investigates the significance not only of the songlines, that mythic and incorporeal map of Australia, but also of his own travels, especially those among the nomadic peoples of Africa, pulling everything together to form a grand theory of footwalking, and much more.

And all this springs from an obsession with what the Eskimo call "the Great Unrest", a conviction that human beings, just as birds do, feel an irrepressible urge, from time to time, to migrate, to slough off attachments, to get on the move and stay there.

More specifically, Chatwin conjectures that "Natural Selection has designed us — from the structure of our brain-cells to the structure of our big toe — for a career of seasonal journeys on foot through a blistering land of thorn-scrub or desert."

The narrative of Bruce's journey is interspersed with digressions such as a visit to a solitary priest who has carved above the door of his hut the apt legend: "Foxes have holes, birds of the air have nests, but the Son of Man had no place to lay his head."

When Bruce finally returns to his own narrative, it is to conclude with Arkady's wedding, but the true romance of this always enchanting, sometimes infuriating book is not that of Arkady and Marian but the one between an Englishman and the wilderness. The journey of the one within the other leads to the only happy ending the traveller can honestly aspire to, a happy death.

In the bush, Bruce and his companions visit three old men at a ritual site; they have sung their way back where they belong. Three old men who knew where they were going, "smiling at death in the shade of a ghost-gum."

JUNE 26, 1987

BLACK MONDAY

£50 BILLION WIPED OFF SHARE VALUES

A RECORD £50.6 billion rout on the London Stock Exchange yesterday was followed by a fall on Wall Street which far exceeded the 1929 crash.

But despite fears that the continuing collapse on Wall Street would force London shares even further down today, the Government said it would push ahead with the world's biggest share sale, the £7.2 billion BP offer.

On a day which made previous "Black Mondays" in the City look like minor hiccups, more than five times as much was wiped off shares as in the previous biggest fall, on August 6. The causes were fears about the dollar and the US trade deficit combined later with reactions to the American attack on an Iranian oil

platform in the Gulf. The attack caused a worldwide sell-off in stock markets, from Japan to New York.

At one stage the *Financial Times* Stock Exchange 100-share index was more than 300 points down, a greater percentage fall than the 12.8 on Wall Street on the day of the great crash in 1929. The New York Dow-Jones index fell by 22 per cent as President Reagan huddled in the Oval Office with his top advisers.

By the close in London, an only too brief lull in Wall Street's headlong plunge had brought the FT-SE 100 index back a little to close at 2,052.3, down 249.6 on the day and a fall of 10.8 per cent. One experienced dealer said "The bull market has been well and truly shattered." Senior government sources said that stock markets were volatile and what had happened yesterday was not justified on fundamental grounds. Ministers believed that the economies of the world were in "great shape".

OCTOBER 20, 1987

MRS THATCHER SERVES HER TIME

THE LONG RUNNING PREMIER

BY HUGO YOUNG

TOMORROW, MRS THATCHER becomes the longest-serving prime minister since Asquith. Not, strictly speaking the longest of the twentieth century. There is Salisbury still to beat. When he retired in 1902 he'd held the job, off and on, for thirteen and a half years. Mrs T will need to win another election and carry on until Christmas 1992 to pass Salisbury. . . .

Such longevity in office is a very large fact. Eight years and eight months. It's an achievement on its own, separate from its consequences. The consequences matter greatly. But the sheer length of it, in the friendless world of political leadership, deserves serious remark. A generation of opponents routed: a generation of rivals eclipsed: half a generation of voters upon whose consciousness no other prime minister has impinged. To my children, a male leader, royal or political, will come as an offence against nature. So this has been an extraordinary story. But we should disentangle the remarkable from the banal. In the Thatcher mythology, the fawning astonishment usually starts too early.

It was not extraordinary that she became a politician. On the contrary, this is what she was born to be. Her lineage and formation allowed of few other possibilities. Politics infused the atmosphere in which she was reared by her father, alderman and leading citizen of Grantham. The political life, with its parallel attractions of service and of power, was the only life set before her as a model superior to that of shopkeeping.

Thus far, she was in no sense an aberrant case. Her origins accorded closely with those of the majority of Conservative leaders. A political family handed down the tradition of political action from one generation to the next. Unlike some of her contemporaries, she may never have exactly imagined she was born to rule, or at least to be Prime Minister. But her father laid out the path of duty just as clearly as any grandee who placed his sons on the road to Parliament. Through Oxford and beyond, released by the alderman, his child never for a second deviated from this ambition.

Nor was it extraordinary that, once at Westminster, she should do well. Women had before. Ambition, diligence and her husband's wealth were duly rewarded. She was an opportunist who took her opportunities, and ascended the greasy pole unencumbered by obstacles of her own making, such as blind faith or awkward conviction. In Macmillan's government she did what she was told, in Heath's she acquiesced in every twist that circumstance made necessary.

Although the mythology allots her the part of affronted critic, silently fuming at Heath's corporatist and inflationary errors, the truth is more congruent with the normal pattern of ambition. She swallowed it all. A prudent careerist could do no other. Her mentor, Keith Joseph, has said that he "only become a Conservative in April 1974". He meant, of course, a nineteenth-century liberal. The timing of the Thatcher conversion, the prelude to leadership, was identical.

This is where the story at last became extraordinary. She was elected leader, in circumstances well known. It happened at a time when the Conservative Party needed careerist pragmatism to be supplanted by something else. She had no difficulty in adapting. So began thirteen years at the head of the party, and the eight years, eight months, which have ensured her, as nobody anywhere will dispute, a dominent place in any history of twentieth-century Britain.

That history will not be written for many years. The effect of the Thatcher era, for good and bad, will be a matter of argument never resolved to general satisfaction. And in explaining why it lasted so long, much must be attributed to highly adventitious factors such as the state of other people's politics and the state of the world, not to mention large doses of plain good fortune. But the personal contribution remains massively visible in the three relevant organisms: the country, the party, and herself.

It is in part a tautology to say that an eight-year leader personifies the country's mood. And after so long, one cannot perfectly distinguish the contributions of leader and of country to a common ambience. Did she bask in a receptive climate, or did she set the temperature herself? Equally far beyond the reach of a firm answer is how long the mood, whoever created it, will last. Only when the leader has gone can we see whether attitudes changed, or merely behaviour.

All the same, no leader can last this long unless she speaks for some deep national sentiments. Three seem particularly conspicuous in her case. British masochism saw her through the unemployment crisis. British bloody-mindedness took on and won the Falklands war. A shared Little Englandism has been the reliable guide to most foreign crises.

These are enduring British traits which this leader has tapped more simply and openly than any predecessor in any party. She has done the same thing in more particular ways. It is hard to think of a single important issue on which, whatever her government may actually have done, her personal attitudes are not populist and universally known to be so. On Europe, on the Bomb, on South Africa, on hanging, on culture, on intellectual life, on welfare scroungers, on union bosses, Maggie could rarely be accused of failing to speak, alas, for Britain.

In the same vein, she has changed some conventional assumptions: again, one may hazard, in conformity with deep national prejudices. In the old order, fairness, equality, the benign State and the dispersal of power were common shibboleths. Fairness has been displaced by success, social justice by the business imperative. This has not been without benefits. But the key quote, a shocking but truthful epitomé, was delivered to *Woman's Own* a couple of months ago: "There is no such thing as society", our leader said. It followed hard on a snort and drivel about caring, a phrase hastily withdrawn on the eve of the election, but immediately validated nonetheless.

So that is a first contribution to this long survival. To produce a stronger economy, she has appealed to some of the worst insticts of the British: insticts, however, which already existed. She articulated something new, but also stayed close to something already there. If Baldwin personified a national mood of quietism and complacency in the 1930s, Mrs Thathcer spoke with utmost eloquence for the materialism and self-interest of the 1980s.

Next there was the party. In eight years, age has not withered it nor custom staled its capacity to unite. Quite the opposite. Conservatives are more united after eight years than they were before the first began. This distinguishes the Thatcher party from most of its predecessors, especially the Liberal Party of HH Asquith himself, whose departure confirmed its disintegration. . . .

This is the product of formidable leadership. By dint of willpower, and consistency seasoned with well-judged deviations, the party's priorities have been remade and only a single Tory MP deserted to the Social Democrats.

And then there was herself. She was a big problem. Many people, looking at her eight years ago, doubted whether she could survive half the distance, not least because she was a woman, her one undoubted claim to historic uniqueness.

Instead, one can see more clearly that her sex has been a key to much that she has got away with, a positive aid to durability.

It has made policies easier to sell. A woman found it easier than many men might have done to persuade the country to take its medicine, to talk her way throiugh social outrage, to present her economic policy as a simple exercise in household management, running a balanced budget, not spending what you haven't earned etc etc.

It has made people easier to sack. No leader has sacked more ministers with less cause. Such ruthlessness was necessary, as she saw it, for the accomplishment of her mission. It has been visited upon scores of inconvenient presences, and somehow made more palatable by the lady's simpering complaints about how much she detests wielding the hatchet.

Finally, her sex has greatly helped the artifice of presentation. She does not mind being made up, and will do anything for the camera. Her reputation for honesty and directness, which is not false, masks an apparently artless guile. It complements the more admirable personal qualities: the forensic skill, the mastery of detail, above all else the inexhaustible enthusiasm for work which few men wanted to do for eight years (see Wilson and Macmillan), even when they had the chance.

Groping beyond Asquith for her place in Conservative history you can soon make some connections. But the resemblances seem much thinner than the differences.

Like Peel she was a provincial, but quite unlike him she despised consensus politics. Like Joe Chamberlain she hated her party aristos, and she still sustains the illusion of herself as some kind of belligerent outsider. But he would surely have scorned the narrowness of her nationalism.

She is interested in science, like Balfour, but hardly a ruminant philosopher. She would like to be Churchillian, but the embarrassing frequency with which she stakes this claim disqualifies her from the league. Besides, the nation has never loved her, nor ever will.

With Macmillan it is hard to see any similarities of either character or outlook. Heath, of course, ought to supply the umbilical connection. But apart from all their other ruptures, the very thing which seems to bind them, their humble origins, in fact most signally divides them. Where Heath spent his adult life escaping from his past, hers has been presented as the source of all political wisdom.

In his history of the party, Robert Blake writes of Disraeli: "At least there must be agreement that he remains the most extraordinary, incongruous, fascinating, fresh and timeless figure ever to have led the Conservative Party." One day it may seem right to withdraw at least some of those adjectives and reallocate them to Margaret Thatcher.

JANUARY 2, 1988

ANOTHER LONG LOOK BACK

THE REAGAN YEARS

BY ALEX BRUMMER

AS RONALD REAGAN journeyed triumphally from Texas to California in the closing hours of Campaign '88, tipping his Stetson to the crowds lining the streets for a glimpse of the Gipper on his last hurrah, it was plain that, whatever his failings, the American people are both forgiving and adoring.

More than any other modern President since John Kennedy, Mr Reagan has restored the ceremonial funcitons of the presidency. Although his popularity slipped during the Iran-Contra debacle, it is now back at its peak and the Reagan era is being hailed as one in which America found heart and confidence again. Although we have come to know over the years that everything sensible that Mr Reagan says is scripted, down to small talk with child visitors to the Oval Office, his engaging style of saying it, his natural sense of humour, and his goodwill always come through.

Intellectually, he has never left Hollywood. Even his own favourite nickname, the Gipper, based on his role as the ill-fated quarterback in the film Knute Rockne, All American, was culled from silver screen archives. As Mr Reagan formally handed the baton to Vice-President George Bush in New Orleans this August he used his famous catchphrase once again: "Win one for the Gipper."

Mr Reagan's record is likely to be debated by historians for years. There have been achievements: the INF [intermediate-range nuclear forces] treaty with Moscow; the moves towards settling conflicts in Afghanistan, Angola, and the Gulf; successful military operations in Grenada and Libya; the reduction of inflation and interest rates; and the longest period of sustained economic growth in the post-war era. In short, he has provided the agenda of peace and prosperity on which Mr Bush seeks the White House.

However, the roots of these accomplishments, particularly on the foreign policy side, are more tangled than the conservative fans of Mr Reagan would admit.

Moreover, economic prosperity has been built on a fragile base which means that young Americans may be required to pay the cost for generations to come with depressed living standards.

While American conservatives would argue that the US's new relationship with the Soviet Union was built on the firm defence policy of the Reagan team and on the modernisation of the strategic triad of the intercontinental MX missile, the Trident 2 submarine and the B-1 bomber, together with research on Star Wars, critics might argue that he was simply lucky.

He was the American President who happened to be in office when the most important changes in the Soviet Union since the revolution were set in motion. There could have been no INF deal without Mr Gorbachev as there could have been no movement on Afghanistan or Angola without the newly elevated Soviet President's contribution. However, Mr Reagan's conservative credentials enabled him to achieve the extraordinary rapprochement with the Soviet Union more easily than might have been possible for a Democratic President.

But whereas Mr Reagan has been reasonably successful in managing big-power relations, he has often failed in his dealings with the little countries. He began his presidency with the return of the fifty US diplomats held in Iran. But he has nothing to compare in the Middle East to the Camp David accord won by President Jimmy Carter. In Lebanon he was forced to retreat after the loss of 241 marines.

His amateur attempts at freeing hostages in Iran brought the greatest crisis of his presidency — the Iran-Contra affair.

Mr Reagan has had good fortune with the economy. After the oil price shocks of the 1970s he came to office when an age of cheap energy was just beginning. This, together with the firm grip on monetary policy imposed by Mr Paul Volcker of the Federal Reserve — the other towering American figure of the 1980s — meant that the spiral of ever-higher inflation and interest rates was broken.

Under the guise of supply-side economics, the movement born in California where resentment of high taxes was at its peak, Mr Reagan built prosperity on an old-style Keynesian boom. But instead of using the fat years of prosperity to pare back the deficits and federal debt he allowed them to burgeon, creating a domestic debt legacy of $2,100 billion — or 43 cents for every dollar of US income — which will take generations to eliminate.

Moreover, the value of the dollar became caught up in the nationalist burst which Mr Reagan brought to the presidency, sending it soaring to new heights on the international markets and pricing US goods out of competition.

The result was a decline in basic heavy industry and agriculture and a foreign investment and takeover binge in the US which has created a bizarre value system. The Ivan Boesky affair and the Michael Deaver lobbying scandals provided grim evidence of a society which had abandoned self-discipline and a value system out of kilter. It has also given rise to a fierce strand of economic populism, and potentially isolationism, should the next Administration begin the long task of correcting fiscal and trade imbalances.

The darker side of the Reagan legacy is already being explored in popular books such as Landslide by the reporters Jane Mayer and Doyle McManus; Day of Reckoning by the Harvard economist Benjamin Friedman; and Rendezvous with Reality by Murray Weidenbaum, the former Reagan chief economic adviser. Such works, written even before the old campaigner has ridden off to the sunset years at his ranch, lack the perspective history will bring. President Truman left office widely despised: in the 1988 campaign he was the President whose name was most invoked by both parties as the epitome of fighting American values.

NOVEMBER 9, 1988

TIANANMEN SQUARE

THE HORROR OF A PEOPLE ATTACKED BY ITS OWN ARMY

BY JASPER BECKER

IT WAS ONLY by the time we arrived at Fuxingmen Bridge, the last bridge in the west before the city centre, and heard the steady crackle-crackle of small arms fire and the intermittent thud-thud of heavy machine guns that the enormity of what was happening dawned on us.

It was 1 a.m. and in the warm June night air the usual crowd in vests and summer skirts were waiting on the flyover crossing the second ring road.

Before we took the scene in, a plump middle-aged woman was carried through the crowd. She was shaking with shock with a large gash across her forearm, and was bundled into a taxi. As the gunfire approached, the crowd behind became frantic and started ramming six articulated buses across the road into the hedgerows on either side.

Until then a tour of the suburbs had revealed the by now usual and farcical attempt by the army to enter. Out in the east towards the airport a few platoons of troops in battle-dress were shepherded by an excited crowd into barracks.

Swinging west along the third ring road, we found more convoys but now also signs of violence or force. The mood was sombre and edgier than it had been a fortnight ago when the soldiers had first come.

But even on Saturday afternoon there were ominous signs of the terror to come. Tiananmen Square was the usual spectacle of red flags blowing gaily, but behind the Great Hall of the People a thousand troops were surrounded by a jeering crowd and the mood was ugly. Occasionally a student emerged holding aloft a captured helmet or showing off a bloody wound.

Littering the street towards Fuxingmen were half a dozen smashed-up army trucks or buses. Troops were trapped in one. Another was crammed full of gear and an AK-47 machine-gun had been erected on top as an exhibition. The stream of cyclists drifting up and down were in high spirits, but there was an air of hysteria.

At around 2 p.m. police loudspeakers had warned the crowd it was illegal to steal equipment from the People's Liberation Army, amid announcements that the troops would not use force but were there to protect the people.

Then eight hundred riot police stormed out of Zhongnanhai, the leadership's compound, firing tear gas and laying about them with clubs. The mêlée lasted half an hour and the police left.

Later, by the square, more troops were hemmed in a crowd by the Revolutionary History museum. Students with 'V' for victory T-shirts led the troops and onlookers in singing the Internationale.

Then at 7 p.m. troops began pouring in. Forty trucks pulled into the eastern approach to the square just by the main diplomatic compounds and were stopped again. The soldiers clutched their guns and twisted nooses in their hands as they were loudly berated by angry grandmothers.

Leading them were trucks of toughs in plain clothes with yellow hardhats, wooden clubs and iron bars. They were surrounded by a crowd of five hundred and several were almost beaten to death as they tried to escape. Unaware of this, diplomats brought their families out to watch the troops.

All of this had failed to give us an intimation of what was in store. As the gunfire at Fuxingmen came closer, we began to run back in fear as the crowd began to set fire to the buses.

A tyre on our jeep had been slashed, but we rumbled down the street dodging in and out of the road barriers until we arrived at the Minzu Hotel, where an angry band of youths stormed our jeep, hurling stones and rocking us until we established our identity.

We dashed across to the hotel entrance, where a crowd was savagely beating a soldier. Another had found safety in the hotel and the crowd was trying to smash the doors. A police car was burning nearby.

The road was littered with broken glass and bricks. Just before, a detachment of riot police had been attacked, and the air was thick with tear gas and smoke.

The sound of gunfire and explosions grew closer and we tried to get into the hotel, finally finding a back entrance.

Chinese students demonstrate in Tiananmen Square

First, a tank came past, then a dozen armoured personnel carriers, followed by hundreds of trucks from which troops fired constantly.

The crowd melted away but there were constant tracers and sparks as bullets ricocheted across the road. Some of the bullets were just "firecrackers", but others left holes in the lobby or dining-hall windows. Lines of soldiers with clubs followed the trucks and buses.

On the truck stood a soldier cradling a machine-gun. Some trucks were adorned with red banners saying, "the army loves the people".

From a window we could see shadowy figures flitting through the dark hurling stones, and after an hour the last trucks moved down. One man siphoned off petrol from our jeep and hurled a Molotov cocktail, setting himself on fire.

Others smashed open the cars, including ours, trying to find transport to carry the wounded away. Later we found blood drying on the pavement, smeared across the car doors and drawn into circles under the hotel's revolving doors.

When the last truck had vanished towards the square, the crowd emerged clutching stones and sticks and moved off in pursuit.

Gradually the chants of "Tu Fei, Tu Fei" — the old nationalist cry of "Communist bandit" — grew louder and louder. Then they stopped and men in tears began singing the Internationale. People tore down the red pro-government banners draped down the sides of the hotel and burned them.

More and more wounded were being taken to hospital nearby. We went to the small People's Hospital and it looked like an abbatoir. There were bodies on benches and beds or on blood-soaked mattresses on the floor. Many had gaping bullet wounds on the chest, legs, or head.

A doctor, voice hoarse with emotion, told us that three hundred wounded had come in.

"Most were so bad we sent them elsewhere. There were 35 seriously wounded and seventy others. Four have died,

including a nine-year-old girl shot through the throat," he said.

Students had rescued badly beaten soldiers and we saw one covered in blood who was clearly not going to live.

It was the same story at the nearby post office hospital. I began to feel sick. Another doctor said twelve people had died under his hands; out of three hundred injured, thirty had died. There was not enough blood, and many bled to death as the exhausted staff could only operate three times in an hour. He thought fifty had died in every one of the twenty major hospitals in the capital.

The horror only worsened as we stood outside the hotel and people told us more and more stories. At the central post office, a journalist from the state news agency had been beaten to death, a family had died in their homes by stray gunfire, another man in his bathroom, a girl by a tear gas shell as she looked out of her window; four police had been dragged out of their car and beaten to death.

Students had been bayoneted to death, others had set fire to two armoured personnel carriers and trucks, tanks had crushed to death eleven students who had left the square and were lagging behind the others, more students had been crushed to death in their tents. People showed us huge shells, six inches long and half an inch in diameter, as well as .303 bullets.

"How could the Communist Party do this? How could they shoot children?" asked a worker in blue overalls. Others pleaded with us to tell the world what happened. The West must stop all investments, they said, and condemn their government. No one, not even the Japanese or the Kuomintang or the warlords, had ever done this and this was their own government. But many were mute with horror. Nobody could find the words.

"All we wanted was some democracy," said a student who had been whipped across the face, his shoulders shaking with anger.

JUNE 5, 1989

Viel Glück + Frieden für
ein neues Deutsch-
Ost-grüßt-West Land

THE FALL OF THE BERLIN WALL

ALL TO HAIL, AND ALL TO PLAY FOR

BY ANNA TOMFORDE AND MICHAEL FARR

THEY CROSSED THE border with incredible joy, amazement, tears and good humour. They sang and sparkled, above, below and beside the Berlin Wall. It was one of those very rare, absolutely electrifying, moments when the ordinary lay people take over and all the professionals — from prognosticators to border guards — get quietly out of the way. From the sidelines we should now be thinking big, electric thoughts about a future where so much, as yet barely definable, is possible. Germany is a country on the verge of reunification in spirit — never mind too much yet about the jurisdictional details. Something will take shape, probably closer to confederation than a total merging of frontiers and institutions. The process under way simply sweeps aside the natural hesitations of history (from Mr Gennadi Gerasimov yesterday in Moscow to the ex-army paper-seller up the road) about seeing one Germany once again. It also sweeps aside, with only a touch-wood percentage of remaining doubt, any real chance of tanks or troops or anyone else standing in the way. The victims of Beijing died so that everyone else would realise that this is now the unacceptable and dead-end alternative.

The crumbling of the Berlin Wall also signifies definitively, beyond the powers of any assemblage of international strategists to deny, the end of the superpowers' cold war in Europe. Those flickering black and white images of the Berlin airlift can go back to the film archive room. Europe has emerged from the post-war transition which was no less transitional for lasting over four decades. The long-obvious truth is now openly revealed. Politics, internal and external, not weapons, kept Europe divided. Counting missiles and armoured personnel carriers was never a more mature exercise than collecting train numbers. Our own former Defence Secretary, Mr George Younger, seen briefly yesterday going on about the "absolute preponderance" of Soviet troops in Europe, needs to take a deep breath and have a word with his American friends, who have themselves fallen into reflective silence. Anyone who now proposes to modernise short-range nuclear weapons should have his (or her) head examined. Does anybody currently believe in any conceivable scenario which would set the Warsaw Pact in motion, or the Soviet army on its own? If the Wall can come down, so can the alliances. Perhaps it will need a deal of tact, and tactical redeployment of generals without jobs. But we should start the advance planning for the decommissioning of the deterrence machine now. And it would be sensible to do it together, in bilateral pact discussions. Indeed it may be prudent for the European chunks of the alliances to get together at the double, before they find themselves abandoned by the superpowers who — from Moscow or Washington — may see the point of commitment in Europe transformed overnight into a negative asset.

There is no denying that the centre of European gravity is going to shift as a result of the German earthquake. No one can be quite sure that some new fault line will not appear. It is very important not to encourage, in appearance or reality, a situation where East Germany simply joins "the Western camp". That would be to create a fresh imbalance — another reason why the dissolution of one monolith must be accompanied by that of the other. It would be the surest way of providing Mr Gorbachev's critics — apparently at the moment disarmed like everyone else by the speed of events — with destructive ammunition. The Soviet Union (unlike, we should note, the US) has always insisted that it is a European power, and will be rightly alarmed if a new Germany merely enlarges the other Europe. It is preferable to see (and we can hardly prevent) the re-emergence of a Germany linked to the rest of Europe, but essentially its own arbiter. Since that was the sovereign role we deliberately created for West Germany, we can hardly deny it now to the East as well.

There are shadows in many minds; of course there are shadows. But West Germany, over forty years, has developed the most prudent of democratic credentials, the most wise and cautious of voting patterns. Germany with its entirely new human face is the formidable economic power on the European — and world — scene. If reunification is a challenge, it can only be met by more and wider European cooperation. As the horizons enlarge, even 1992 begins to appear a somewhat limited concept which will move sharply down the agenda in Strasbourg next month. Looking even further ahead (but if ever there was a stimulus to vision it is now) we begin to understand the potential behind the idea of Mr Gorbachev's common European home. A Europe where national rivalries are subsumed by economic co-operation, where military budgets are cut to ceremonial levels, where the wealth is at last available not only to tackle long-neglected evils at home but to pay for a genuine fight against poverty, injustices and ecological disaster in the rest of the world.

NOVEMBER 11, 1989

1990 | 1999

THE STATE WE'RE IN

WILL HUTTON

LIKE A RUSSIAN doll, the task of reform has many layers. We need employment, which requires more capital stock and higher investment, which will be the most effective instrument for the social objective of bringing the marginalised back into the fold. And that in turn will involve the redistribution of income, perhaps even of work. Yet all these measures depend upon a recognition that rights . . . must be accompanied by responsibilities. Without lower consumption there can be no investment for the future; without taxation there can be no infrastructure of public support from which all benefit.

Corrective economic and social policies and institutions that embody them presuppose a system of values; and that demands a political constitution in which public values and common interests can be defined.

This implies nothing less than the root and branch overhaul of the Westminster version of democracy. If markets require boundaries and rules of the game, they must be set by public agency – but if such intervention is disqualified by the belief that any public action necessarily fails, then the initiative cannot even reach first base. The state must act to assert common purpose; but unless the state enjoys legitimacy and expresses the democratic will, it can make no such claim.

JANUARY 21, 1995

THE RELEASE OF NELSON MANDELA

A MAN WHOSE TIME HAS COME AT LAST

BY DAVID BERESFORD

IT WAS 4.16 p.m. South African time on Sunday, February 11, 1990, when he finally came out of prison twenty seven years, six months and six days after he was captured in the little town of Howick, supposedly betrayed by a CIA agent.

As it happened, the timing was all wrong. President F. W. de Klerk had promised he would be out at 3 p.m., so he was one-and-a-quarter hours late. Which, when you think about it, is a little strange for a man who must have been longing to get the hell out of it for more than a quarter of a century. But then that was just one small element in a surrealistic day and, besides, he was having a cup of tea in the prison with his family.

But by the time Nelson Mandela made that magnificent, if fleeting appearance at the gates of Victor Verster prison the air was electric with all the waiting and the excitement. The press had been there in growing numbers from about 8 a.m.

Others were gathering as well; a crowd of well-wishers swelling to some two thousand who danced and sang their way through the day.

There were about a hundred uniformed police standing at the prison gates; a few dozen loitering under pine-trees on an adjoining rugby field; two truckloads overlooking the scene from a mountainside; groups of plain-clothes men in surrounding vineyards and troops in nearby bushes.

The end of the long wait was heralded, inevitably, by the networks when four of their helicopters, tipped off by radio, came hurtling over the hills and went zigzagging over the ground like an angler's floats signalling a shoal of hooked fish.

In this case it was a joint catch and as realisation dawned on the waiting crowd that it was Mr Mandela's car they were tracking, on its way from his prison bungalow, the shouts and cheers reached hysterical proportions. The car drew up and he stepped out to give a clenched fist salute before taking the hand of his radiant-looking wife, Winnie, and advancing towards the gates 10 yards away, which symbolised freedom. The photographers stampeded and jumped upon each other with the air of desperation born of the fond belief that fame and fortune lay in a clear shot of Nelson Mandela.

After shaking a few hands their target made a strategic retreat to his car and was whisked off in what was just one of the strange sights of yesterday: the "desperate criminal" and "bloodthirsty terrorist" of yesteryear protected by motorcyle police with all the pride of a presidential escort.

They took the back roads to Cape Town where Mr Mandela was to address a rally which was a pity, because the 50 kilometres of the national road from nearby Paarl to the mother city was lined by well-wishers waiting to glimpse the living legend.

When the cavalcade reached the city it found a huge, seething crowd of sixty thousand gathered on the Grand Parade in front of the city hall. On a porch under a huge ANC flag the two anti-apartheid clerics, the Reverend Frank Chikane and the Reverend Allan Boesak, had urged patience as the hours passed. The heat in the middle of the crowd was almost unbearable, even in the evening. Fainting youths were passed over heads and hauled up to the podium for air.

A water main was broken open and people scrambled for handfuls of water. On the edge of the parade ground the crowd surged now and then to the thud of gunshots as police in adjoining streets fired at alleged looters.

In one corner a mobile medical clinic tended the injured lying on stretchers, some of them children.

The crowd waited on, heedless, for the man. And then suddenly he was there, to a bellow of welcome. Gaunt in his grey suit and donnish in spectacles, he read his prepared speech, concluding by recalling his speech at the Rivonia trial so long ago: "I have fought against White domination and I have fought against Black domination. I have cherished the ideal of a democratic and free society in which all persons live together in harmony and with equal opportunity. It is an ideal which I hope to live for and to achieve, but if needs be, it is an ideal for which I am prepared to die."

Then the crowd broke into the hymn, Nkosi Sikelele i'Afrika, and the waiting was forgotten in the moment: Nelson Mandela had returned to his people.

FEBRUARY 12, 1990

MRS THATCHER HEADS BACK TO THE PAVILION

BY MELANIE PHILLIPS

AND SO NOW they're all chaps together again. The captain has been bowled middle stump while attempting to hit the ball out of the ground. Cricketing metaphors can be rescued from uncomfortable female appropriation. The masculine ethos of public life can reassert itself untroubled by this vexatious business of coming to terms with a woman in power; a woman, moreover, who refused to be a gentleman. For whoever wins the Tory party leadership, whoever wins the next general election, it will now be men fighting each other by the rules of a game they all understand.

If she'd been a man, she would never have got away with half of it; she understood this and played it for all she was worth. Her gender was the supreme weapon with which she wrong-footed her cabinet, the Opposition and the media, producing the extremes of drooling sycophancy and spineless wimpishness in a world of public affairs where a woman who stepped outside the role men expected her to play left them effectively emasculated . . . .

The misogyny which greeted her appointment as Conservative leader has not disappeared but has been coated by a thin veneer of respectability. The arguments against Mrs Thatcher's policies and style have been inextricably bound up with the confused hostility provoked by her gender.

It has been said that she was the most extraordinary Prime Minister Britain has had. It is probably nearer the mark to say that the profound effect she had upon national life was due rather more to the extraordinary reactions she provoked among those around her.

NOVEMBER 23, 1990

A MARCH ON THE MILD SIDE

REJOICE IN VICTORY! we were once adjured. But there was very little of that in the City of London yesterday as the boys from the Gulf got their welcome home. It was a gentle, muted occasion — beneath the sort of lowering skies which suspended missions over the Mansion House just as they had suspended them over Iraq. In every respect, that seemed aptly judged. No tickertapes and weeping presidents and whooping patriotism. The troops were led by a notably thoughtful soldier, Brigadier Patrick Cordingley. They were glad to have acquitted themselves with high efficiency. But their thoughts were also with those few on their own side who died; the thousands upon still uncounted thousands amongst their out-gunned adversaries who perished; the Kurds in the north and the refugees in the south, huddled in apprehension; the returning strut of Saddam; and, maybe, the squat figure of Kuwait's Crown Prince on the rostrum, saluting the return of freedom with a new law which allows his government to deport without trial any foreigner alleged to have committed a driving offence. A long parade of thoughts.

This was a different kind of war: co-operative effort for a purpose. The narrow aim was to return Kuwait to the Emir. The broader aspiration, pavilioned in adjectives, was to help create a better world. Any present accounting would be of narrow victory and broad failure. There is no glowing Middle East peace process. There is no golden enhancement of UN authority (rather, dismay at its bureaucratic nit-picking).

There is nothing yet you could call democracy in the Gulf. There is Saddam. There is unchartable misery to come for his citizens and his shattered country. Few, in truth, expected a new dawn once the guns fell silent. But even those who expected little must be sadly disappointed.

Nothing of this reflects on the troops who marched yesterday with some dignity. They were professionals assigned to a specific task, and proud in its accomplishment. But the dignity of the occasion, all of a piece with British reflections in the wake of war, makes a creditable study in contrasts. Britain's political leadership, declining to rejoice, gained no lasting garlands: the khaki was already threadbare before the word "election" could be whispered. America's leaders, meanwhile, are bathed in continuing glory and much triumphalism. They rejoice perpetually: they have defined military victory alone as a line under the affair, seeking to shut out the cries for help of those left behind. That is, to some extent, understandable: exhausted reaction after vast effort. But it is also the line of failure drawn. The Gulf, at this point, is only a defining event in that it defines American attitudes towards the wider role its rhetoric hails. That stance lacks stamina. Its attention span is perilously short; its need to declare an end and move on intense. There is no new world order in any of this. And that, down the damp streets of the City yesterday, was perhaps the abiding memory.

JUNE 21, 1991

ENTER YELTSIN, EXIT GORBACHEV

FAREWELL TO THE SOVIET UNION

BY MARTIN WOOLLACOTT

THE TWENTIETH CENTURY came to an end at 7 p.m. Moscow time on December 25, 1991. The moment when Mikhail Sergeyevich Gorbachev, the last leader of the Soviet Union, ceded place to Boris Nicolayevich Yeltsin, the first ruler of the new Russia, seems a marker of far more importance than any on the horizon eight years from now.

It is as if the business of our century is over ahead of the calendar. The two enormous conflicts which have characterised it, that between Capitalism and Communism, and that between the old empires and the new powers — struggles that have interacted through the decades — have ended. "Bolshevism," as Winston Churchill in 1918 imperiously demanded it should, has finally "committed suicide."

The other great fight, that between the Anglo-Saxon powers and the newcomer states of Germany and Japan, has terminated with it. The Soviet Union's eclipse has been the basis for Germany's emergence as the main European power: without it Germany's renaissance after the disaster of the Second World War would have remained incomplete. As for Japan, America's industrial decline and the end of the Cold War has created the space in which the post-1945 renewal could be rounded out into real power.

Of course, certain facts remain unchanged. The Russian empire is, from one point of view, the last old empire to disappear, going the way of the British and French empires, its allies in two world wars. Yet those maritime domains were essentially different from Moscow's land empire, which in some sense will continue.

The struggle between Boris Yeltsin and Mikhail Gorbachev was often perceived as an ideological contest —

between a nationalist and an internationalist, between an ex-Communist and a Communist. This was overdone. Both men were ex-Communists, but one was in a position to repudiate the party and the past more completely than the other. And both believed that Russia's historic influence over neighbouring peoples ought to be preserved, but Yeltsin could offer a more neutral and hence more acceptable version of union.

The struggle was something else as well — an epic, perhaps a tragic, contest between two men of utterly incompatible temperaments. For Gorbachev, Yeltsin was impetuous, wilful, a bully boy, the ultimate wrecker. For Yeltsin, Gorbachev was the "lover of half measures and half steps", who wished to appear as a "wise, omniscient hero" but who was in fact a devious manager and manipulator of men.

Yeltsin has now harried Gorbachev from office; yet those who criticise should remember Yeltsin's own humiliation in 1987, dragged from a hospital bed to be abused and cast into the political wilderness. In the hour of Yeltsin's revenge it is worth recalling what he wrote in his autobiography: "Our huge country is balanced on a razor's edge and nobody knows what will happen to it tomorrow." That is as true today under Boris as it was under Mikhail.

Yet, in saluting Mikhail Gorbachev, a man to whom we all have reason to be grateful, we have at the same time to accept that after the coup the division of power in Russia between two rival leaders and governments was unstable. That dualism was dangerous — one man had to win, and Gorbachev had to be the loser. Russia is a safer place, and the world with it, because that rivalry has ended.

DECEMBER 27, 1991

ESCAPE FROM SARAJEVO

THE DEATH OF JORDI PUYOL

BY MAGGIE O'KANE

JORDI HAD HIS doubts on Sunday morning. He wanted to leave. At 12.10 on Sunday afternoon a mortar bomb dropped out of the sky like a shot putt and killed him.

He was from Barcelona, 25 years old and wore his thick black shiny hair in a ponytail. It was his first job and he told his friend, Santiago, who had a bit job with Associated Press, that he wanted to be a war photographer. His newspaper had put up $1,000 for the trip. $100 for each picture. His last picture was a shot of a man fishing in the river in the centre of Sarajevo with a burnt-out building rising above.

MORTAR BOMB

The mortar bomb came as mortar bombs do in Sarajevo, falling out of the sky from no particular place with no particular logic except terror. David Brauchli, the 27-year-old photographer, had a bullet-proof vest. Jordi had none.

"Fuck, I've been hit," he said. "The blood is coming out of my chest."

David crawled into a doorway with shrapnel in his groin and leg. "Help us," he shouted.

Jordi died quickly, losing consciousness on the pavement. David Brauchli was operated on immediately and sur-

vived. The city had been under blockade for six weeks and the hospital had run out of oxygen so there was no general anaesthetic. The local anaesthetic did not work as it should so the nurses tied his hands to the edge of the operating table.

The men in the beds beside him and the nurses kept asking: "When is the Sixth Fleet coming to help us?"

On Monday they took Jordi's body to the mortuary and laid him down beside a woman who had turned black. "These days people just can't get to the hospital to collect their dead," his doctor said . . . .

In the end we took the coffin in . . . [a] . . . civil servant's chugging blue Zastava, laying the rough brown chip-board from the passenger seat into the back of the car. At 2.30 p.m. a Catalan journalist, Eric Hanck, pulled away from the Belvedere Hotel on a twelve-hour journey from Sarajevo to the coast with the naked body of his dead photographer and friend, Jordi Puyol, wrapped in plastic and sprayed with formaldehyde.

On the road out we passed the burnt-out trams in Titova Street, where the corpses of nine soldiers had rotted for four days, then passed the crossroads and the burnt-out electrical switching station. On the road from the city the first of the

women and children from the children's convoy trying to escape from the city were turning back. They knew it was hopeless.

She was in her middle thirties with two children walking back to the city along the main road in the rain. She had two brown-paper bags and the children were carrying blankets that dripped on to the wet pavement. The children's convoy had been stopped at the Serbian militia checkpoint.

NO WAY OUT

There were 3,500 women and children in the convoy. The mile-long queue would wait all day in the rain to be turned back as night fell. In the back of each car were children sitting amid bursting suitcases. Round the cars the Serbian militia in blue uniforms and green camouflage carried Kalashnikovs and strolled up and down past their little hostages.

It took twelve hours to get to the coast. Tony Smith of the AP in a smashed-up car led us through the checkpoint saying: "We have one wounded and one dead." The coffin was our passport.

MAY 21, 1992

HEIRS TO HEARTBREAK

THE REAL CASUALTIES OF THE ROYAL SPLIT

BY LOUISE CHUNN

THE PICTURE ON the cover of yesterday's *Guardian* was a sad sight for anyone. But for a parent whose children have had to endure a marital split, it was a heartbreaker. As their mother, the Princess of Wales, drove them back to boarding school, Harry, 8, stared vacantly out of a rain-splashed car window, while 10-year-old William looking suddenly older, the way kids do — had his hand to his mouth and his head bowed, in a pose not unlike his father, the future King of England.

So, what about the children? In the rush to damn the royal former partner for one sin or the other . . . it's very easy to forget that there are two boys who are old enough to read the headlines too. Any of the dozens of books stacked high on the self-help shelves of your local bookstore will tell you that breaking up a marriage is hard to do "properly". And if you get it wrong, they pull no punches about just how screwed up the children can be.

Feeling the eyes of the world, and its press, on them during the dismantling is not going to help in trying to achieve the recommended civilised separation. But if the differences of Charles and Diana were what split them apart — he dour and self-obsessed, she flighty and "modern" — their views of how to bring up their children together were likely to cause much the same problems as they will now they live apart.

So while the body language of that sad little snap said a lot yesterday, the clothes that these two boys are dressed in has been telling us all the truth for years. We didn't have to wait for the leaks and tapes; any self-respecting royal-watcher should have known it was all over for the tweed-bound Charles when the kids started wearing baseball caps and trainers. Rather than get together in their father and son Simpsons tracksuits (potbellied Homer for dad, radical dude Bart for Wills and Harry) to kick around a football in the back garden, Charles and his boys have never been seen looking "natural".

In the dark days of the Second World War, the British got a lift out of knowing that the little princesses were just perfectly behaved and more expensively dressed versions of their own progeny. But nowadays the princes, when photographed in the presence of their father, look as though they are from a different age. They wear jackets and white shirts and ties. They wear proper trousers and funny hats. They wear shoes you have to polish, with laces you have to do up.

Mum's the with-it one. She knows what kids like. It's what other kids like, and television dictates. Diana's perfectly happy to kit them out in American sportswear — naff slogans, lurid colours and all. Partly, it's because of her youth. She is, after all, a great deal closer to their ages than Charles, and her own upbringing, for all its privilege, must have been groovier than his. (Whose wasn't?) But she also appears to be prepared to enter into the world that children inhabit. Charles does not. So while she took them to one of those massive amusement centres off the M25, he took them shooting. The two activities lie at the opposite edges of a child's universe. The modern is not necessarily better than the traditional; but they are hugely different . . . .

If they each use their children to express their obvious dislike of each other, they make it impossible for the children to be loyal to both parents without acrobatic changes on the trips between Kensington Palace and Highgrove.

No one wins in this battle, least of all the kids. If Charles and Diana consult the self-help books, they'll read that divorce is not an end to couples compromising, but only the beginning. Such advice may not apply when considering the much more political position of royal children from broken homes who stand to inherit the crown — but they should.

JANUARY 14, 1993

RWANDA: NEVER FORGET

THE LIES THAT FOLLOW GENOCIDE

BY CHRIS MCGREAL

RWANDA'S FORMER MINISTER of Information, Eliezer Niyitegeka, looks more comic than intimidating. He wears a dazzling white suit, Afro-hair-style and has an AK-47 slung across his shoulder. He last set foot in Rwanda in mid-July. He and the other ministers of the ousted Rwanda government have taken refuge over the border in Bukava, Zaire. Not for them the miseries of Goma's refugee camps. Many have set-tled into the Hotel Riviera, where com-forts include pornographic movies after midnight. The exiled regime's offices are furnished with computers and a satellite phone. Here they are attempting to rewrite the history of the Rwandan genocide.

Perhaps as many as a million people died in three months of anti-Tutsi pogroms. Hutus who opposed the slaughter were exterminated as well. The ministers in exile who presided over the killings are now the targets of UN investigators piecing together evidence to put them on trial for genocide — they are also at the top of the list of people the new Rwandan government wants to execute if it can lay hands on them first.

Foremost among them is the ousted president, Theodore Sindikubwabo, a paediatrician who set in motion the slaughter of Butare's Tutsis. His prime minister, Jean Kambanda, travelled Rwanda using the language of murder understood by all. The commerce minis-ter — once imprisoned for murdering his wife; the justice minister — herself mar-ried to a Tutsi; the youth minister — who openly encouraged children to kill; all of them are preparing a common defence, intent on obscuring the world's already confused view of Rwanda's calamity.

The time may come when the former ministers run for cover, along with the army chiefs settled into a Protestant evangelical mission in Goma, and the other alleged Rwandan war criminals scattered, as yet unfettered, across Africa and Europe. But for now they are on the offensive.

"Why do you want to talk about these dead Tutsis? What about my human rights? I can't even go home. Do you know there are people in my house in Kigali who are not even paying rent?" Niyitegeka challenged me.

"Neither of the two groups, the RPF nor us are saints. We know that massacres have been on both sides. I don't see any difference," deposed Prime Minister Kambanda argued. But the main purpose of the defence is to ensure that one of the swiftest and most organised mass murders of modern times is seen, not as a political act, but as an African tribal bloodletting that nobody could predict and nobody could prevent. Among those keen to obscure reality is Eliezer Niyitegeka.

Niyitegeka comes from Kibuye province in the far west of Rwanda, bor-dering Lake Kivu's placid expanse. Like most of once-crowded Rwanda, its ter-raced hills are shorn of trees so every scrap of available land can be made use of. It was once home to one of the highest con-centrations of Tutsis in the country . . . .

As the killing machine cranked into gear across Rwanda, the wheels started turning in Kibuye. Slowly at first, indi-vidual opponents of Hutu extremism, both Tutsi and Hutu, were picked off. The province's Tutsis knew it was wise to keep a low profile. But many thought they had nothing to fear personally. Then Niyitegeka descended on his home province.

"I went there to stabilise the situa-tion. The problem was that the RPF had given the Tutsis weapons and there were infiltrators everywhere. Nobody pre-pared a massacre of the Tutsis, but we had to kill the infiltrators. If there were prepared massacres they were the mas-sacres by the opposition, the RPF, not us," he now claims.

In fact, the speeches he gave in towns and villages, broadcast by Radio Rwanda and the notoriously extremist RTLM radio, had a far from settling effect. "I have trust in our armed forces. They will defeat all our enemies. And you, the population, should join the armed forces to eliminate every kind of

enemy, wherever they may hide," he said in a speech broadcast on RTLM. For those such as the Hutu mayor of Kibuye town, Augustin Karara, the message was clear.

"When Eliezer was moving around he was encouraging the people to kill. He couldn't say it openly. He would say they were doing very good 'work' or they should 'get to work'. Such a message meant killing Tutsis. He was on very good terms with some mayors where a lot of people were killed. He praised them openly for their 'work'," Karara said.

On Sunday, April 17 Karara noticed new faces on the streets. "Groups of men were discussing something. Some came from outside town. They went around collecting men. Some came willingly, they were enthusiastic to kill. Others were forced to go. Then the army passed out guns and the church was surrounded. The governor went up there but he didn't try to stop it. A lot of people think he was

behind it. The militia and the army and police took part. Not all, but those that didn't stood by. Those who escaped the bullets and grenades were cut up with machetes," he said.

"They wanted me to buy beer for the killers to make the killing easier. Afterwards there were some people who were still alive and wounded. I took some people to the hospital. The militia asked me what I was doing with those 'inyenzi' [cockroaches] but let me take them. Then they went there and killed them," Karara said.

The next day the scene was repeated at the stadium. Probably ten thousand people were killed.

In Kibuye, now plants are thriving on top of a mass grave sloping behind the church. But they cannot stifle the stench that still permeates the building. The church walls are scrubbed clean but the outbuildings remain as they were on the day of the massacre. Bloody hand-

prints and footprints speckle the walls like a child's painting. Recent rains washed away the topsoil from another mass grave near the stadium, exposing the rotting corpses. The UN used bulldozers to cover them over again.

Augustin Karara was replaced as mayor by the RPF. After a long interrogation it cleared him of any role in the massacres. He was one of many brave Hutus who did what they could to protect Tutsis at considerable risk to themselves, disproving the extremists' claim that the killing was nothing more than tribal warfare.

Those in Kibuye town who did not flee still shy away from discussing the genocide, and more particularly what occurred at their church. But Karara says that quietly and slowly they are beginning to face up to it.

"Now they feel ashamed. They are very ashamed. It is very shameful," he said.

DECEMBER 3, 1994

NIGHTMARES ON CROMWELL STREET

THE WEST TRIAL

BY DUNCAN CAMPBELL

PERHAPS THE WESTS are our Mansons, turning what was happening sexually in the country at the time into a distorted image of itself. In the same way that Manson manipulated foolish women, so Fred did with the sad succession of women who married or wanted to marry him and whom he despised or killed. Every generation has its demonic figures and Fred and Rose may now be ours, our Mansons from the Forest of Dean, where Dennis Potter always hinted they might be lurking.

As each witness in the trial appeared, I would make a brief note beside their names in my notebook so that I could recall them after their evidence. Most notes just indicated "fair hair/ponytail/leather jacket" or "smart/ black hair/fringe/Welsh". But flipping through seven books' worth of trial, I noticed how often the phrase "dead eyes" cropped up. So many of the people who had survived, the "lucky" ones — if it is lucky to escape with just a few years of sexual abuse or with only being tied up, gagged and raped rather than murdered and beheaded — were clearly deadened by their experience.

So does it deaden everyone who touches it or reads about it? The jurors were offered counselling at the end of the case and I imagine some will take it, for they looked weary. We are not allowed to interview them and we know them only by the nicknames we gave them — "Julie Andrews", "the old codgers" and so on. Relatives of the victims and police officers have also been given help. Even the journalists covering the case were offered it, though there were no takers.

But of course, the case invades the brain. On a mundane level, I can't now dissociate masking tape from the masks that gagged the murdered girls, see a DIY sign without thinking of Fred, the DIY king of Cromwell Street, or spot a hitch-hiker without a thought of the cheery bell-bottomed teenagers in their maxi-coats and platform shoes who disappeared. Of course, it invades dreams: one of the few women reporters who covered the whole trial dreamed of leaving a supermarket with bags of shopping and being approached by Fred West with an offer of help. I dreamed of sifting through earth and finding fingers buried in it while a little girl sat beside me and wept. We have heard horrible things but there are horrible things all around us and to hear them is not to suffer them or to love someone who has suffered them.

So I feel a terrible irritation when I turn on the late-night television and see the commentators — for some strange reason in this secular society they tend to be chaps with their collars on back to front — who have been wheeled on to talk about the Moral Issues, and hear those phrases rolling off the conveyor belt. The Heart of Darkness, the Nature of Evil, the Loss of Innocence. For this was not a case which can be simply placed in a little box labelled "evil" that can then be closed and locked away....

NOVEMBER 25, 1995

A PEOPLE BETRAYED BY PARLIAMENT

BECAUSE WE BELIEVE in elections fought in the light, not in the dark, we are publishing today a summary of evidence submitted to Sir Gordon Downey on the cash for questions scandal. This is an issue which goes to the heart of parliamentary democracy. The facts the report reveals are, in short, that a number of MPs now offering themselves for re-election have secretly confessed to, or are plainly guilty of, criminal offences of bribery, corruption, and cheating the Inland Revenue. Secret confessions, we now know, have been made to flagrant breaches of the parliamentary law on declaration of interests, and some of the evidence given to a parliamentary select committee has been shown to be lies.

Had things been handled differently, Sir Gordon's full report could have been published by Parliament itself. We would have much preferred that to happen. But yesterday it was clear that in spite of the forces anxious for publication — not just the opposition parties, but Sir Gordon himself, his masters, the Committee on Standards and Privileges, and even Conservative MPs who figure in the investigation — John Major and his Government remained obdurate, wholly indifferent to the public's right to know. This affair began with concealment — concealment from Parliament and the public of the secret and squalid motives which led MPs to table their questions: the cash which companies and their lobbyists were ready so freely to put in their pockets. Now it culminates in a further concealment. John Major — honest John, as he used to be advertised, who began so well, setting up the Nolan committee, backing Sir Gordon's appointment, declaring on television that his report must be available before the election — has now decided instead on an election fought in the dark. For reasons which — insultingly — he has never even attempted to justify, he fixed the timetable for the election in such a way that Sir Gordon's report, which he himself had demanded, could not be published before the nation went to the polls. Since then he has sneeringly resisted every attempt to rewrite these arrangements.

Whose rights are infringed by this concealment? Most immediately, those of voters in those constituencies where MPs at the heart of Sir Gordon's investigations are offering themselves to the voters. The whole basis of the British electoral system cannot work if voters are denied essential information about those who aspire to represent them. The interim report published yesterday fulfils that requirement in the case of fifteen named MPs — eleven Conservative, three Labour and one Liberal Democrat — whom Sir Gordon exonerates. The failure to arrange publication of the rest of his findings denies that essential safeguard in ten other constituencies. In eight cases the MPs involved (though some are not standing again) have been identified; in two cases, they have not. What are the voters to make of it? Either way, someone is wronged. Where these MPs are innocent, they have to fight the suspicion that they may be guilty. Where they are guilty, the concealment may save them from the retribution they deserve at the hands of electors. The electoral process is thereby frustrated: and needlessly frustrated, since but for John Major's obduracy, none of this need have occurred.

The injustice done to the rest of us is less specific, but it is real. Part of the context of the Government over the past few years has been sleaze. But without the Downey report, the electorate cannot judge how grave that offence has been. Either way, someone is wronged. The Prime Minister's failure to use the options before him to let the public see the report have fed the suspicion that the findings looked bad for his party. And the details we give today confirm that they do. John Major sought to dismiss the whole affair yesterday as an "opposition stunt". That is not how most voters are likely to see it.

It is already clear that the procedures the House instituted when seized by shame and remorse over earlier allegations will need substantial amendment. They need to reflect the comfort of members less, and the rights of the public much more. Parliament, as for a while it seemed to accept, is on trial in this matter: its attachment to self-regulation will stand or fall by its resolution. For ourselves, we remain convinced that an independent commission against corruption, safe from interruption — or in this case disruption — by parliamentary prorogations or committees with in-built government majorities can alone provide the safeguards required in an honest democracy; can alone ensure that issues like these are resolved in the light, not the dark. We believe that Parliament holds its privileges not for itself but on trust for the people who are represented there. In this matter the Prime Minister and Parliament itself have singularly failed to protect the essential rights of the voter. It is because we believe that this balance needs to be redressed that we today publish the essence of Sir Gordon Downey's investigation.

MARCH 21, 1997

THE AMORAL ARCHITECT OF HIS OWN RUIN

LEADER COMMENT

JONATHAN AITKEN'S REVISIONIST biography of Richard Nixon is a revealing text for those seeking clues to the extraordinary downfall of talented, complex but ultimately amoral men. Aitken aptly describes Watergate as a "Shakespearean tragedy", a phrase which equally well captures the scale of his own terrible undoing. In the space of six weeks he has lost his political career, forfeited a fortune in legal costs and seen his 18-year marriage founder. He must now face the consequences of being caught out lying on oath in the High Court and of weaving a determined conspiracy to pervert the natural course of justice.

Aitken's life, like that of Nixon on the morning of Friday August 9, 1974, is in ruins. His epitaph for the former president could well stand as his own: "Even the most generous explanations for his conduct do not bring him exculpation. In his frenzied efforts to fight his way out of the quicksand . . . he made himself guilty of many 'crimes' — among them deceit, negligence, bad judgement, mendacity, amorality, concealment and a disastrous reluctance to face up to personal confrontations with the individuals who were creating the worst problems."

Aitken's overall empathy with his subject is a matter best left to the psychologists. But it is extraordinary that any man could write a 600-page book on Richard Nixon and yet not learn the fundamental lesson of his tragedy: beware the cover-up. Aitken's own downfall was caused by a cover-up, a lie about a weekend in Paris in 1993. We still do not know why it was so vital that he should have lied so doggedly and consistently about that weekend, but it was emphatically the lie, not the trip, that finished him.

That initial lie ensnared not only him, but his family, for it was vital to Aitken to be able to pretend that his wife paid his bill at the Ritz Hotel in Paris. In fact, as we were eventually able to prove, Mrs Aitken spent the weekend in Switzerland with their daughter Victoria. Thus was Aitken's 17-year-old child also sucked into an ever more desperate conspiracy. It would be inhuman not to feel sympathy for the Aitken family as they contemplate the wreckage of their lives. But it is hard to feel much compassion for a man who would send in his own daughter to tell lies on oath — a serious criminal offence which could even have cost her her liberty — to save his own skin. Such behaviour in any father, never mind a Privy Counsellor, is repulsive. That is why the police should send for the court papers with some urgency.

This is the fourth libel case the *Guardian* has been forced to fight in as many years in pursuit of what we modestly considered to be the public interest. In the absence of effective regulations governing the political process the media has found itself sucked into a vacuum. In the absence of the criminal law, the libel law has been used as a weapon both of disclosure and of control. The libel laws can indeed be effective in searching out the truth — though they should be reformed and never again should a defendant be denied the fundamental right to a jury. But they are a poor substitute for the thoroughgoing Corruption Act of the sort that is now promised, though long overdue.

As the evidence spilled out in Court 10 the impression grew ever stronger of the dismal complacency at the heart of a government which had already dealt feebly with a succession of revelations by this and other newspapers. As with Hamilton and Smith, the Aitken affair was treated as if it were a matter of footling consequence. It is painfully clear that Sir Robin Butler set about his inquiries into the *Guardian*'s initial allegations with all the ferocity of a spaniel. Once his case was closed Jonathan moved on and up. Just as Tim Smith was promoted after admitting taking £25,000 from a company under investigation by the DTI, so Aitken was elevated to the Cabinet. Why on earth not? We had the least corrupt parliament in the world, and anyone who said otherwise was a conspiracy freak or else simply out to undermine the Great Institutions of State.

In court Aitken was perfectly frank about his inclination, if not his right, to lie to journalists, notwithstanding his own distinguished former career as a reporter. Truth and openness — causes so important that famously he stood trial at the Old Bailey in their defence — were trifles to be jettisoned once on the other side of the fence. Mendacity and secrecy destroyed him. We take no pleasure in the ruin of a man with many talents and qualities. We did our best to avoid the anticipated outcome. But ultimately it was he who unsheathed the sword of truth, and he who was inevitably impaled on it.

JUNE 21, 1997

A TIME FOR CELEBRATION

BY JONATHAN FREEDLAND

"FEW NOW SANG England Arise, but England had risen all the same ." So wrote AJP Taylor of the 1945 election in which the Labour Party first claimed a working majority in the House of Commons. Forty-two years on, Edward Carpenter's socialist song is even less often sung now than it was then. England Arise would not get past first base as a New Labour anthem. And yet its words — "the long long night is over" — express our first feelings this morning. For England arose yesterday, because without a change in the heart of England there can never be a change of government either. And Scotland arose too, for whom the wait has been grimmer and the possibilities this morning correspondingly brighter. Wales too is once more a waking dragon today. Northern Ireland? That's another matter. We await today's declarations before assessing that thorny question in this new political era.

Taking office ... Tony Blair and his wife, Cherie

But the long-awaited deed has at last been done. The Conservative defeat, though less cataclysmic than some of the more extravagant polls predicted, is nevertheless emphatic. It is therefore the significant first stage in the creation of a different kind of Britain from the Britain that we have all become so used to. What Hazlitt once wrote of the Bourbons — "When a government, like an old-fashioned building, has become crazy and rotten, it stops the way of improvement, and only serves to collect diseases and corruption" — also reads like an almost perfect description of the condition of the Conservatives. Their government had to go because it was a bad government proposing obnoxious policies and because it was in the grip of an increasingly hysterical rage against Europe in all its forms. But it also had to go because it had governed too long and too loosely for the good of democracy and of politics . . . it was essential that the Conservatives were defeated and, after the longest period of continuous single party rule since the 1832 Reform Act, at last they have been. Perhaps there is a God, after all.

How will the general election of May Day 1997 be seen in ten years' time? As the moment when the electorate finally nerved itself to put a stake through the heart of the living dead of Thatcherite Conservatism? Or as the moment when Britain at last gave itself the chance to construct a modern liberal socialist order and, by so doing, caught the mood of the troubled Western world?

If the early indications were a good guide to the emerging story of the night, then the true answer to that question is finely balanced. As in 1992, the final result in 1997 seems likely to show that when the voters got into the polling booths more of them decided to stick with the Conservatives than had admitted as much to the opinion pollsters. Polling organisations which had suspected this are, to that extent, vindicated by these results. But the more important conclusion from this is political. Even when offered every possible assistance in making the switch from Conservative to Labour, lots of voters still stuck with the Tories. Even after a campaign of enormous professionalism and assurance, the Labour share of the poll is nothing like as large as it was a month ago. Polls which suggested, some months back, that Labour would get the votes of well over half of the electorate have been proved wrong in the end. Labour has done its job well and conclusively, but its mandate is constrained by the same factor which should have constrained the Conservatives for so long — namely, that a majority of the electorate have voted against the party which forms the government. That is one reason why Labour must stick to its pledge to hold a referendum on our unsatisfactory electoral system.

That said, this is not a moment for emphasising the problems which lie ahead. There will be lots of time for that. This is a moment for celebrating the fact that a degenerate Conservative Party has been despatched into opposition, and for marking the first Labour election victory for almost a quarter of a century. When Labour was smashed by Margaret Thatcher in 1983 and 1987, that prospect hardly seemed possible. That it has happened is a tribute to many unsung people, but also to Neil Kinnock, in particular, to John Smith and, of course, to Tony Blair. We greet their election with a congratulation, a cheer, and a surge of hope that it can live up to the expectations which so many millions have placed in it.

MAY 2, 1997

A TIME FOR MOURNING

PRINCESS DIANA'S BODY BROUGHT BACK FROM FRANCE

BY JONATHAN FREEDLAND

IN THE END, they let her go quietly. No drum, no funeral note — only a dumb silence as the body of Diana, Princess of Wales, returned to the land she might have ruled as queen.

There was no crowd to meet her, none of the hordes of flag-wavers she so delighted in life. Instead the flat, grey tarmac of RAF Northolt, windy as a prairie, a line-up of dignitaries — and a hearse.

She had made the journey from Paris by plane, on an RAF BAE 126. They kept the coffin in the passenger cabin, within sight of her two sisters, Lady Jane Fellowes and Lady Sarah McCorquodale, and her former husband, the Prince of Wales.

The skies themselves seemed to make way for her arrival, the clouds parting like an honour guard. Once the plane had landed, it nudged toward the welcoming party hesitantly, as if weighed down by its tragic cargo. Waiting there was the kind of receiving line Diana met every day. In the middle, arms by his sides, fists clenched tight, the Prime Minister. A cleric stood close by, bright in scarlet cassock.

Eventually the plane door opened, and the Prince appeared head down, hands clasped behind his back. He was guided by the Lord Chamberlain, the Earl of Airlie. In another context it might have been a standard royal visit: Charles shown round a new factory or hospital wing. But he had come on a more baleful duty. He took his place in line — as he has done so often.

By now, the team of coffin bearers, each one in the crisp uniform of the Queen's Colour Squadron, had completed its precise march toward the other side of the aircraft. At the stroke of seven o'clock, the hatch opened revealing a glimpse of colour, the Royal Standard clinging to the hard, square outline of the coffin. It seemed an unforgiving shape: just a box, with none of the curve or sparkle of the woman whose body lay within.

Princess Diana's coffin, decked with lillies

The silence of the air was cut, and not just by the sound of distant traffic — which rumbled on, as if to prove that the clocks never stop, even for the death of a princess.

The air was filled with the chickageev, chickageev of the thousand camera lenses pointed at the scene ahead. Even now the world's telephoto eye was still staring at her, more focused than ever. Despite everything, everyone still wanted a piece of Diana. The cameras kept up their din, but there was an eerie silence from the men who held them. Once they would cry out, "Diana! Diana!" — urging her to look their way or to flash just one more of those million-dollar smiles. But there was no shouting yesterday. And no smiles either.

The bearers of the body inched their way to the hearse. They stood, swivelled on their heels, and clasping tight with their white gloved hands, lowered the coffin as smoothly as a hydraulic pump. They were about to turn away, but a bit of the flag was still spilling out; it had to be tucked in, just like the train of one of Diana's more lavish ball gowns.

The sisters stepped forward, each one turning to curtsy for the man whom Diana had once loved. Charles kissed each one before they stepped into the royal Daimler. The next car was filled with bouquets.

The Prince himself did his duty, talking to each one of the VIPs who had stood beside him. Tony Blair clasped both royal hands in a double handshake, nodding intently. Charles made a gesture with upturned palms, as if to say "What Can I Do?" He thanked the RAF guard and disappeared back inside the plane, heading for Balmoral and his newly bereaved young sons . . . And then, on the final day of August, the sky darkened, and the wind whipped harder. It felt like the last day of summer, and the beginning of a long winter.

SEPTEMBER 1, 1997

TELETUBBY TIDINGS

SAY EH-OH TOPS THE CHARTS

SHORTLY BEFORE 7 p.m. last Sunday the nation learned its fate. For the next two weeks we are doomed to a peculiar form of aural torture: the constant repetition of a sugary jingle lisped by four mutant psychedelic gonks. Say Eh-oh is almost certain to top the charts right up to Christmas. Move over shepherds, wise men and kings! Here come Tinky Winky, Dipsy, Laa Laa and Po with their festive cheer of custard, toast and hugs. Tele-tubbies! Tele-tubbies! They bring you good tidings of great joy. Shame about the music.

The new wave of Teletubbymania hits a country which is barely recovering from its bout of Barbiemania. For weeks now some of us have not been able to get it out of our heads. "Come on Barbie, Let's go party! Ah-Ah-Ah-Ah! Life in plastic, it's fantastic! Ooo-oo-ooooh! Oooo-oo-oooh!" It is, of course, a relief to escape from the hermetic world of Ken and Barbie. But it is little comfort to find oneself instead in an acid green Orwellian landscape watched over by a sinister windmill and a troop of menacing rabbits.

It would be some comfort if the success of these two songs were solely attributable to the innocent choice of the under-tens. But we know that a large proportion of Teletubby fans are in fact students who chill out in Laa Laa land before retiring to bed. Dozens of websites deconstruct the meaning of the Teletubbies — their sexuality, their politics, their potency as narcotic metaphor. One Media Studies lecturer has described them as the biggest campus cult of the decade. Their only rivals are, indeed, Ken and Barbie. Or, possibly Alan Partridge. Or even Mrs Merton. Post-modern irony is clearly becoming not only the dominant cultural force in Britain today, but also a formidable commercial force. Aha! And Eh-oh!

DECEMBER 10, 1997

THE COMING OF PARA-RELIGION

A NEW FAITH

BY DAVID MCKIE

THIS IS AN age forsaking religion: or to put it another way, taking up irreligion — though the two are not quite the same.... [For] we shouldn't assume that those who are not religious can be classed as anti-religious. As religion declines, so we see the growth of what might be called para-religion. Paramedics resemble medics, but not in some of the senses that matter most. Para-religion resembles religion, but with even more crucial exemptions. You can see the rise of para-religion in music: the astonishing success of music which would once have been thought antique or alien, propelling composers from Abbess Hildegard of Bingen to Gorecki and Part and John Tavener into the Classic FM charts.... You can see it even more powerfully in the surge of grief and commitment which followed the death of Princess Diana, with some of the kerbside interviews couched specifically in terms more often associated with gods than mere mortals...

But of course this isn't religion. It's religion with the awkward, unwelcome, non-negotiable bits left out. It's the balm without the demands and the obligations and even the fear. And in this it resembles much else in an age which constantly says: don't make things too difficult. Concert promoters, I saw it reported this week, are turning against the symphony, which audiences find too long and demanding...

The poet of para-religion is Philip Larkin, not a religious man but infected by a kind of religiousness with nowhere to go. I shall shun the more famous poems and cite a lesser one.

What are days for?
Days are where we live.
They come, they wake us,
Time and time over.
They are to be happy in:
Where can we live but days?

Ah, solving that question
Brings the priest and the doctor
In their long coats
Running over the fields.

DECEMBER 18, 1997

THE MONICA AND BILL SHOW

THE CLINTON INQUISTION

BY POLLY TOYNBEE

HOW DID IT come to this, the ultimate humiliation, the President of the United States starring on the Jerry Springer Oprah Winfrey Show of all time? Whatever the founding fathers meant by high crimes and misdemeanours, they were very clear about cruel and unusual punishment. This was slow torture by excruciating embarrassment.

"This material is unsuitable for children," the television news presenters warned sanctimoniously. It was unsuitable for us all. Sixty-eight per cent of Americans said so too — they never wanted the tapes broadcast. And 55 per cent said they wouldn't watch them in any form.

But of those who did watch, many may think a little better of their president and a great deal worse of his grotesque persecutors. As the hours of inexplicably crackly, ill-filmed tapes rolled on, the sense of unreality grew.

Surely not? Not this? The precise legal status of "the insertion of an object into another person's genitalia"? If once in a while — but surprisingly rarely — Mr Clinton protests, isn't that what victims of gross invasion of privacy have a right to do? You can watch people goaded week after week on people-freak shows, but this, for God's sake, is the President.

Despite all the gleeful advance briefings predicting the tapes would kill Bill Clinton, the Republicans may have blundered badly. The President keeps his cool remarkably well under obscene and prurient questioning.

The disproportion of this groping investigation into a pathetic and tacky affair defies belief: "Did you give her a box of cherry chocolates?" Now we wait to see if the good sense of the voters holds up. So far, the majority still say he's doing a good job, and now his character may even emerge enhanced. He sounds human, warm and a great deal better than his prosecutors. He is, for instance, kind and affectionate about Monica — no more "that woman" stuff. Sure, he quibbles: "It depends on what the meaning of 'is' is" was a gem that will live for ever.

SEPTEMBER 22, 1998

WEE GIRL POWER

THE SPICE GIRLS HIT GLASGOW

BY PAT KANE

IT'S THE BEST noise I've ever heard at the end of a gig. Nine thousand voices and 18,000 feet, screaming and stamping — except they all belonged to eight-year-old girls. A strange tumult, very large but very light — like the last echo of a much grander roar.

I watched the massed lassies waving their thousands of light-sticks at the departing Spice Girls, and it felt like some gigantic feminist cult meeting, a youth rally for the Wannabe Party.

This was, very tangibly, Wee Girl Power. But the power to do what?

A cynic would say: to consume the Spice Girls. The first things to hit the eye were the endorsements projected across the stage, and Pepsi, Impulse and Kodak songs were given pride of place in the middle of the set.

Even when the Girls are at their best — Scary doing boxercise, Posh slinking away in her off-the-shoulder numbers, Baby skipping around like a size-14 Lolita, Sporty hitting her migraine-inducing high notes, Ginger trying to stay in her dress — their Spice is a resolutely banal, workwomanlike thing, the songs as solid and dull as fleet cars. Yet when mere perspiration inspires sheer devotion like this, you have to ask what little girls understand about the Fab Five that adult males don't.

It's essentially this: boys are always rubbish, girls are always great — whether they're vamps or victors. This was a night of militant matriarchy, led by the decidedly woman-shaped Geri, who strode through the proceedings with an almost matronly authority . . . The last song was Mama I Love You, with childhood snapshots of the Spices beaming out across the hordes.

This gig was handled like a pier-end panto — except the dames wore Versace and the set was more cyber sci-fi than Brothers Grimm. Mel B (Scary) and Mel C (Sporty) did a Puss In Boots skit, where they pretended to run from the rest in order to perform a high-kicking version of Sisters Are Doing It For Themselves. Sporty leapt about in a Scotland football top, Girl Power slogans slammed out of the video screen.

Widow Twanky mainlining on Camille Paglia: you had to smile. "I think this side of the hall is berrah than the rest!" screamed Scary Spice in her dulcet Yorkshire tones. "Lemme 'ear yer Zigga-Ziggah!" Oh, we heard.

My eight-year-old dragged me out of the hall a few times — and on the way, close to the front, I saw two extreme sights: a hall full of ecstatic schoolkids, glitter-haired, united in sheer girliness, and a stage full of evidently exhausted hoofers, their banter misfiring and forced, working hard for the money. That's the story of pop — not girl power but fan power. As long as wee lassies want to hand-dance among themselves, the Spices will be around.

APRIL 6, 1998

AIDS STILL OUT OF CONTROL

COMPLACENCY MISPLACED

BY SARAH BOSELEY

THE AIDS EPIDEMIC is out of control in many parts of the world, wiping out gains in the quality of life, infecting 11 men, women and children every minute and killing 2.5 million people last year, a United Nations report said yesterday.

Clare Short, the International Development Secretary, said at the report's launch in London that complacency in the West about Aids was misplaced. Infection was rising almost everywhere, even in the United Kingdom, Europe and the United States, which could afford costly drugs to keep the disease under control.

"The figures we are contemplating today are truly terrible," said Ms Short. "They are wiping out some of the development gains for which we have worked so hard, measured in increased life expectancy and reduced infant mortality."

The report by the joint UN programme on HIV/ Aids (Unaids) said half of the 5.8 million people infected by the HIV virus last year were children and young people aged 15 to 24 — some because they were born to women with HIV, some through sex and others through using dirty needles to inject drugs.

EDUCATION VITAL

There has been a 10 per cent rise in infection worldwide. In Britain, according to the charity Aids Care Education and Training, the 12,000 people living with HIV in 1992 rose to 20,000 this year, and it anticipates at the present rate the figure will reach 30,000 by 2002.

In sub-Saharan Africa, where the picture is worst, 34 million people have been infected and 12 million of them have died. Last year there were 4 million new infections and 5,500 deaths every day. Half of those infected are women.

Education and condom use are vital in changing attitudes — and in Uganda, Botswana, Namibia and Swaziland, the tide of the epidemic has been turned, the report said.

But Ms Short said: "It needs to be as easy to get hold of a condom in a poor country as it is to get a can of Coca-Cola."

NOVEMBER 25, 1998

A BLESSED GOOD FRIDAY

NORTHERN IRELAND'S PEOPLE GLIMPSE PEACE AT LAST

THESE MEN AND women did noble work. Tired after thirty hours without sleep, their fatigue from thirty years of war proved greater. In the name of the people of Northern Ireland, they reached out to their deadliest rivals — and made peace. It took the deaths of more than three thousand people, the serious wounding of some thirty thousand others, but yesterday the two sides of that long and bloody conflict joined together to declare, "Enough."

The Easter snow never let up, the air outside the Castle buildings stayed bitter and frigid — but still Sinn Fein's chairman described it as "a beautiful day." And so it was. Inside the Stormont building, men whose adult lives had been filled with talk of armed struggle and no surrender were now sharing a joke, paying warm tribute to each other. Usually hard-faced men came to speak, only to find a catch in their voice. One delegation was spotted in the middle of the night, its members quietly hugging each other.

The emotion was earned, as was the universal declaration that Stormont had witnessed history in the making. There are important caveats. But no one should lose sight of the scale of the achievement. After three decades of conflict — and an antagonism that has endured for centuries — Unionism and nationalism, loyalism and republicanism, Protestants and Catholics may finally have found a way to live together.

This is no mere pact between governments, nor some worthy accord among moderates: it is not a re-run of Sunningdale or the Anglo-Irish agreement. This is an agreement backed by those who represent the men of violence, standing at opposite extremes. Gerry Adams was smiling yesterday, apparently with the blessing of the IRA army council — but so was Gary McMichael and David Irvine, the men who speak for the convicted killers of hardline loyalism. It is as if the Middle East peace process had brought together Hamas and the Jewish settlers of the West Bank:

it is an extraordinary feat of diplomacy.

The politicians yesterday counselled against euphoria, rightly warning that the task of reconciliation has only just begun. Prudence would suggest waiting a while before handing out plaudits. Even so, it seems right to credit those who pulled off what so many — until very recently — said was impossible.

In Northern Ireland, John Hume, Gerry Adams and David Trimble have all earned a place in history. Mr Hume for having the courage to stand with Sinn Fein early, encouraging them to choose politics over warfare. Mr Adams led the republican movement away from violence and towards a compromise on its core doctrine of a united Ireland: Sinn Fein has now formally accepted the partition of Ireland — an historic break.

Mr Trimble proved the most obstinate negotiator in the last moments yesterday, but he showed political strength, too — persuading a party which has made intransigence into an article of faith to compromise. The Ulster Unionists' acceptance of the new Ministerial Council of the North and South grants the Republic a governmental stake in Northern Ireland for the first time. Until now Unionism has regarded the South as an alien, if not enemy power.

Outside the province, London and Dublin can allow themselves a weekend of congratulation. Bertie Ahern buried his mother on Thursday, then headed to Belfast for two sleepless days cajoling and arm-twisting the parties towards an agreement. Tony Blair was pivotal, luring David Trimble back to the peace table just when the entire effort seemed doomed. All that was possible thanks to the dogged, indefatigable work of his secretary of state, Mo Mowlam. Her human touch attracted much criticism these last months, but now she is vindicated: she succeeded where every predecessor had failed. Thanks in part to her, Tony Blair has won the prize that had eluded every British PM since Gladstone. It is

the crowning achievement of his first year in office.

All the participants were lucky, too, in their chairman. George Mitchell's years of senate deal-making stood him in good stead, as did the presence of his two, largely unsung co-chairs from Canada and Finland. It helped that the trio was backed by an American president who believed in the Northern Ireland peace process before almost anyone else. Bill Clinton took a lot of flak for granting Gerry Adams a US visa in 1994 — a move which, with hindsight, seems only to have helped. John Major and Albert Reynolds authored the first framework document which made yesterday possible. The deal may be done, but peace is never a done deal. The lesson of peace processes elsewhere — whether in the Middle East or South Africa — is that the signature is just the start.

There will be opposition, whether through Ian Paisley's planned No campaign for the referendum on May 22 or the rejectionist violence, likely to be committed by those paramilitaries who stayed outside. The alphabet soup of terror — from INLA to the LVF, CAC to CIRA — will be determined to break public confidence. The peacemakers must stand firm. There will be challenges from within, too — starting with conflicting interpretations of what the 67-page document's details all mean.

Several of the parties must now have the plan approved by executives and members. Some Unionists might baulk at the early release of prisoners; some republicans may recoil at the return of decommissioning. Both sides are bound to find it hard to sit together with old enemies: imagine it, a Unionist and a Sinn Feiner, side-by-side in an Ulster cabinet. Failure is a possibility. But so, now, is success. The people of Northern Ireland at last have an opportunity to live their lives in peace. It is a time for gratitude, and even the odd private prayer. For this was a blessed Good Friday.

APRIL 11, 1998

A HUNDRED DAYS TO MILLENNIUM

BY JOHN VIDAL

IN THE PAST century, we have had an official celebratory diet of dreary royal weddings, anniversaries, coronations and funerals. We have been told by the state to come together over the end of great wars and the death of leaders. But that's about it. For December 31, however, we are being expected to participate rather than to sit back and enjoy the uptight pageantry of empire. We can watch millennium night on the box, but everyone from the churches to the town halls and the government is desperate to welcome us to their bash.

Indeed, we are being effectively told to let rip. Forget the corporate Dome Experience, the shiny new constructions and all the millennial tree-planting and embroidery projects. It's quite like old times. Wild, serious celebration in Britain used to be a common affair linked directly with nature. It peppered every rural community calendar, marked the coming and going of seasons, planting and harvest times, the rhythms of the land and the changing of personal circumstance. Buffoonery, feasting, dance, misrule, drunkenness, obscenity, mirth, reversal of role and gender, heightened spirituality and sexuality, mockery and monkey-play were essential ingredients of the celebration of agrarian life. The difference is that then it needed no sanction or encouragement by the authorities.

Indeed, celebration was mostly a great two fingers to the established order. And now what do we have? Quite hilariously, one of the most self-avowedly Christian, puritan, uptight governments Britain has known, one which never ceases to extol the virtues of social obligation, which gives us few laughs, makes us work the longest hours in Europe and gives us the fewest public holidays, is sponsoring at vast expense, an enormous pagan midwinter festival of dance, fire and light.

There is a Christian and spiritual element, of course, but the tradition being most heavily drawn upon for the millennium celebrations is deeply rooted in the ancient, wild north European celebrations of life in the bleakest part of the year. Their magnification into the national-scale collective experience we are being lined up for suggests that the authorities have looked back and seen on the deepest level a great mess, and peered ahead and seen worse to come. The wise response, echoed throughout history by almost every society enduring hard times, is to let rip, symbolically throw away the old, celebrate the new and start over. But the old endures. Just as pagan celebration links time to nature, so dawns, sunsets, but above all music, fire and light are to be the central themes of the British celebrations.

Most of what will happen on millennium night will be tame enough — no wild, naked dances in the embers of sponsored bonfires, please; stand well clear of the bangers, ma'am, and enjoy Cliff Richard in the park, you Brummies — but it has to be seen in an unpredictable urban context. Millennium night will be marked by a series of mega raves, concerts and events in all major cities with fierce drumming, massive sound systems and giant crowds. The power of orchestrated sound, light and dark is unpredictable. The British may be officially stodgy, but as the recent Carnival in the City, the road protests, the Reclaim the Street parties and our football culture show, there is a wild, raw edge.

The great light show will be stuffed with significance: ancient symbolism about the rejection of the past, junctions of time, crossing thresholds, the arrival of the unknown and fear of the future. There will be *son et lumière* shows aplenty, great beacons on hundreds of hilltops and rivers of light. In Scotland, always the truest and wildest when it comes to celebration, there will be burnings of hated figures and symbols of the past, a direct link to Indian and other cultures which ritually wash away the past at the start of each year. It is intended that every Christian church be bathed in light, that every laser beam in the land should point skywards, and that giant projections be beamed on to buildings. The finale will be a truly staggering display of fireworks in many cities. The Mersey is to become a river of light; a long stretch of the Thames will be lined for miles with a 40 ft. wall of fire, culminating in a monstrous £20 million of rockets exploding above the capital. This is brave, dangerous, potentially subversive stuff for an establishment which has no experience of grand public celebration.

There must be some worried people just beginning to appreciate what may happen. Half of Britain primed to go wild after months of marketing and official hype? A drug- and booze-crazed populace dotted with extremists? People gathering in millions to dance to live music in all the major

The Millennium Dome . . . corporate experience or carnival culture?

cities? Has Mr Blair not been warned that one of the prime functions of carnival is to express the dark underbelly of society, and that history suggests grand celebration often unleashes orgies of disorder which rulers must then stamp on fiercely? Besides, the best parties always get out of control, and end in official tears and recriminations. You can already hear the official tut-tuts, the "steady-chaps-time-to-go-home-now" appeals on television, the police sirens, the corporate exhortations to get back to work and the economists' stultifying calculations that the celebrations have cost Britain billions in lost productivity and ruined our chances of hosting the World Cup. The Y2K bug may prove not to have been a technological glitch so much as a very human, atavistic impulse to crash brains everywhere at symbolic moments, a mental, even elemental need for chaos and disorder at times of change.

But bizarrely, the government may have got it right. The occasional celebration in culturally repressed societies is a way of maintaining social order, letting off steam and bringing people, minorities together. The great Lord Mayor shows on the Thames were symbols of political and temporal power, but they were also riotous, chaotic celebrations by the many river and boat communities. Ken Livingstone and the GLC were applauded for their parties in the parks; the Notting Hill carnival helps bond the Black community. Councils understand that huge firework displays are investments in place. Equally, football passion gives towns a rare sense of communal identity, and the recent eclipse had the effect of getting all of Britain to log off its computers, head outdoors, stare into the sky and experience a brief moment of wonder and togetherness.

But not all will be grand chaos by any means. Behind the mega experiences and the orchestrated urban mayhem will be hundreds of smaller events for which communities are even now preparing, intended to define interest groups or place. Blair's hunch that the overlong demise of state celebration in Britain may have actually contributed to Britain's social disintegration could pay off. Mark the moment, however meaningless, and you separate time, in this case a miserable century

of dreadful deeds and failures from a blank, deeply uncertain future. The millennium celebrations should, therefore, be recognised as a deliberate political move to maintain order and refresh a fractured, atomised society.

In constitutional terms, it is one more triumph of Westminster over the Palace. The millennium celebrations fit wider shifts in British culture, too. Almost without noticing, celebration has changed in Britain in the past decade, moving towards a more global, southern-style, urban, theatrical, eclectic model. Today it is more costume-based, artistic, imaginative and participatory. And there are signs that it is fusing cultural influences.

What may have started with music flooding in from Africa or South America, has moved into theatre and now carnival. The rather heavy British indoor pub and club culture is being slowly and surely exchanged for an outdoor street world where architecture, design, dance, food and music are all lightening up. British celebration is following, looking outwards to the age-old carnival spirit of light rather than the dark Victorian pageants that have dominated this century.

For millennium night, the Thames will be lined with dozens of stages where there will be artistic "experiences" and bands playing music from almost every ethnic group found in London. Already the artistic community can see that the celebrations will define popular culture for some time. There is in the land, says almost everyone involved in the preparations, a great, untapped desire in people to be together, to express themselves, to hold hands, and to belong to something greater than themselves and to define place, community and spaces. Some of this is certainly hype and wishful-thinking, and there are millions who will turn the lights out at 11 p.m. on December 31, 1999, and wake up the next morning as if nothing had happened. But as the millennium countdown begins in earnest, we should be prepared for the unexpected and a few tectonic shifts in the old order. At the very least, it should make the British, whoever we are, see the place and ourselves in a new light.

SEPTEMBER 18, 1999

GuardianUnlimited

Acknowledgements

The publishers would like to thank the following agencies for the photographs used inside this book. In certain cases, the following acronyms have been used when crediting photographs: Associated Press (**AP**), Camera Press (**CP**), Consolidated Communications (**CC**), Filed Photo from Guardian archives (**FPGA**), Guardian (**G**), Hulton Getty Picture Collection (**HGPC**), Mary Evans Picture Library (**MEPL**), Pacemaker Press (**PP**), Press Association (**PA**), Popperfoto (**P**), Topham Picturepoint (**TP**), United Press (**UP**), Universal Pictorial Press & Agency (**UPPA**), VinMag Archive (**VMA**).

CHAPTER 1 - p3 The Dunottar Castle, HGPC/ p5 Manchester Town Hall, MEPL/ p6 Machine Gun, MEPL/ p7 Battle of Spion Kop, MEPL Picture Library/ p8 Boer soldiers, HGPC/ p9 British concentration camps, HGPC/ Buffalo Bill's Wild West Show, MEPL/ p10 Sketch of Oscar Wilde, MEPL/ p11 Queen Victoria's funeral cortege, HGPC/ p12 Queen Victoria HGPC/ p13 Funeral of Queen Victoria HGPC/ p14 Sketch of hare, FPGA/ Hillare Belloc MEPL/ pp16 & 17 Pictures of the Potemkin mutiny, HGPC/ p18 Brough Golf Club, HGPC/ p19 Belfast riots, 1907, HGPC/ p20 Bleriot's Channel flight, HGPC/ p21 Halley's Comet, Science Photo Library/ p22 Devon and Somerset staghounds on Exmoor, Frank Craig (MEPL)/ p23 Emily Davison, MEPL / p25 Winston Churchill at The Sidney Street Siege, HGPC/ p26 Pictures of The Sidney Street Siege, Jan 3rd, 1911, The Illustrated London News Picture Library.

CHAPTER 2 - p29 Polar Bear at London Zoo, Ted Hamilton-West (G)/ p 31 Soldiers at Victoria Station, HGPC/ p 32 'Shell burst', WWI, HGPC/ p33 German Pioneers laying gas projectors, TP/ pp34-35 Prepared for gas attack, HGPC/ p36 Battle of Passchendaele, CP/ p38 Charles Montague Doughty, HGPC/ p39 Rolls Royce Armoured Car, TP/ pp40-41 Battlefield at Mercken, HGPC/ p42 British Western Front in France, P/ pp44-45 Casualty of War, HGPC/ p46 Observation Balloon on the Western Front, R.M. Paxton (MEPL)/ p47 Switch room of the old National Telephone Exchange, circa 1900, HGPC/ pp48-49 German prisoners in a 'cage', Dernancourt, TP/ p51 Buckingham Palace on Armistice Day, Spencer Arnold (HGPC)/ p52 Armistice in London, HGPC.

CHAPTER 3 - p55 Vladimir Lenin, 1918, UP/ p56 Michael Collins TP/ p57 Lord Carnarvon at the entrance of Tutankhamen's Tomb, HGPC/ Tomb of Tutenkhamen, HGPC/ Goldmask of Tutenkhamen, Ronald Sheridan Ancient Art and Architecture Collection/ pp58-59 Hitler during an election speech, 1933, by Heinrich Hoffmann/ p60 Rose Macauley, FPGA/ p61 Burnt-out bus at the Elephant & Castle, during the General Strike, HGPC/ pp62-63 Still from Ben Hur, MGM, 1925/ p64 Wall Street Crash, TP/ p65 Advert for the film 'Potemkin', VMA/ p66 C.P. Scott, G/ p67 Manchester Guardian, G/ p68 Unemployment demonstration, 1930's, FPGA/ p69 Unemployed man on a street corner in Wigan, HGPC/ p70 Gandhi on the Salt March, 1930, HGPC/ p71 Prisoners at work, Dachau, 1938, AKG London/ Jewish shop, Berlin, 1933, MEPL/ pp72-73 Jesse Owens, HGPC/ p74 'Curly Top', 20th Century Fox/ pp76-77 'Guernica', by Pablo Picasso, 1937, ©Succession Picasso/DACS 1999/Museo Nacional Centro de Arte Reina Sofia, Spain/Bridgeman Art Library/ p78 Neville Chamberlain making his 'Peace with honour' speech, 1938, HGPC.

CHAPTER 4 - p81 James Joyce, Zurich 1938, HGPC/ p83 Hitler in Langemarck, 1940, HGPC/ p84 Sigmund Freud, London 1938, Supplied by Mrs Anna Freud/ p85 Christopher Isherwood, left, and W.H. Auden, by Howard Coster, COI/ Winston Churchill arriving in Downing Street, 19 August 1941, HGPC/ p86, 87, 88 & 89 Dunkirk homecoming, June 5th, 1940, HGPC/ p90 New Bishop of Coventry enthroned in wrecked Cathedral, AP/ p91 Attack on Pearl Harbour, AP/ Japanese pilots, 'Winds of the Gods', December 7th, 1941, HGPC/ p92 Rommel, HGPC/ Land girls, TP/ p93 GI's dancing with girls, HGPC/ p94 Allied paratroops over Southern France, August 1944, CP/ p95 D-Day, Normandy landing, June 6, 1944, FPGA/ pp96-97 Sword Beach, Normandy, PA/ p98 Liberation of Paris, HGPC/ Liberation of Paris, HGPC/ p98 Dresden after the raids, February 1945, HGPC/ p99 Prisoners at Buchenwald, April 1st, 1945, HGPC/ p101 Liberating American troops discover ashes of holocaust victims at Buchenwald, AP/ p102 Big Ben - victory night , May 19th, 1945, HGPC/ p103 Remains of Hiroshima, HGPC/ p104 Hiroshima atomised, August 6 1945, AP.

CHAPTER 5 - p107 Still from Great Expectations, HGPC/ p108 India celebrates her independence, August 21, 1947, HGPC / Kon Tiki expedition, HGPC/ p109 Gandhi's funeral, February 4, 1948, HGPC/ p111 Berlin food drop, HGPC/ pp112-113 Preparing for the Berlin food drop, HGPC/ p115 Yeats' funeral, October 9, 1948, HGPC/ p116 Queen with newborn Prince Charles, December 21, 1948, HGPC/ Duke of Edinburgh and Prince Charles, April 9, 1949, CP/ p117 Ezra Pound, HGPC/ B-29 Superfortress Bomber, TP/ p119 Humphrey Bogart, CP/ p120 TV Family, VMA/ p121 Al Jolson, 1930, HGPC/ p123 Returning the Stone of Scone to Westminster Abbey, FPGA/ p125 American soldier using Flame-Thrower, HGPC/ pp126-127 Prisoners of War, 1950, HGPC/ p128 Just What Is It That Makes Today's Homes So Different So Appealing, 1956 ©Richard Hamilton 1999. All rights reserved DACS/ p130 Albert Elnstein's warning speech, HGPC.

A CENTURY OF IMAGES - 1972 Vietnam War: Children flee from a napalm attack, Corbis-Bettmann/ 1912 Emily Pankhurst, Corbis-Bettmann/ 1916 Battle of the Somme, Imperial War Museum/ 1939 'Gone with the Wind', Selznick Int. Pictures/MGM/ 1945 Churchill greets the jubilant crowd, Rex Features Ltd./ 1966 World Cup victory, Corbis-/Bettmann/ 1969 Buzz Aldrin's first step on the Moon, July 20, Corbis-Bettmann/ 1972 US casualties in Vietnam, Tim Page (Corbis)/ 1985 Live Aid Concert, Neal Preston (Corbis)/ 1997 Tributes to Diana, AP.

CHAPTER 6 - p151 Lana in mink, 1955, HGPC/ p152 Drink Milk campaign, 1950, HGPC/ p153 Girls in milkbar, 1950, HGPC / p154 Derek Bentley, HGPC/ England cricket victory, HGPC/ England cricket victory, HGPC/ p155 50's Beauty, HGPC/ Kinsey, 1952, HGPC/ p156 Still from 'Roman Holiday', with Gregory Peck and Audrey Hepburn, 1953, HGPC/ p157 Barbers shop/Gregory's haircut 1950s, HGPC/ p158 Hemingway on safari, 1954, HGPC/ p159 Roger Bannister, 1954, HGPC/ p160 Samuel Beckett, 1950, HGPC/ p161 JB Priestley, HGPC/ p162 Hungarian uprising, November 12, 1956, HGPC/ p163 Hungarian uprising, 1956, HGPC/ pp164-165 Elvis signing autographs, HGPC/ p166 ElvisPresley, CC/ p167 Egyptian independence, Nasser, TP/ p168 Girls in chemistry lab, HGPC/ p169 Soviet Sputniks, HGPC/ p169 Telex trouble, BT archives/ p171 Sharpeville massacre, March 1960, HGPC/ pp172-173 Sharpeville massacre, HGPC/ p174 Racial Discrimination, HGPC/ p156 Nikita Krushchev, HGPC.

CHAPTER 7 - p177 Liz Taylor in 'Cleopatra', HGPC/ p179 Marilyn Monroe, HGPC/ p180 US Blockade of Cuba, TP/ p181 Nelson Mandela, HGPC/ p183 Christine Keeler, HGPC/ p184 JF Kennedy, Jackie & Caroline, FPGA/ p185 Dallas Motorcade HGPC/ p186 Beatles on stage, HGPC/ p187 Beatlemania, Corbis-Bettmann/ p188 Lord Todd, CP/ p189 Truman Capote, HGPC/ p190 Ian Brady, May 6, 1966, HGPC/ p190 Myra Hindley, HGPC/ p192 Che Guevara, Channel 4 photo/ p193 Hippies in the park, HGPC/ p194 Campbell Soup, by Andy Warhol,1962,©The Andy Warhol Foundation /DACS, London 1999. Trademarks Licensed by Campbell Soup Company. All rights reserved/Saatchi Collection/Bridgeman Arts Library/ p195 Andy Warhol, HGPC/ p196 Enoch Powell, Channel 4 photo/ Martin Luther King, HGPC/ p197 Martin Luther King, HGPC/ pp198-199 Man walking on moon, Corbis/AFP

CHAPTER 8 - p203 Bloody Sunday, 1972, HGPC/ pp204-205 Injured man is carried away, having been shot by a member of the Parachute Regiment, 1972, PP/ p206 Jonathan Aitken, HGPC/ Germaine Greer, HGPC/ p207 Otter, Tony McGrath (G)/ p208 Idi Amin, June 1974, FPGA/ p210 Watergate panel, HGPC/ p211 Richard Nixon, HGPC/ pp212-213 Muhammad Ali, HGPC/ p214 Sheikh Ahmed Al-Yamani, Saudi Arabian Minister of Petroleum & Mineral Resources, FPGA/ p215 Cars, Denis Thorpe (G)/ p216 Thatcher voted leader of Conservative Party, HGPC/ p217 Churchill's People, BBC/ p218 Sex Pistols, Virgin Records/ p219 'Grease', Paramount Pictures/ p220 Vietnamese Boat people, HGPC/ p220 Star Wars, close up of Obi Wan with light sabre,1997 Lucas Film Ltd/ pp222-223 Star Wars, 1997 Lucas Film Ltd/ p224 Margaret and Denis Thatcher outside No. 10, HGPC/ p225 Thatcher at Tory Headquarters, HGPC/ p226 Ayatollah Khomeini, Abbas/Magnum.

CHAPTER 9 - p 229 Lord Soames stepping down as Governor of Rhodesia, Neil Libbert (G)/ p230 Grafitti on a wall in Coventry, June 1983, Denis Thorpe (G)/ p231 BullRing Shopping Centre, Birmingham, FPGA/ MPs join protest against unemployment, Gary Weaser (G)/ p232 Falkland's war, HGPC/ 'Gotcha' The Sun, News International Syndication/ p233 Miner's Strike,1984, HGCP/ pp234-235 Police face pickets at Orgreave, Don McPhee (G)/ p236 Freddie Mercury, Live Aid, 1985, HGPC/ p237 Bob Geldof in Ethiopia, 1984, Central Independent TV/ pp238-239 Starving children in Ethiopia, 1984, HGPC/ p240 Big Bang, 1986, PA/ p241 Black Monday, 1987,TP/ p242 Margaret Thatcher, HGPC/ p243 Thatcher holding t-shirt, Don McPhee (G)/ p244 Ronald and Nancy Reagan, HGPC/ pp246-247 Student faces tanks in Tiananmen Square, 1989, Jeff Widener (AP)/ p249 Tiananmen Square, June 1989, Bob Gannon (G)/ pp250-251 Fall of the Berlin Wall, 1989, HGPC

CHAPTER 10 - p255 ANC leader Nelson Mandela is released from prison, February 1990, AP/ p256 Thatcher leaves Downing Street, Ken Lennox (Mirror Syndication International)/ Gulf War Parade, TP/ p257 Yeltsin and Gorbachev, 1991, Yuri Gripas (G)/ p258 Sarajevo, Bosnia 1992, Reuter/ p259 Princess of Wales driving Princes William and Harry away from Kensington Palace, January 12, 1993, PA/ pp260-261 Victims of the massacre in Rwanda, December 1994, FPGA/ p263 Dead by the roadside near Goma, Zaire, December 1994, Martin Argles (G)/ p264 Policeman standing guard outside No.25 Cromwell St., 1995, UPPA/ pp266 & 267 Jonathan Aitken, Sean Smith (G)/ pp268-269 Tony Blair following the Labour Party election victory, May1997, P/ p270 Tony and Cherie Blair outside No. 10, Sean Smith (G)/ p271 Welsh Guards carrying Diana's coffin in Westminster Abbey, Johnny Eggitt (G)/ p272 Teletubbies 'Crackers', BBC/ p273 The Spice Girls performing at the 1997 Brit Awards, UPPA/ p274 Soldier and young boy in Northern Ireland, 1994, PP/ p277 Solar Eclipse, August 11, 1999, Corbis/AFP/ p278 The Millenium Experience, NMEC/SHAM.

FRONT COVER - (Photographs not credited elsewhere) **Margaret Thatcher**, Denis Thorpe (G)/ **Tony Blair**, All Action Pictures/ **Winston Churchill**, Rex Features Ltd..

INSIDE BACK COVER - Top: **Alan Rusbridger**, Jill Mead/ Bottom: **Giles Foden**, G.

Additional Photography by Scott Wishart

Every effort has been made to trace the copyright holders. Guardian Newspapers Ltd apologise for any unintentional omissions.